Preventing Racism at the Workplace

A report on
16 European countries

DÉPÔT
DEPOSIT

EF/96/23/EN

Preventing Racism at the Workplace

A report on 16 European countries

by John Wrench,
Centre for Research in Ethnic Relations,
University of Warwick;

Danish Centre for Migration and Ethnic Studies,
South Jutland, University Centre, Esbjerg.

European Foundation
for the Improvement of Living and Working Conditions
Loughlinstown, Dublin 18, Ireland
Tel: +353 1 282 6888 Fax: +353 1 282 6456

Cataloguing data can be found at the end of this publication

Luxembourg: Office for Official Publications of the European Communities, 1996

ISBN 92-827-7105-9

© European Foundation for the Improvement of Living and Working Conditions, 1996

For rights of translation or reproduction, applications should be made to the Director, European Foundation for the Improvement of Living and Working Conditions, Loughlinstown, Dublin 18, Ireland.

Printed in Ireland

Preface to the report on Preventing racism at the workplace

The "Joint declaration on the prevention of racial discrimination and xenophobia and promotion of equal treatment at the workplace" agreed by the European social partners at the Social Dialogue Summit in Florence in October 1995 sets out a range of means that can make a positive contribution towards preventing racial discrimination at the workplace.

The "Joint declaration" asks for the support of the European Foundation for the Improvement of Living and Working Conditions in the follow-up of the Declaration. This publication wants to be a first contribution to this process.

The publication which covers all European Union member states and Norway is the result of putting together 16 national reports. This has been a formidable challenge that the author, Dr. John Wrench, has been able to respond successfully. The reader has in its hands a well written and structured report of the present developments and possible future strategic options on preventing racism at work.

We are grateful to the authors of the national reports and the many commentators that reviewed the national and the European reports. To them and to Dr. John Wrench our most sincere gratitude.

Clive Purkiss   Eric Verborgh
Director   Deputy Director

PREVENTING RACISM AT THE WORKPLACE

A report on 16 European countries

	Introduction	1
1.	**Background: Migrant Workers in Europe**	3
	1.1 Legal Categories of Worker in the EU	3
	1.2 Definitions of Racism and Discrimination	5
	1.3 Terminology in Different Countries	6
	1.4 Different Migrant/Ethnic Minority Groups in the EU	10
2.	**The Labour Market, Inequality and Discrimination**	30
	2.1 Factors Influencing Inequality	30
	Developments in the economy and the labour market	31
	Characteristics of migrants and ethnic minorities themselves	31
	Discrimination in national and EU policies	32
	Processes of direct and indirect discrimination	33
	2.2 Legal and Administrative Discrimination	34
	Legal discrimination against non-EU nationals	34
	Discrimination against EU nationals	39
	2.3 Evidence for Racial Discrimination	40
	Statistical evidence	40
	Discrimination testing	41
	Research into the actions of employers	43
	Indirect discrimination	48
	Employment agencies	50
	Evidence from migrants and ethnic minorities	51
	Individual cases	53
	2.4 Discrimination and the Informal Economy	54

3.	National Policies against Racism and Discrimination	60
4.	Company Policies against Racism and Discrimination	85
5.	Trade Union Policies against Racism and Discrimination	97
6.	**Obstacles To Progress**	119
	6.1 A Lack of Information and Research	119
	6.2 Problems of Attitudes and Knowledge	124
	6.3 Weaknesses in Legislation and its Implementation	132
	6.4 Broader Developments in the Economy and the Labour Market	138
7.	**Conclusions And Strategic Options**	142
	7.1 Problem Areas Revealed by the National Reports	144
	7.2 Areas for Action	146
	Improvement of the rights of third-country nationals	146
	EU directive on racial discrimination	147
	EU initiation of a code of practice	149
	Member state action on citizenship rights	150
	Anti-discrimination legislation at member state level	151
	Voluntary measures against discrimination by employers and trade unions	154
	More information and research	164
	General employment protection	167
8.	**References**	171

ABSTRACT

In 1994 the European Foundation for the Improvement of Living and Working Conditions (Dublin) launched a project "Preventing racism at the workplace". It commissioned a report from researchers in each of the 15 EU member states, plus Norway, on measures against racism and discrimination in employment in each country. These reports provided overviews of existing research in the field. They described the circumstances of ethnic minorities and migrants in the labour market, provided summaries of national, company and trade union policies on ethnic minorities/migrant workers, listed obstacles and facilitators to present and future integration, and suggested strategic options to enhance anti-discrimination policies.

This report brings together material from the 16 national reports. It identifies obstacles and facilitators in the implementation of policies, and considers future strategies at both member state and EU level that could improve the prevention of workplace racism and discrimination. It concludes that an effective anti-discrimination law for the EU should cover *everyone* who works within its borders: citizens, other EU nationals, and third country nationals. The principle must be that everyone within a state's jurisdiction is protected against 'racial' discrimination, broadly defined to cover discrimination by 'race', religion, colour, and ethnic or national origin.

Evidence for racial discrimination

The national reports show how the migrant and visible minority population in the EU is disproportionately represented in poor and insecure work and amongst the unemployed, even the second and third generation migrant-descended population who have been born, raised and educated in a member state. One reason for this is discrimination. However, the concealed nature of processes of discrimination in the labour market leads to the danger of underestimating the extent of labour market racism at any one time. The national reports set out a number of different ways that such acts and their effects come to notice.

Statistical evidence: After holding constant other variables, such as education, age, sex, occupational level, and region, researchers in the UK and the Netherlands have still found higher unemployment rates for ethnic minorities than white nationals. It is clear that only a small part of this can be accounted for by the level of education and other characteristics. Similarly in Sweden, when other variables are held constant, refugees from the Middle East, Asia and Africa are found to do less well in finding work than those from Eastern Europe. Such findings strongly suggest, therefore, that racial discrimination is still a factor which operates in the labour market. Complementary and more direct evidence comes from a variety of other sources. One of these is "discrimination testing".

Discrimination testing: This method utilises two or more testers, one belonging to a majority group and the others to minority ethnic groups, all of whom "apply" for the same jobs. The testers are matched for all the criteria which should be normally taken into account by an employer, such as age, qualifications, experience and schooling. If over a period of repeated testing the applicant from the majority background is systematically preferred to the others, then this points to the operation of discrimination according to ethnic background. Tests carried out in the UK and the Netherlands have shown repeatedly that white applicants are far more likely to be successful than are equivalently qualified applicants from a visible minority background. Unfortunately, although this method is one of the most important and effective means of demonstrating the existence of the problem, it has still not been widely applied in other EU countries.

Research into the actions of employers: In the Netherlands, interviews with employers demonstrated prejudice against foreign employees and a regular preference for white nationals. Respondents interviewed for the French report were quite open about their refusal to recruit persons from North Africa and Africa generally, some stating that employment of immigrants "would detract from the firm's image". The UK report described employers who would refuse to recruit ethnic minorities for some jobs, arguing that it was not they themselves who were prejudiced, but their workforce or their customers. The Danish report describes employers' reluctance to take on foreigners as apprentices for jobs such as plumbers, as they felt customers would not like such a person in their house. A study of managers representing the largest firms in Norway found that almost 80% thought that managers do discriminate against immigrants in recruitment.

Indirect discrimination: Indirect discrimination in employment exists with job requirements or recruitment practices which, although applied equally to all, in practice treat members of one ethnic group more favourably than another. The exclusion resulting from indirect discrimination can be either accidental or intentional. The most common example of indirect discrimination was the recruitment of family members of existing employees. Thus, in a largely white workforce, this excluded ethnic minorities. This was found in the UK and Portuguese reports for the recruitment of apprentices, and in many instances in the Netherlands. In Denmark, many companies where employers used to recruit new employees through the Labour Exchange now mainly recruit new workers by asking their employees to find someone. In Germany it was found that one reason for the under-representation of migrant young people in the modern sectors of industry in Nordhrhein Westfalen was the practice of recruiting the children of employees.

Preference for the children of staff in the major public services is described as an "unwritten law" in France, widely subscribed to and encouraged by the trade unions. In Finland, it is estimated that internal and informal network recruitment are the main methods for finding employees, with employment agencies being informed about less than 30% of all vacancies. This practice, common in many other countries too, means that migrants and ethnic minorities are excluded from the recruitment pool.

Employment agencies: Officials of the Danish Labour Exchange informed a researcher 'off the record' that they take notice of the wishes of employers when they specifically ask not to be sent immigrants and refugees. The French report describes the use of coded messages written into job offers placed with temporary employment agencies which signify "no foreigners". Officials in a UK agency which specialises in finding jobs and training for school leavers and young people, described employers who would refuse to interview Asian youngsters on hearing their name, or specify 'We want a white youngster'. Many officials would voluntarily direct ethnic minority young people away from firms and schemes where they suspect they will be rejected.

Discrimination and the informal economy: The issue of discrimination southern EU member states - Italy, Spain, Portugal, and Greece - is different from how the problem is seen in other European countries. It concerns the super exploitation of large numbers of migrants, whether undocumented or not, in poor or illegal work, suffering conditions which would not be tolerated by native workers, but which they are not in a position to reject. Immigrants are actively preferred and recruited because they are cheaper, more vulnerable, and more pliable - they are less able to resist over-exploitation in terms of work intensity or working hours.

Similarly in Austria the particular legal regime that immigrants work under makes them attractive to employers because they are forced to accept working conditions far worse than those tolerated by Austrians. Immigrants in these conditions experience a perverse kind of "positive discrimination" in the selection process and then in work suffer the "negative" discrimination of conditions which indigenous workers would not tolerate. Where work is illegal, immigrants themselves are often reluctant to bring to public attention their conditions; sometimes trade unions work to expose abuses in the media, but there has been relatively little academic investigation of racist and discriminatory practices within the workplace.

Obstacles to progress

The national reports have pointed to the existence of a number of problem areas. (Not all of these apply equally to all the European countries studied.)

1. Inadequate specific information and research on the employment circumstances of migrants/ethnic minorities, and on the occurrence of discrimination.
2. The occurrence of overt racism towards migrants/ethnic minorities, and direct racist exclusion from employment opportunities
3. Practices at work of indirect discrimination. These include the use of family

connections and informal 'acceptability' criteria in recruitment.
4. A general ignorance and lack of awareness of the problems of racism and discrimination in employment on the part of many employers and trade unionists.
5. Hostility and misunderstandings on the part of employers and unions about equal opportunity and equal treatment policies, and anti-discrimination practices, as well as misconceptions about the nature of racism and discrimination.
6. Broad ideologies of resistance to anti-discrimination measures. These might be rooted in economic or market theories; alternatively they could be related to philosophies about the principle of racially or ethnically specific policies as opposed to universalistic measures.
7. Weaknesses in existing legislation against discrimination in employment in many countries, and problems with the implementation of legal and administrative measures against discrimination. Sometimes there is the absence of political will at a national level to implement the legislation which exists.
8. The lack of social, economic and political rights of 'denizens' and the related effects of 'discrimination in law' which excludes non-nationals from certain jobs.
9. The absence of anti-discrimination measures at European Union level.
10. Broader developments which undermine progress towards anti-discrimination protection, such as the spread of illegal/undocumented work, structural unemployment, etc.

Areas for action

The national reports have shown that discrimination operates in different ways and at different levels. Some of the action which needs to be taken is that at the EU level; others are at member state level. The report concludes that there are eight main areas for action:

1. Improvement of the rights of third-country nationals: The first issue is that of the anomalous status of third country nationals in the EU, and the discrimination and disadvantage related to this. There now exists a two-tier workforce - one with the right to work anywhere in the EU, and the other restricted to a single EU country. The distinction between EU nationals and legally resident third-country nationals will become wider as more opportunities develop across the EU single market for jobs, business and cultural activity, but third-country nationals will not be able to move in order to take advantage of them. The national reports have given many examples of the ways in which this disadvantage is experienced. It is important that denizens are given full rights of employment and mobility across the EU.

2. EU directive on racial discrimination: This report has shown the problems stemming from the wide variation in anti-discrimination legislation between member states. Across EU countries, measures to combat discrimination are variable in their scope and effectiveness, and in some cases hardly exist. Many member states are at quite different stages of developing law and practice to deal with racial discrimination in employment, and in some cases protection is wholly inadequate. Member states are unlikely to introduce measures which are truly effective unless encouraged to do so by a directive at the European level. A directive would lay down a common basis in goals to be achieved through legislation, whilst allowing each national government the flexibility to deal with its own particular problems

3. EU initiation of a code of practice: Codes of good practice against discrimination in employment are currently in use in the UK and the Netherlands. A code gives guidance to help employers and others to understand the law, and sets out policies which can be implemented to help to eliminate racial discrimination and enhance equality of opportunity in the workplace. A code can give practical guidance to explain the implications of a country's anti-discrimination legislation, and can recommend measures to reduce the possibility of unlawful behaviour occurring. In order to encourage the adoption of such a code at member state level it would be possible for the EU to initiate a code of practice to combat racial discrimination in employment, similar to the code it initiated on sexual harassment.

4. Member state action on citizenship rights: In those countries where it is not easy to achieve citizenship, there are employment disadvantages which are unacceptable, particularly when this applies to legally-resident people born in an EU country of migrant parents. There is a need for greater official tolerance of *dual* citizenship. Even when legally-resident foreign workers do not want to become naturalised citizens of their new society, a new status of denizenship could be granted to them, similar to those of dual nationals, entitling them to all the rights of citizenship within their country of residence, including the right to participate in national elections.

5. Anti-discrimination legislation at member state level: The national reports revealed weaknesses in existing legislation against discrimination in employment in many countries. Sometimes there is the absence of political will at a national level to implement the legislation which already exists. One consequence of having anti-discrimination legislation that is weak, or weakly applied, is that there remains little pressure on employers to adopt more 'voluntary' measures such as the use of codes of practice, or positive action, in those countries where such measures are officially allowed or encouraged. A starting principle of domestic legislation should be to make racial discrimination a criminal and/or a civil offence. Legislation must include both a strong prohibition of racial discrimination in all its forms, together with a committed prosecution policy. It is also important for legislation to recognise the distinction between direct and indirect discrimination.

6. Voluntary measures against discrimination: As well as laws against discrimination, there is a need for the stimulation of a range of social policy initiatives against racism and discrimination, including equal opportunities programmes, codes of practice, positive action, education and information provision, and training. The law can be used not just to prohibit, but to allow, to encourage and to facilitate. It can provide a stimulus for organisations to undertake 'voluntary' action, such as adopting equal opportunity policies.

7. More information and research: The report describes how national reports were hindered by incomplete national statistics, and more specifically by lack of research on the experiences of migrants in employment, and on discrimination. In many countries there was relatively little or no such research to refer to, little public awareness of discriminatory practices, and therefore little debate as to their implications for social exclusion. The acceptance of a notion of 'no problem here' means there is little incentive for research, the absence of which then reinforces the idea that there is no problem. Until broader awareness of the various processes of discrimination and exclusion are identified and discussed, there can be no progress in related social policy developments against exclusion.

8. General employment protection: Even with the best measures, anti-discrimination law and practice will have a limited impact in the context of a general degradation of work. Anti-discrimination protection can only be effective in the context of reasonable minimum standards of employment protection. At an EU level this issue has been addressed through the Social Charter and the social chapter of the Maastricht Treaty. Even in a country with strong anti-discrimination legislation, if standards of general employment protection are weak, then in practice the anti-discrimination measures are significantly undermined. In some countries with higher standards of general employment protection these often benefit migrant workers along with indigenous workers, but if anti-discrimination measures are absent or weak, then its migrant and ethnic minority workforce are unable to seek protection those extra disadvantages suffered only by visible minorities.

Without a high general standard of employment protection, the existence of anti-discrimination laws will emphasise divisions in employment, with only those people with relatively secure jobs and the protection of a trade union being in a position to insist on their rights. Those more vulnerable and disadvantaged workers in marginalised employment with the least access to the law will find anti-discrimination legislation almost irrelevant. Clearly, what is needed are both elements: general employment protection measures, and more specific anti-discrimination measures in all EU member states.

INTRODUCTION

In 1994 the European Foundation for the Improvement of Living and Working Conditions (Dublin) launched a project "Preventing racism at the workplace in the European Union". It commissioned a report from academic researchers in each of the then 12 member states on measures against racism and discrimination in employment in each country. Later, reports from the new member states - Austria, Finland and Sweden - were added, plus one from Norway, which requested participation in the project although not a member of the EU.

The national reports were written by the following:

Austria	August Gächter, Institut für Höhere Studien und Wissenschaftliche Forschung, Vienna
Belgium	Albert Martens, Katholieke Universiteit Leuven
Denmark	Jan Hjarnø, Danish Centre for Migration and Ethnic Studies, Sydjysk Universitetscenter, Esbjerg
Finland	Elina Ekholm, Maarit Pitkänen, University of Helsinki Vantaa Institute for Continuing Education
France	Véronique de Rudder, Maryse Tripier, François Vourc'h, Unité de Recherches Migrations et Société, Université Paris 7
Germany	Nora Räthzel, Institut für Migrations und Rassismusforschung e.V., Hamburg
Greece	Rossetos Fakiolas, National Technical University, Athens
Ireland	NEXUS Research Cooperative, Dublin
Italy	Giovanna Campani, University of Florence; Francesco Carchedi, PARSEC, Rome; Giovanni Mottura, University of Modena; Enrico Pugliese, University of Naples
Luxembourg	Serge Kollwelter, Association de Soutien aux Travailleurs Immigrés, Luxembourg
Netherlands	Mitzi Gras, Frank Bovenkerk, Willem Pompe Institute, University of Utrecht
Norway	Jon Rogstad, Institutt for Samfunnsforskning, Oslo
Portugal	Maria Leonor Palma Carlos, Genoveva Calvão Borges, Instituto de Estudos para o Desenvolvimento, Lisbon
Spain	Lorenzo Cachón, Departamento de Sociología, Universidad Complutense de Madrid
Sweden	Maritta Soininen, Mark Graham, Statsvetenskapliga institutionen, University of Stockholm
UK	John Wrench, David Owen, Centre for Research in Ethnic Relations, University of Warwick

These reports did not generally include original research, but provided overviews of existing research in the field. They described the circumstances of ethnic minorities and migrants in the labour market, provided summaries of national, company and trade union policies on ethnic minorities/migrant workers, listed obstacles and facilitators to present and future integration, and suggested strategic options to enhance anti-discrimination policies. This report brings together material from the 16 national reports in order to produce an overview of policies in each member state directed to prevent racism and discrimination at the workplace. The report attempts to identify obstacles and facilitators in the implementation of policies, and to consider future strategies at both member state and EU level that could improve the prevention of workplace racism and discrimination.

The major body of factual material in this report is taken directly from the 16 national reports. Only in some cases of missing information have I gone to other sources to fill the gaps. The organisation and analysis of the material is my own. In particular, Chapter 7 (Conclusions and Strategic Options) is to be seen as my own interpretation of the implications of the material in the 16 national reports, and does not necessarily represent the views of the Foundation or of the other national reporters. Nor does the content of each of the national reports necessarily represent the views of the government or social partners in that country. In some cases - for example, the Netherlands and Germany - employers' and/or trade union representatives have disagreed with some parts of their national reports and have therefore provided appendices to be attached to these reports. Only a small part of each national report is reproduced in this consolidated report. The full national reports themselves, with all their statistical detail for each country, can be obtained directly from the Foundation in Dublin.

John Wrench

Centre for Research in Ethnic Relations
University of Warwick

Danish Centre for Migration and Ethnic Studies
South Jutland University Centre, Esbjerg

1. BACKGROUND: MIGRANT WORKERS IN EUROPE

1.1 LEGAL CATEGORIES OF WORKER IN THE EU

The working population of the EU can be divided into five main categories in terms of legal status:

1. Citizens living and working within their own country.
2. Citizens of an EU member state who work in another country within the Union.
3. Third country nationals who have full rights to residency and work in a member state.
4. Third country nationals who have leave to stay on the basis of a revocable work permit for a fixed period of time
5. Undocumented or 'illegal' workers

1. Citizens living and working within their own country.
These citizens have full rights in law: socio-economic rights (e.g. guaranteed access to the provisions of the welfare state) and political rights (e.g. the right to vote and be eligible to stand in national elections).

2. Citizens of an EU member state who work in another country within the Union (EU denizens).
Citizens of an EU member state have the right to live and work in another member state, and bring in close relatives regardless of their nationality. They can move and reside freely within the EU, and can vote and be eligible to stand in local and European parliament elections. They in theory enjoy the same rights as the nationals of the country they have moved to. However, in practice they may find themselves with less rights than nationals of that state, in, for example, being denied equal access to some public sector jobs.

3. Third country nationals who have full rights to residency and work in a member state (non-EU denizens).
As nationals of a non-EU country these workers have almost all the rights of a full citizen, but there are important exceptions. They may be formally excluded from access to some public sector employment. They do not possess EU citizenship rights - for example, the right to move to another member state. They may only visit another member state for a maximum of three months and have no permanent right to work or reside there.

4. Third country nationals who have leave to stay on the basis of a revocable work permit for a fixed period of time
These are similar in position to those in category 3 but with fewer rights and a weaker position in the labour market. Often category 3 workers began as workers in this category. A permit may be for a few months for a restricted activity or geographical

area, or for several years, for any activity or area. Some from this group will over time fall into category 5 of 'illegal' workers when (a) they remain in the country after their work permit runs out or (b) they take work in a field not covered by their existing permit.

5. Undocumented or 'illegal' workers

These may range from recent political refugees whose status has not been recognised, to people who have worked in the EU for many years without any legal rights to residence or employment. There are more of these workers in the south of Europe than in the north, although it seems that illegal work is growing in countries of the north too.

Visible minority status

The above five categories reflect formal status, and a continuum of rights ranging from full rights and privileges of citizenship in category 1 to relatively few rights in category 5. However, formal citizenship constitutes only one of the major dimensions of status in the EU. Another major dimension also produces a hierarchy of inequality, but informally: this is the criteria of ethnicity or skin colour, which identifies a person as a member of a 'visible' minority. Visible minority status cuts across the citizenship divisions listed above and produces new gradations of inequality. Thus even those people with full and formal citizenship rights can suffer disadvantage in the labour market on the grounds of colour.

All the above five categories of legal status can therefore be further divided into two: white and non-white, or visible minority. In the first two categories, EU citizens living in their own country, and EU citizens working in another EU member state, the non-white groups form a minority. In the next three categories they are more likely to form a majority. In all categories, generally speaking, the non-white workers are likely to suffer disadvantage at least relative to the white members of that legal category. Paradoxically, the relative disadvantage suffered through racial discrimination for citizens in categories 1, 2 and to a lesser extent, 3, constitutes a more visible and serious social issue precisely because they have more formal rights. They have justifiable expectations of fair and equal treatment and are more likely to be in positions where they are in competition in the labour market with white workers. An increasing proportion of visible minorities within these categories will have been born and educated in an EU country. Further down the hierarchy, it becomes less easy to demonstrate the extent to which the relative disadvantage in employment experience is a result of racial discrimination, partly because the disadvantage on formal and legal grounds is greater and more obvious, and because workers in these categories are less likely to be competing with white nationals in the same labour market. By the time we get to the category 5 workers in the illegal labour market, it is difficult to separate out the effects of 'racism' from the straightforward exploitation of a relatively powerless group of workers. To talk about racial discrimination in the conventional sense is less appropriate as these workers are often in a different labour market to 'normal' citizens. Nevertheless, it is clear that racist beliefs can be drawn upon as an ideology of justification for exploitation which occurs at this level.

1.2 DEFINITIONS OF RACISM AND DISCRIMINATION

The international convention whose object is to prevent racism and racial discrimination is the International Convention on the Elimination of All Forms of Racial Discrimination, (ICERD) which was adopted by the UN Assembly on 19 December 1965. The first part of it defines what is meant by racial discrimination:

> 'The term 'racial discrimination' shall mean any distinction, exclusion, restriction or preference based on race, colour, descent or national or ethnic origin, which has the purpose or effect of nullifying or impairing the recognition, enjoyment or exercise, on an equal footing, of human rights and fundamental freedoms in the political, economic, social, cultural or any other field of public life' (Banton, 1994).

More narrowly, discrimination in employment can be said to occur when migrants/ethnic minorities are accorded inferior treatment in the labour market or in the workplace relative to nationals/whites, despite being comparably qualified in terms of education, experience or other relevant criteria.

This is not the place to go into an academic discussion on the meanings of the concept racism. It is argued that there are qualitatively different racisms in different social contexts and historical periods, and according to whether the exclusionary doctrine or practice is directed against culturally or biologically defined difference (Miles, 1993). Certainly in Europe there is great variety and complexity both in the ideologies of exclusion and in the groups who are victims of its practical manifestations. Often, racism and discrimination are manifested against non-white formerly colonised peoples, as in the UK. Sometimes racism is expressed as anti-foreigner, rather than, for example, anti-black, hence the frequent use of the terms 'racism and xenophobia' together. In Germany the main issue is seen to be 'discrimination against foreigners'; and the word 'racism' (Rassismus) still tends to be limited in its associations to anti-Semitism and the Nazi ideology (although the word Rassismus is coming to be used in a way closer to the British use of the term 'racism' - Dummett, 1994). Sometimes there can be discrimination in European countries against people with very little - or no - phenotypical difference, as exhibited, for example, in hostility to the Jews in Austria, to southern Italians in the north of Italy, or to gypsies, Romany or Travellers in Spain, Italy or Ireland. It has been argued that the prejudices which came to the surface during the 'head-scarf' issue in France are less 'racist' in a strictly defined sense, but 'anti-Islam'.

Criteria which mark a group for unjustified inequality in treatment may vary in different member states (Rex, 1992). For example, in many countries a visible minority group characterised by a different native language represents a target group for prejudice and for differential treatment. Turks or Moroccans in Germany or the Netherlands constitute groups which are visibly and linguistically different, and sometimes language is used to justify exclusion from jobs or promotion opportunities. However, there are also migrant groups who speak the same language as that in their new country, such as Surinamese in the Netherlands, West Indians in the UK, and Algerians in France, and it is by no means clear that these suffer less discrimination than the others. Furthermore, in Germany there is one recent migrant group who despite not speaking German and being seen to have a different culture, are *not* seen as posing a 'problem'. These are the Aussiedler, the so-called 'ethnic Germans' - populations from Eastern European countries, mainly from Russia and other areas of the former Soviet Union and Poland, whose ancestors left for the East some four to eight hundred years ago. When issues of migration are discussed in Germany, and problems of integration raised, the only groups that attract the attention of politicians and social scientists are workers from the former countries of recruitment, and asylum-seekers.

Another example of a criteria which elicits qualitatively different treatment in different countries is 'blackness'. Whereas in some European countries, such as the UK, some of the worst prejudice is directed at black people, in France the worst form of discrimination is suffered not as much by black African and Caribbean groups as by North Africans.

It is important that academics continue to develop more sophisticated analytical tools to distinguish the full complexity of the different exclusionary ideologies and racisms which operate in different national, cultural and historical contexts. However, from the point of view of this report these distinctions are less important. There are similarities between all of these different forms of prejudice and discrimination, and, more importantly, common practical and policy implications. For the purposes of this report the following definition of racism will be assumed (see Vasta, 1993):

> 'Racism' will be considered to be the process whereby members of social groups categorise members of other groups as different or inferior on the basis of real or imagined physical or cultural characteristics, and which serves the purpose of legitimating inferior treatment, exclusion or exploitation.

This report addresses the issue of employment discrimination covering all the five legal categories of worker, and addresses both the formally-based and informally-based sources of inequality described above, including the operation of racism and discrimination in all its various forms. The report concludes that an effective anti-discrimination law for the EU should cover *everyone* who works within its borders: citizens, other EU nationals, and third country nationals. The principle must be that everyone within a state's jurisdiction is protected against 'racial' discrimination, broadly defined to cover discrimination by 'race', religion, colour, and ethnic or national origin. The European Convention on Human Rights is based on a similar principle of universal coverage (Dummett, 1994).

1.3 TERMINOLOGY IN DIFFERENT COUNTRIES

International comparisons undertaken by research workers run up against the problem of a lack of uniformity in the terminology used in different societies. As the French authors state, these differences are often rooted in theoretical - or, more exactly, epistemological - differences, and often derive from preoccupations of an essentially political nature. This is most certainly the case as regards immigrant populations and their descendants, and cultural, ethnic or 'racial' minorities. The official or semi-official terminology each country employs to classify such population groups is clearly directly linked to the nation's history and 'founding myths', to its colonial past and to the associated conditions on which nationality is conferred. Thus not only is there different terminology in different countries; the varying historical and cultural overtones of these terms means that it is difficult to find a universally acceptable way of describing those social groups which are relevant to this report. The terms alien, foreigner, immigrant, migrant, or ethnic minority are all used (sometimes differently) in different member states.

In the **UK** the words 'migrant' or 'immigrant' are rarely used. Common usage employs the term 'ethnic minorities', which generally means those visible minorities who migrated from the ex-colonies (mainly in the Caribbean and the Indian sub-continent) after world war two, and their descendants. In the UK most ethnic minority residents are full British citizens; therefore, to talk of them as 'foreigners' is incorrect. The term 'immigrant' is seen to be misleading, and almost insulting, particularly for those who were born in the UK. The term 'Asian' is conventionally employed to refer to people from India, Pakistan and Bangladesh. Some British academics use the term 'black' to describe both Asian and Caribbean groups; however, the British Census does not adopt this usage of the term black, restricting it to 'Black-Caribbean', 'Black-African' and 'Black-Other'.

In the **Netherlands** the concept 'ethnic minorities', as used in government documents, refers to ethnic groups which are target groups of the Dutch minorities policy, and includes non-nationals as well as nationals. The central objective of this policy is to increase the integration and participation in Dutch society of those migrants who are considered to have settled permanently in the Netherlands. The ethnic groups who are targeted by this policy are characterised by occupying a predominantly low socio-economic position and by being considered poorly 'integrated'. They are: the Antilleans, the Surinamese, the Turks, the Moroccans, the Spaniards, the Italians, the Yugoslavs, the Greeks, the Cape Verdians, the Moluccans, the Portuguese, the Tunisians, refugees, gypsies (and even 'caravan dwellers' who, whilst not constituting an ethnic minority, are nevertheless a target group of Dutch minorities policy on the basis of their relative social deprivation). Another term sometimes used in the Netherlands is that of 'allochtones' (non-indigenous), which refers to people of a different socio-cultural origin coming from a foreign country, whatever their current nationality.

Although the term 'ethnic minorities' is used in the UK and the Netherlands, in many other countries the use of this term would be inappropriate. 'Ethnic minorities' refers instead to long standing ethnic groups within their own nationalities, such as German speakers in Northern Italy, or Basques in Spain. Often official usage will allow the use of the term only in this narrow context. For example, in **Greece** there is only one officially recognised ethnic minority: the religious one of the Greek Muslims in the northern part of Greece. Of the other groups with a different identity living in Greece, the official position is that by and large many of them have been assimilated, and the remainder are too small. Therefore the term 'ethnic minority' does not apply to any of them. The term is not used to refer to the more recent groups of migrant workers, and as in **Spain, Italy** and **Portugal**, these are generally referred to as 'immigrants' or 'foreign workers'. This is also the case in **Norway**, where a new official definition of immigrant was formulated in 1993 to include persons with two foreign-born parents, allowing both first and second generation immigrants to be covered.

In **Sweden** the word "immigrant" is used. Sweden has traditionally attempted to avoid the creation of 'ethnic minorities', which have been seen as contrary to the aims and spirit of the country's integration policy. Even Sweden's indigenous minority, the Samer or Lapps, are not accorded full ethnic minority status although some minor concessions have been made to their demands. This is also true of the Finnish population in Sweden. The Finns are by far the largest immigrant group with long historical connections as part of a colonial past. While the Finnish group has come further than any other immigrant group in having some of its demands accepted, it is still not regarded as an 'ethnic minority' by the authorities. According to the Swedish National Immigration Board (SIV), there is no generally accepted definition of "immigrant" in use today. The widest definition includes all who are born in another country and their children, though many in this category would not define themselves as such. A narrower definition covers foreign citizens born abroad.

In **Denmark** the word 'immigrant' is commonly used. The Danish definition of an ethnic minority is a group of people indigenous to Denmark but with close cultural and linguistic links to another nation. The only minority in Denmark recognised by law is the old indigenous German population in South Jutland, which has certain rights such as the right to speak their own language, start their own schools, participate in local Danish elections, own newspapers and access to other media and, finally, the right to maintain religious and cultural connections with Germany. No other ethnic, religious or linguistic group has been granted similar wide ranging minority rights. Consequently, no group of immigrants has been recognised as a minority.

In **Luxembourg**, reference is usually made to 'immigrant workers', a term which continues to be used to describe all non-Luxembourger workers despite the creation of the European Union. The use of the term 'ethnic minority' is rare. For the **German** government, only German nationals can be ethnic minorities. Those officially recognised are German gypsies and the Danish and Sorb minorities. Turks and other immigrant groups are not recognised as constituting an 'ethnic minority'; official German usage is likely to employ the term 'foreigner' (Ausländer). The writer of the German report prefers to use the term 'migrant workers', even though the majority of the population to which she refers are not migrants any longer; they have become settlers. In addition, their children and grandchildren have not migrated from anywhere - they were born in Germany and have lived there ever since. Nevertheless, the use of 'ethnic minority' is inappropriate in Germany not only because of its very specific official usage, but, more importantly, because populations of migrant origin in Germany do not define themselves as 'ethnic minorities'. Whenever they voice their demands in public, most of their organisations stress their members' status as immigrants (Einwanderer). This has to be understood as a conscious reaction against the government's position that Germany is not a country of immigration. It is likely that, in the future, the term 'migrant', which is increasingly used by social scientists and also in public discourse, will replace the term 'Ausländer', as blanket use of the term 'Ausländer' becomes discredited.

Another contrast in terminology usage between the UK and Germany is the idiosyncratic British use of the word 'race' or 'racial' minorities. 'Race' is usually used in the UK as a social construct, with no correspondence to any biological reality. Many British writers prefer to use the term in inverted commas so as to emphasise this point. However, whereas in the UK and USA it is largely accepted that 'races' are a social construction and not a biological fact, this qualification would still not legitimate its use in Germany, where 'race' has a clear biological meaning and is therefore hardly ever used, (except by self-confessed racists). Similarly in **Austria**, any reference to 'race' as a distinguishing criterion is regarded as indicative of an extreme right-wing political stance and therefore avoided by most people. In daily life there is little use of the word "racism"; instead there is the expression "hostility to foreigners" (Ausländerfeindlichkeit) or xenophobia. The Austrian report focuses primarily on 'foreigners' - persons of non-Austrian citizenship - rather than 'immigrants', which would also include naturalised immigrants. It does not conern itself with the ethnic minorities created in the late 19th century in the process of centralisation and nation-state formation. These are to be found in agrarian areas along the southern and south-eastern border. They are distinct from the rest of the population only in the language habitually used, although it is safe to assume they all also speak German.

In **Ireland** there are few immigrants as such, and these are not perceived as a social issue. Instead an ethnic minority group is seen to be most relevant to this report, namely the indigenous Travelling Community, which is now accepted as a distinct ethnic group based on their values, beliefs, customs and nomadic way of life. These are acknowledged to have suffered from endemic levels of prejudice and discrimination which have contributed to extreme disadvantage and social exclusion. Similarly in **Spain** gypsies constitute an important ethnic minority. This minority is important both because of the large number of people who constitute this group and also because of their social and cultural impact in Spanish society. The number of gypsies living in Spain is similar to or even higher than that of foreign residents in Spain. They are the least valued group in Spanish society, and thus the most vulnerable to discriminatory practices (CIRES, 1992). However, unlike Ireland, there is a large and increasing immigrant population in Spain. Immigration has become a new 'social fact', experienced as a problem by Spanish society. The presence of the new immigrants - the 'real' foreigners - has led to the creation, in the Spaniard's mind, of a social image of a new 'them' as different from the previous historical 'them' in Spain, the gypsies (Calvo, 1990; Martín et al, 1994). Thus the Spanish report analyses the issues involved in the integration of foreign workers in terms of 'immigrants' rather than 'ethnic minorities'.

In **France** the term 'immigrant' (immigré) is the category most favoured by popular usage, the one most frequently used in political speeches, in media presentations, and in conversation. Its legal or accurate meaning contrasts with its social usage. Official statistics define 'immigrants' as foreign persons, or persons who have acquired French nationality, born outside Metropolitan France, which includes in particular - although they are neither foreign nor French by acquisition - persons with French nationality by birth, born in the Overseas Departments and Territories (in particular, the French Antilles). However, this statistically precise meaning of the term contrasts with its meaning in everyday usage. The word 'immigrant' has long been used effectively as a synonym for 'immigrant worker', denoting someone who comes to work temporarily in unskilled labour. The employment crisis has added new social overtones: the 'immigrant worker' is now gaining new pejorative overtones of simply an 'immigrant' as a competitor in the arena of unemployment relief and a 'profiteer' of social welfare provision. In fact, both French nationals and foreigners who may never have actually migrated, including children of 'immigrants', who are themselves French nationals, are routinely classed as 'immigrants'.

In France the concept of 'ethnic minority' is very little used. Ethnicity is not a historical reality defined as such in France, and its implications continue to be denied or disguised by means of other categories, at least officially. This reflects the French universalist, republican tradition which does not easily allow for ethnic difference, in contrast with some other Northern European countries.

In **Belgium**, like France, there is a difference between the strictly accurate meaning of the term 'immigrant' and its conventional usage. Although in its broader sense it means 'people originating from a foreign country', sociologists and others define immigrants more narrowly as non-Europeans who have usually, but not always, come to the host country as foreign labour and who often find themselves in a disadvantaged social position. In Belgium, the term is usually used to refer to immigrants from the Maghreb and Turkey. Another term sometimes used in Belgium is that of 'allochtones' (non-indigenous), which is used in the Netherlands and, by extension, in the Flemish-speaking part of Belgium.

Generally, in this report, the terms used will be 'migrants' and/or 'ethnic minorities'. The term 'visible minorities' will also be used. However, when this report quotes from the individual national reports it will use the same terminology employed and deemed suitable by the authors of those reports.

1.4 DIFFERENT MIGRANT/ETHNIC MINORITY GROUPS IN THE EU

It is not the task of this report to set out in empirical detail descriptions of the various migrant groups or ethnic minorities who exist in each EU member state (and Norway). We should note from the start that the 'problem area' of this report is not the migrants themselves but the policies of the member states. What defines groups as relevant to the subject of this report is how they are regarded and treated in different member states. Those particular social groups which are most relevant to the considerations of this report will vary from member state to member state, not just because the countries from which migrants originate are different but because, as shown above, the same ethnic minority group may be perceived and treated differently in different member states.

Britain, France, Belgium, Germany, the Netherlands, Sweden and Austria have, relatively speaking, the largest migrant or visible minority populations. Denmark, Greece, Ireland, Luxembourg, Portugal, Finland and Norway have relatively smaller and more stable migrant/visible minority populations, although Portugal and Greece, along with Spain and Italy, have been experiencing an increasing influx of often 'illegal' migration. The most numerically important third country nationals resident in the EU come from Turkey, Morocco, Algeria, Tunisia, the former Yugoslavia, the Indian sub-continent and the Middle East. There are also significant numbers of foreign-born residents who are not third country nationals in that they hold the citizenship of their country of settlement: these include immigrants from the Indian sub-continent, the West Indies and other countries of the New Commonwealth in the case of the UK; Indonesians and Surinamese for the Netherlands, from Guadeloupe and Martinique for France, and from the Cape Verde Islands for Portugal.

Brief summaries of the circumstances of migrants and ethnic minorities within individual countries and in their labour markets is set out below:

1.4.1 AUSTRIA

The population of non-Austrian citizenship in the 1991 census stood at a little over half a million, out of a total population of close to eight million. It is now estimated to be at about 715,000 with about 600,000 thereof requiring a residence permit.

For most foreign nationals, access to employment is dependent on some kind of permit being issued by the Public Employment Service over and above the residence permit required for legal residence. Some categories of foreign nationals do not require a labour market permit, the most important being refugees granted asylum for an indefinite period of time, citizens of member countries of the European Economic Area plus (since 1994) their third-country citizen spouses and children under the age of 21.

Foreign nationals, in order to be an active part of the labour force, require both a residence permit and a labour market permit. There are four different kinds of labour market permits, none of them permanent. Access to the labour market is tightly controlled. The law sets an absolute ceiling to the foreign labour force, (currently nine per cent of the total labour force). Ceilings are regularly exhausted, meaning that no new permits can be issued. This leaves many legally-resident people without the possibilty of legal employment. The victims are primarily women returning to the labour market or entering it for the first time after raising a family, young immigrants with less than three years of residence (unless they are Bosnian refugees), and people remaining unemployed after their unemployment benefits have run out. All of these persons hold valid residence permits but remain excluded from legal gainful employment.

Foreign nationals are largely employed for wages rather than salaries. In 1994 more than three quarters of women and almost 90% of men received wages whereas less than half Austrian nationals, both among men and women, receive wages. Median wage rates of foreign nationals are on average about ten per cent below those of Austrian wage recipients. One fifth of foreign nationals belongs to the lowest ten per cent income group (corrected for hours worked). The reason is not unequal pay for equal tasks but systematic allocation to low-paying occupations

There is a substantial degree of concentration by industry. Eleven industries, covering about half the overall labour force, employ about 95 per cent of foreign nationals. The highest proportions are in declining factory industries such as garments, textiles, and leather, but also in other factory industries like food, chemicals and the vast metals industry complexes. Outside the factories, construction, and increasingly agriculture, are of importance, and in services it is transportation, hotels, restaurants and especially cleaning services that have relatively high shares of foreign workers. About one third of all firms in Austria employ foreign nationals (Pichelmann et al, 1994).

Unemployment
Unemployment rates vary substantially between Austrian and foreign nationals, and among foreign nationals by permit held. The unemployment rate of foreign nationals usually given in Austria is inflated because it relates the total number of foreign unemployed to only the permit-holding employed. It was reported to stand at 7.1, 7.4, and 8.9 per cent in 1991, 1992, and 1993 respectively, and at 8.0 per cent in 1994. It was about 1.5 per centage points higher for Turks than for Yugoslavs (Biffl, 1995).

At first sight the unemployment characteristics of the foreign labour force seem to be unusual in a European context, and unlike those exhibited by imigrant workers in other EU member states. For example:

- Among men the unemployment rate of the permit-requiring labour force is smaller than that of the total wage labour force.
- Unemployment rates of holders of medium-term, geographically restricted permits have been falling while those of holders of longer-term unrestricted permits and of workers dependent on a short-term single-job permit have been rising.
- The unemployment rate of holders of longer-term unrestricted permits, among men, now exceeds that of all other groups, and among women it exceeds the average of the permit-requiring labour force.
- One third of the foreign labour force is unemployed at least once per year, as opposed to one fifth of the Austrian nationals in the labour force. However, the average duration of unemployment *within* the year is only three quarters of the average duration among Austrian nationals.
- Long-term unemployment increases together with the security of residence. The less a group's right to legally reside in Austria is tied to employment and income, the higher is the share of the long-term unemployed in their total unemployment.

However, these patterns can only be understood by reference to the particular national immigration and work permit policies characteristic of Austria. These put serious pressure on foreign nationals, once unemployed, to find new employment quickly, otherwise they risk becoming 'illegal' and face deportation. Thus they have to accept whatever conditions are offered in order not to remain unemployed for too long. This explains their absence in the statistics for long-term unemployment. (See Section 2.2.1).

1.4.2 BELGIUM

In 1946, an Italo-Belgian protocol made provision for Italian workers to emigrate to Belgium to work in the coal fields. Later Belgium called on other countries to provide labour, firstly Spain and Greece and then Morocco and Turkey. During the period of major economic expansion in the 1960s, several sectors were faced with an acute shortage of unskilled labour. The result was very intensive (and semi-illegal) recruitment of unskilled workers from North Africa and Turkey, whilst migration from Spain, Portugal, Greece and, to a certain extent, Northern Italy continued.

The immigration of unskilled workers was halted in 1974, as in many other West European countries. Since then, the increase in the foreign population in Belgium has been due mainly to the birth-rate and the immigration of relatives of people already established in Belgium. New work permits for immigrants are being granted mainly to highly skilled workers (e.g. North Americans, Japanese, Scandinavians). At national level, one in ten inhabitants is non-Belgian. Some six per cent of the population are EU nationals and four per cent come from outside the EU. Of the ten main groups of foreign nationals in Belgium, only two are non-EU nationals, that is, Moroccans and Turks, who together represent 2.3% of the total population.

The labour market
Most foreign workers have been channelled towards low-skilled or unskilled jobs in a limited number of sectors (coal-mining, iron and steel, textiles, construction, domestic work, catering, and cleaning). It is in the industrial sector that foreign employees are proportionally the most numerous, and particularly so in the processing of ferrous and non-metallic minerals, as well as the manufacture of metal products (and construction). In the service sector, however, outside 'hotels and catering' and 'recovery and repairs', there are few foreign employees.

In most sectors, the concentration of foreign employees is increasing. This is a result both of the attraction (in absolute figures) of foreigners towards some sectors (chemical products, office machinery, food products, paper, recovery and repairs, etc.) and to the withdrawal of Belgians from these jobs. Foreigners and migrants of foreign origin are mainly employed as manual workers, are in unskilled or semi-skilled (manual) jobs; concentrated and restricted, within enterprises, in particular sections and departments.

A survey discovered that the conditions experienced by Maghrebian and Turkish workers - the two groups who are the main victims of intentional discrimination - are marked by certain regularities: they tend to be employed below the level of their real skills; they tend to work in unskilled and/or temporary work, and they follow fragmented and insecure 'career paths'.

Unemployment
The unemployment rate among foreigners remains, on average, more than twice as high as that among Belgians (23.2% as against 10.1% in 1991). There is a particularly heavy increase (both in absolute figures and proportionally) in unemployment in the Moroccan and Turkish population. The uneven distribution of foreigners and immigrants, by comparison with Belgian workers, becomes apparent when sectors and enterprises are undergoing restructuring, and in the case of mass redundancies and enterprise closures (see the example of the Limbourg coal-mines closure in Section 7.2.1). Immigrants are often disproportionately concentrated in these old heavy industries, vulnerable to closure.

1.4.3 DENMARK

In January 1994, there were 189,014 persons of foreign nationality in Denmark which is 3.6% of the total population; 29% of these were nationals of other Nordic countries, other EU countries or North America. The remaining 71% came from non-Nordic and non-EU states. In spite of the fact that the issue of first time labour permits has been suspended since November 1973, the number of foreign nationals in Denmark increased from almost 90,000 in 1974 to over 189,000 in 1994. This is due to family reunion, natural increase and the granting of asylum to an increasing number of refugees. The majority of labour migrants from non-Nordic and non-EU states have come from Turkey, the former Yugoslavia, Pakistan and Morocco. In some groups with foreign nationality, such as migrants from Pakistan, it has been common to take Danish citizenship. From 1979 to 1993, 82.5% of the Pakistani nationals residing in Denmark were given Danish citizenship, compared to only 8.9% of the Turkish citizens in the same period.

The labour market
When these labour migrants started to come to Denmark in the late 1960s and early 1970s the majority were employed in manufacturing industries, especially in metal industries, in positions which did not demand skilled qualifications. Some also found work in the food-processing industries, plastic and glass goods manufacturing, and in market gardening. Some of these industries were hard hit by the recession from 1972-1982. The metal industry in particular lost many jobs, and though the employment situation has improved, foreign nationals have not been able to regain their employment. During the 1970s and 1980s, migrants started to take over other types of jobs which Danes no longer wanted to do because of low pay, inconvenient working hours, or dirty and unhealthy conditions (such as cleaning, washing-up in restaurants etc.) Some have since become bus and taxi drivers, and some have started their own businesses such as small shops, restaurants, pizzerias, newsagents and greengrocers. Finally, some have become bilingual employees in schools and kindergartens.

A study published in 1986 concludes that the migrants have a labour market of their own. A far higher proportion of foreigners are employed as unskilled labourers compared to the labour force as a whole, and there are relatively few salaried employees. In addition to this, foreign workers' safety conditions at work leave much to be desired. Research carried out in the Århus Region established that employers with many immigrant employees were often in serious violation of the working environment laws. The worst violations were found in firms where immigrant workers were concentrated on a single work function. In some workplaces there is a clear tendency towards an ethnic division of labour. Immigrants and refugees primarily get the menial, dirty and unpleasant jobs, with few possibilities of changing to better positions. The Danish report describes how in some firms, people talk of 'work for Turks, work for Pakistanis and work for Danes'.

Unemployment
On January 1 1993, foreign nationals comprised 2.5% on the Danish labour market but nearly seven per cent of all unemployed. Unemployment is for some nationalities 3 to 4 times higher among immigrants than among Danes, and 50-75% have unstable

employment and are hit by periods of unemployment every year. Immigrants are affected by unemployment more often and for longer periods, and if they become unemployed, they have greater difficulty in finding new employment. Studies of the age distribution of the unemployed have shown that half the unemployed Turkish nationals are under 30 years of age compared to about 30% for Danish nationals. For foreign nationals from third countries the rate of unemployment increased in the period 1987-1991 for the 16-23 age group, while the opposite tendency was the case for Danish citizens. Younger Turks in particular suffer unemployment. Many leave school without passing the final exams, and 90% of the 16-24 age group have no education which provides them with recognised qualifications on the labour market.

Self-employment
In order to overcome the burden of unemployment and discrimination, many immigrants try to set up as small shopkeepers, grill bar owners, etc. However, this also means that the decision to become an entrepreneur springs from avoidance behaviour and not from entrepreneurial vocation as such. This, in turn, is reflected in the higher than average number of failures of migrant businesses and the precarious existence provided by most of these undertakings.

1.4.4 FINLAND

The population of Finland is more homogenous than the population of most European countries. The largest minority group are the Swedish speaking Finns, differentiated from the majority population on linguistic rather than ethnic grounds. Of a total population of just over five million, about six per cent (roughly 300,000) are Swedish speaking. The "old" ethnic minorities in Finland are Sámi and Romany populations, and smaller Jewish and Tatar groups. The new ethnic minorities are migrants. In the 1980s the Nordic countries were the most important countries of origin for migrants; in the 1990s the growth of immigration is largely due to the inflow of refugees, especially from Somalia, and to the arrival of ethnic Finns from the former Soviet Union. Migrants increased rapidly in number over the 1980s and 1990s in Finland. Nevertheless, by the end of 1994 the proportion of migrants in the total population - 1.2 per cent - was probably the lowest in Western Europe. Citizens of the former Soviet Union and Russia are the largest group of migrants, followed by Estonians and Swedes.

The labour market
In 1994 there were about 22,000 foreign workers in Finland, representing only 0.9 per cent of the total labour force. About half the foreign labour force hold work permits - citizens of the European Economic Area and Nordic countries do not need work permits. About two thirds of the immigrant workers in Finland come from other European countries. Immigrants seem to work in the 'peripheral' areas of the Finnish economy, rather than the 'core', and immigrants from Western Europe tend to obtain better positions than those coming from Africa, Asia, and Eastern Europe.

Unemployment
In Finland the unemployment rate rose rapidly, from 3.5 per cent in 1990 to 16.9 per cent in June 1995, and the unemployment rate for migrants increased dramatically

over this period. The unemployment rate for migrants is more than double that for Finns. The highest rates occur for Somalis, Iraqis and persons from the former Yugoslavia. In 1992 the unemployment rate for refugees was over three times that for Finns. According to the Finnish report, unemployment is a far more important issue in Finland than the ethnically segmented labour market, with potentially serious long term social repercussions, including the growth of racism. Self employment is not significant in the employment of migrants.

1.4.5 FRANCE

Since the 1950s the number of foreigners coming from European countries has been in constant decline (a drop of 416,535 between 1968 and 1990), a trend which accelerated after the end of the 1970s, owing mainly to the substantial reduction in the number of foreigners from EU Member States such as Italy, Spain and Portugal. Against this, the proportion of those coming from other parts of the world, North Africa in particular, has shown an appreciable increase. The major visible minority groups in France are Algerians, Moroccans, Asians, Tunisians and Turks. In 1990 France had a million and a half Maghrebians, which included 795,920 from Algeria. The visible minority population is now estimated at over four per cent.

The labour market
The level of qualifications among the 1.7 million foreigners employed in France is markedly lower than that of French nationals: they are to be found, to a higher than average degree, in unskilled jobs and, often, in casual employment. The number of foreigners employed in industry is steadily declining (-25% as against -9% for the total of workers in industry); increasing numbers are to be found in the tertiary sector (+22% as against +16%). Having been employed as unskilled labour in large industrial plants, foreigners are now becoming the main source of labour for small craft, trade and service enterprises (Echardour and Maurin, 1993). Industry no longer relies so much on unskilled labour and many sectors in which foreign workers were strongly represented are in decline.

The sectors in which foreigners find it easiest to get work are precisely those, such as mining and construction, which have the most arduous working conditions and are the least 'modern' (hence most susceptible to restructuring). This labour force is also attractive to sectors where the drive for quick returns is most intense and whose employees are particularly exposed to the vicissitudes of the business cycle. The sectors which employ foreigners are those where unemployment is highest, where people change jobs most frequently and where seniority is lowest. The rising trend of industrial accidents is giving rise to increasing concern, particularly in view of the growth in sub-contracting and the use of illegal labour: immigrants are over-represented in these statistics.

Very few foreigners are employed by the State or local authorities (5.8% of the total, compared with 23.2% for persons of French birth), a sector which offers the most stable employment. They are much more numerous in the categories 'temporary employment' (7.8% compared with 5.7%) and 'private sector employment' (76.4%

compared with 56.0%) They are thus more vulnerable than French nationals to economic fluctuations.

Unemployment
Significantly more foreigners than nationals are to be found in the ranks of the unemployed, whatever their sector of employment or socio-occupational category. Particularly hard hit are workers from non-Member States of the European Union. It is foreigners who have borne the brunt of the loss of close on 100,000 unskilled and 20,000 skilled jobs between 1982 and 1990.

1.4.6 GERMANY

The migrant population which forms the object of public debate and research today, started to come to Germany in 1955. This was due to a policy of recruitment, desired by German industry and initiated by the German government. The first contract was made with the Italian government in 1955, and contracts with Portugal, Spain, Greece, Turkey, Tunisia and Morocco followed. Those workers were recruited as 'guest workers' and were meant to return to where they had come from when they were no longer needed by German industry. Although today it is clear that the majority of migrants living in Germany now are not going to return, to a large extent rotation did indeed happen. Between 1955 and 1973, about 14 million non-German migrants migrated to West Germany, 11 million of whom returned. In 1993, 6.8 million migrants were living in Germany, which was 8.3% of the whole population (81.3 million). About 60% of the migrant population has now been living for 10 or more years in Germany. More than 70% of the migrant population between 15 and 20 years of age has been born and/or raised in Germany. The largest group amongst the foreign population are Turkish: as over a million and a half people, they constitute around one-third of the foreign population. There are also over 300,000 asylum seekers and around 50-70,000 Sinti/Roma.

The labour market
Migrant workers are concentrated in areas of manual work and highly under-represented in areas where non-manual work and more qualified white-collar work is the norm. The fact that migrant workers are also slightly over-represented in the service sector is due to their over-representation in cleaning and catering. These are the sectors with the highest percentage of migrant work. Both sectors are among the sectors with lowest pay, insecure jobs (often seasonal work), and very little prospect of promotion. Another sector with a comparatively high rate of migrant labour is the textile industry. This is mainly due to migrant women working in this sector. Although the situation of migrant workers has slightly improved in the eighties, they are still predominantly found in those sectors of the labour market where manual work is hard, and/or the prospects of promotion or even the prospects for the whole industry are limited. This is true for mining and energy, and the steel, construction and textile industries.

In the same way that migrant men are used to do the work indigenous men have abandoned for better jobs and better pay, migrant women are used for the most disagreeable, dangerous and low-paid jobs which were before done by indigenous women. Compared to the per centage of young migrants among the young population in general (16.7%), young migrants are under-represented in apprenticeship (9.4%). Although this is a higher proportion than in 1992 (7.2%), the proportion of young migrants among young people has also risen.

Unemployment
The employment of migrant workers in Germany increased from 1.6 million in 1985 to 2.2 million in 1995. However, although the absolute number of migrants in employment has been growing, so has the absolute number in unemployment, and the *rate* of unemployment is higher for migrants. Over the late 1980s and early 1990s unemployment among foreign workers worsened in comparison to Germans. The average for this period was 12.86% for foreigners compared to 8.17% for Germans (Forbes and Mead 1992). In 1995 the unemployment rate for migrants was 16%, compared to an overall rate of 9.2%.

1.4.7 GREECE

Only rough estimates can be made about the number of both the size of the foreign population in the country and of their participation in the labour force. Estimates are partly based on the 1991 census figures; however, many foreigners did not register at the 1991 General Population Census. And even the Census fails to show the dramatic increase in the number of foreigners, mostly illegal economic immigrants coming from the former Socialist and the Third World countries since the early 1980's. Most observers put the actual number of foreigners at 450,000-600,000, basing their estimates on observations in various parts of the country. Despite massive deportations and measures taken in 1993 and 1994 to restrict illegal entries, thousands of economic immigrants cross every day the land and coastal borders of the country.

Officially Greece recognises only one ethnic minority, the Muslim minority in Northern Greece. The two main minorities in the country, the Muslims and the Gypsies, count between them about 400,000 people, and these do suffer racism and discrimination.

The labour market
In the last three decades the number of foreigners employed with work permits has fluctuated between 24,000 and 34,000. Over half of them are ethnic Greeks and nationals of other European countries. Over half of the legally employed foreigners are also highly qualified and hold high level jobs. The participation rate of the foreigners in the labour force is put at 70-80% on average. For a large part of the registered foreigners it is much lower, because those of Greek origin holding foreign passports and many of those coming from the other EU countries and the non-EU developed ones are in Greece with their families. At the other extreme, migrants coming from the former Socialist and the Third World countries have a very high participation rate.

Even higher, 95 per cent or more, is the participation rate among the illegal economic immigrants. No matter how many illegal immigrants are arrested and deported by the police, the fact remains that Albanians, Poles and nationals of Third World countries work everywhere in Greece, employed in practically all productive branches. In many construction works, animal husbandry businesses and small retail trade firms about one in three employed persons is a foreigner. Thousands of households also employ foreigners in-house helpers (mainly women for the Philippines but also nationals of both sexes from many other countries), charwomen, baby-sitters and gardeners.

Most minorities are under-represented in the public sector. By law, the overwhelming majority of the public sector jobs are reserved for Greek nationals. Although some nationals of the other EU countries are now employed in the broader public sector (no more than a few dozens), that sector is not open to foreigners. According to the data of the Ministry of Labour about one quarter of the foreigners with work permits are employed in trade, commerce and catering, and about one third in various services. Manufacturing industry and handicrafts employ about 12 per cent of the total, and transport and communications also about 12 per cent. Banking and insurance, construction and agriculture (including animal husbandry and fishing) employ each about 4 to 6 per cent of the registered foreigners.

The Muslim religious minority counts about 50,000 labour force participants and its proportion in the total registered labour force is about 1.2 per cent. Very few Muslims are employed in the various public corporations and even fewer are civil servants; and there is hardly any Gypsy employment in either the civil service or the broader public sector, where the most prestigious, secured and relatively well paid jobs are found. The Muslims in Thrace are in the majority in most farming activities and have low participation in manufacturing industry. In some urban centres they are also in the majority in trade.

Because many Gypsy women do various jobs and Gypsy children take active part in helping their working parents, the about 350,000 Gypsies have an actual activity rate considerably above the national average. The Gypsies engage mainly in small retail trade. They also offer maintenance and repair services which however face a rapidly declining demand. Some engage in producing hand-made goods which also face a declining demand. They are hardly any Gypsy farmers, but Gypsies do much agricultural work as farm labourers, engaging in fruit picking and similar seasonal jobs which require high geographical mobility. It is argued that without the flexible Gypsy employment, many farmers could not bring the harvest in. A relatively small number of Gypsies work in greenhouses and in animal husbandry.

Unemployment
The small number of foreigners employed with work permits do not face any unemployment because their permits are employer and job specific. The holder of the permit can change neither and therefore cannot be without a job. If for any reason the labour contract is terminated, the foreigner must leave Greece.

Self employment
All groups with a different identity mentioned above have a fair proportion of self-employed among their ranks. The Gypsies and the Muslims have a higher proportion, but their self-employed are mainly in retail trade, in personal services and the handicrafts. In contrast, there is a limited number of self-employed at the professional level.

1.4.8 IRELAND

The Irish situation is different in many ways relative to other countries in the EU. For one thing, Ireland has never been a colonial power and has not had the same relationship with ex-colonies that has been a spur for immigration to other European countries. Neither has the country been a particularly attractive destination for immigrants. With high levels of unemployment and low per capita income, emigration has persisted as an endemic social problem and despite a brief phase of inward migration in the late 1960s and early 1970s (largely involving the return of previous emigrants), the problem has persisted. With the recession of the 1980s, both outward migration and unemployment rose dramatically. The peak in emigration was reached in 1988/89, with an estimated net migration of 46,000 people. At the same time unemployment in Ireland rose from about 17% in 1986 to nearly 25% in 1992. As a result of these factors, Ireland is one of the most homogeneous countries in the EU in terms of 'race' and ethnicity.

Ireland has nonetheless over the years attracted numbers of people from European and non-European countries. The predominant groupings are people from either Great Britain, other EU countries, North America, some African nations and a range of Asian countries. These number are not significant in comparison to other countries. However, there are ethnic and racial minorities in Ireland. Perhaps the largest indigenous ethnic group is the Travellers, who are widely acknowledged to have suffered from endemic levels of prejudice and discrimination which have contributed to extreme disadvantage and social exclusion. The last complete census of Travellers was undertaken in late 1986 recording a population of 16,000 persons distributed among 2,800 households. However, more recent figures suggest that the population has been increasing over the past ten years, possibly by as much as thirty per cent.

Information on non-indigenous ethnic or racial groups in the labour market is limited. The statistical information available are not broken down into those employed/unemployed or those available for work and those unavailable for work, for reasons of age, retirement etc. It is known that the Travellers have limited access to skilled or non-manual work, and that they are over-represented amongst the unemployed.

1.4.9 ITALY

For immigrants with regular status, the countries of origin of the four largest visible minority groups are Morocco, Tunisia, the Philippines and Senegal. The 'problem area' essentially concerns these immigrants from the Third World and Romany groups of both Italian and foreign origin (usually from former Yugoslavia or Romania). (The distinction between Italian and foreign Romanies is not always taken into account: the tendency is to assimilate Romany populations with Third World immigrants and to forget that some members of these populations have enjoyed Italian citizenship for many generations.) The number of foreigners applying for (and securing) citizenship each year is very low.

Particular problems come from foreigners whose presence in Italy has never been legalised and legitimised. However, in Italy, the problems relating to immigration have not been associated with national ethnic minorities, which form a long-standing component of the Italian population and are guaranteed rights under the Constitution. Generally speaking, except in the cases of Alto Adige and the Valle d'Aosta, Italy has no sizeable ethnic or linguistic minorities concentrated in any particular area who have established a tradition of autonomy, self-organisation or independent political representation. Italy has no national minorities that are, as minorities, exposed to the risk of discrimination, and such groups are protected by strict and effective regulations at institutional level.

The labour market
Most foreigners who are resident in Italy have a work permit, whilst another sizeable proportion are holders of 'family' residence permits. However, the types of work permit held do not always correspond to the immigrants' occupational status, so that many holders of 'family' permits are economically active. The same applies to higher-education and university students.

About 50% of legally employed immigrants work in industry, 9% in agriculture and the rest work in the service sector (Ministry of Foreign Affairs, Directorate-General for Immigration and Social Affairs, November 1992). Research on the employment of immigrants in industrial and agricultural enterprises has been conducted in the north of Italy (Lombardy and Emilia Romagna). The structure of the (declared) employment of immigrants in these regions has the following characteristics: for the employment of (regularised) immigrants, industry comes top of the list, followed by the service sector (domestic and non-domestic workers) and agriculture. The trend towards employment in industry is increasing (more than 50% of immigrants were recruited during the period 1990-93); there is, however, a difference between the structure of employment in Milan (metropolitan centre), where the service sector predominates, and its structure in the other provinces of the two regions, where industry dominates. Employment in the agricultural sector is declining. However, since employment in agriculture is largely undeclared (as it is in the service sector and construction industry), the statistics are not necessarily an accurate reflection of the actual situation. Research on the agricultural sector also demonstrates that a distinction needs to be drawn between two components of demand: the demand associated with seasonal work (fruit picking) and that associated with the shortage of a national labour supply for specific, usually secure, jobs in stock-farming and horticulture.

The findings of the studies on enterprises in Lombardy and Emilia Romagna contradict the assumption that immigrants are employed mainly in sectors characterised by low levels of technology, structural instability of employment and dependence on market fluctuations. On the contrary, in some cases, there are more immigrant workers in enterprises with high levels of investment and a strong innovative bent. In Central and Northern Italy, the immigrants' living and working conditions and their utilisation of social services are reasonable, and the majority of immigrants enjoy regular employment. However, in Southern Italy and the islands, the living and working conditions and their utilisation of services are less secure:

discrimination against immigrants and social tensions (sometimes caused by competition) are a constant threat. In areas that are characterised by a significant seasonal labour requirement, foreign workers have gradually taken over from nationals. In the agricultural sector, indigenous labour is also used informally. Undeclared labour is an essential condition for the development of agriculture, which is based on illegal employment of the workforce.

Unemployment
The nationalities most commonly registered with Uffici di Collocamento (Employment Office) are Maghrebis (mainly Moroccans, followed by Tunisians), Senegalese and citizens of former Yugoslavia. Some people registered as unemployed are performing temporary, insecure work such as, for example, street selling, until more worthwhile prospects emerge.

Self-employment
According to the number of work permits of this type issued, there are some 20,000 immigrants who are self-employed in Italy. Research indicates that the category of self-employment conceals a variety of activities: from top-level posts and commercial management to street selling. Street sellers occupy a significant place among self-employed workers. Together with female domestic staff, they were the first immigrants in Italy and have since become a structural component of immigrant employment, especially in the South. Generally 'ethnic business' is still under-developed in Italy and is essentially limited to the restaurant trade in various regions, especially in major urban centres.

1.4.10 LUXEMBOURG

Luxembourg originally encouraged Italians to come and work in mines and factories, and foreign worker predominance in the steel industry lasted until World War 1. In later efforts to encourage foreigners to settle and integrate, successive governments tried to ensure that certain criteria were observed, with the result that migrants were predominantly European, white and Catholic. For the most part, foreigners in Luxembourg are European Union nationals, mostly foreign workers recruited in the south of Europe, from Italy, then Portugal, both countries of Catholic tradition. Approximately 30% of the foreigners in the total population are currently in this category with only a small per centage coming from countries outside the European Union. With the exception of a thousand or so Cape Verdeans, very few are non-white nationals. Slightly over 1,000 Cape Verdeans came to Luxembourg with passports dating back to colonial times; however, there are probably another 2,000 who opted for Portuguese nationality when Cape Verde gained its independence, or who have taken out Luxembourg nationality meanwhile.

The labour market
Luxembourg has increasingly provided work for people in the border zones of neighbouring countries. The number of border zone workers has doubled in six years, and they now constitute a quarter of the workforce. Another quarter is made up of immigrants, and native Luxembourgers fill no more than half the available jobs. The economic expansion of the last 25 years has created much new employment in

Luxembourg. Craft jobs have doubled, and the number of people in waged/salaried employment has risen from 150,000 to 200,000 in six years. This has led to reliance on foreign labour. All new jobs have been filled by non-Luxembourgers, who have been essential for the country's economic success. There are large numbers of foreigners at either end of the social scale: they occupy jobs carrying little social prestige and offering low pay (e.g. cleaning, building and catering), and management posts in international firms. In the main, foreign workers are recruited from two social groups: unskilled manual workers and highly qualified white-collar employees.

The iron and steel industry, one of Luxembourg's traditional and most important, remains the preserve of the country's working class. In other sectors of industry, there are significant numbers of foreign workers, and in commerce and catering they are almost as well represented as native Luxembourg workers. Foreign workers are to be found in large numbers in commerce and catering as well as the service sector in general. In the building industry white-collar staff and managers are predominantly Luxembourgers, while building labourers are mainly foreigners. Foreigners are under-represented among the self-employed and white-collar staff, and very few occupy posts in the national civil service. However, a large number of them work as international civil servants, working for international institutions. This reflects the presence in the Grand Duchy of administrative and service departments of the European Union. Building, commerce, banking and other market services employ very few Luxembourgers.

Unemployment
Luxembourg enjoys an expanding economy, with about 4,100 job-seekers (in early September 1994), of whom 2,800 are in receipt of unemployment compensation. It is worth noting that only those residing in Luxembourg may receive unemployment compensation; workers from the border zones do not qualify.

1.4.11 THE NETHERLANDS

In 1990, there were 2,225,000 people in the Netherlands, who, on the basis of their own native country or their parents', were to be counted among the non-native population (Tesser, 1993). This is approximately 14% of the entire Dutch population The concept of 'ethnic minorities', as used in government documents, refers to ethnic groups which are target groups of the Dutch minorities policy (see Section 1.3 above). The main migrant groups covered by this are Antilleans, Surinamese, Turks, Moroccans, Spaniards, Italians, Yugoslavs, Greeks, Cape Verdians, Moluccans, Portuguese, and Tunisians. Eurasians and Chinese are not targeted by this special government policy as these groups are not seen to have a disadvantaged position in Dutch society. There are also gypsies, and 35,000 asylum seekers per year. Approximately 900,000 people belong to the target groups of the Dutch minorities policy The four largest groups of minorities together - the Turks, the Moroccans, the Surinamese and the Antilleans - consist of almost 700,000 persons.

The labour market
In 1991, the entire economically active population, which consists of all 15 to 64 year-olds who either have a job, or are counted among the non-working population,

consisted of over seven million people. The entire ethnic minority economically active population comprised of approximately 560,000 people, of whom about 50% belonged to the target groups of the Dutch minorities policy. The Turks and the Surinamese form the largest categories of the ethnic economically active population (74,000 and 78,000 people, respectively). Third are the Moroccans, with 43,000 people, and fourth the Antilleans, with 24,000 people. The Surinamese and the Antillean economically active population consists of almost as many men as women. The Turkish economically active population consists of little over 25% of women, whilst the Moroccan economically active population consists of little less than a fifth of women (Roelandt et al, 1992).

The position of ethnic minorities on the labour market is poor, especially in comparison with the native population; unemployment among ethnic minorities is high, and they are over-represented in industry, and in jobs at the lowest occupational level. Visible minority men and women are far more likely to be working on a temporary basis than are native Dutch men and women (Roelandt et al, 1992). Turkish, Moroccan, Surinamese and Antillean men are highly over-represented in industry. Furthermore, Turkish and Moroccan men are, relatively more often, working in agriculture and the fishing industry, and are underrepresented in the other sectors, like banking and insurance. Turkish women are mainly working in industry, in parts of the service sector, and in agriculture and the fishing industry. Moroccan women are over-represented in industry, in parts of the service sector, and in the hotel and restaurant business.

Unemployment
The unemployment per centage among ethnic minorities is much higher than that among natives. For native Dutch the unemployment figure is 7% for men and 13% for women; among Turks this is 34% for men and 48% for women; among Moroccans it is 39% for men and 66% for women; for Surinamese it is 27% for men and 35% for women, and for Antilleans it is 32% for men and 48% for women (Roelandt et al, 1992). There is also a discrepancy between the duration of unemployment of natives and ethnic minorities. For job-seekers without a job, 35% of native Dutch had been long-term unemployed, compared to 57% for Turks, 55% for Moroccans, 49% for Surinamese, and 39% for Antilleans (Roelandt et al, 1992).

1.4.12 NORWAY

In 1994, immigrants (i.e. with two foreign born parents) comprised 4.9 per cent (211,200 persons) of the total population in Norway (Statistics Norway 1994). About nine out of ten of all people in the minority groups were first generation. Of all immigrants living in Norway, just over a third were from other Nordic countries, EU countries or from North America. The remainder were from Third World countries and Eastern Europe. From the Third World countries, most of the immigrants in the labour force come from Pakistan, Sri-Lanka, Vietnam and Turkey.

Immigrants constitute 3.9 per cent of the total workforce in Norway. In total, 160,100 immigrants aged 16-74 years were potential members of the labour force (Sivertsen 1995). Of these, 66,400, or 41.5 per cent, were employed, while 10,100 or 11.4 per cent were registered as unemployed. At the same time, 54.7 per cent of the native workers were employed, while 4.8 per cent were unemployed.

Compared to the population as a whole, immigrants from Asia, Africa or South and Central America are over-represented in industries such as manufacturing, wholesale/retail trade/service industries and restaurants, community social and personal services. The per centage of Africans working in manufacturing is very similar to the population as a whole. While the Indians are over-represented in the wholesale industries, Africans and people from South and Central America are over-represented in domestic service. Immigrants from Asia, Africa and Latin America are concentrated in unskilled work and in low-pay sectors, such as cleaning and domestic work, catering and so on. Immigrants from these countries include 80 per cent and 60 per cent of all foreign nationals in these types of industry. One important conclusion that can be drawn is that immigrants seem to be employed within industries with low educational requirements.

1.4.13 PORTUGAL

Portugal is not a major country of immigration. There are an estimated 140,000 foreigners, constituting 1.4% of the population. Since the 1970s immigrants have entered from Africa, and Portuguese emigrants returned from Europe and America. The flow from Portuguese-speaking African countries constitutes the largest number, mainly from Angola, Cape Verde, Guinea-Bissau and Mozambique. The most 'visible' minority is formed by the 28,000 Cape Verdeans who constitute over 40% of the regular foreign population. As well as these there are thousands of other Cape Verdeans who hold Portuguese citizenship. There is a small community of Muslims from Pakistan and Bangladesh who are mainly trades people. Irregular immigration is estimated to be between 60,000-70,000 people. There are also gypsies, and refugees from Romania, Angola and Zaire.

The labour market
The most significant visible minority, the Cape Verdeans, are employed in the building sector; they are also found to a lesser extent in processing industries, in transport, and in the public cleansing department of the municipal councils of Greater Lisbon. Women are employed in restaurants, hotels, shops, and as cleaners and domestic helps. Their position in the labour market is generally insecure, with greater vulnerability to unemployment. About 50% of ethnic minority workers have no employment contract. There is very little information available on those who have Portuguese nationality, but they include a proportion with better 'middle class' and white collar jobs.

1.4.14 SPAIN

It is only recently that Spain has become a country of immigration. At the end of 1993 there were in Spain 580,000 legal foreign residents. The volume of immigrants in 1993 represented only 1.5% of the total Spanish population. From the middle '80s, there has been a significant and progressive increase in the flow of immigrants who have entered Spain. In the '80s, this increase coincided with Spain's entry in the EU and with the economic growth of those years. In those same years there was a radical change in the immigrants' area of origin: around one third of these immigrants came from Morocco (while in 1983 Moroccans only accounted for 2.5% of foreign residents in Spain, in 1993 they represented 17%). Half the foreigners who live in Spain come from other EU countries. Eighty per cent of immigrants are concentrated in Madrid, the Mediterranean Coast and the Canary Islands.

Similar in number to the foreign population is the Spanish gypsy community. Gypsies are not only a social group or ethnic minority, but also a 'marginal ethnic minority' (Calvo, 1990). They constitute the real 'them' in the Spaniards' minds, even though they are Spanish. Surveys always show that gypsies are the most widely rejected group by the Spanish society, suffering negative attitudes even more than Arabs and other immigrants (Calvo, 1990; Izquierdo, 1994).

The labour market
The Spanish report distinguishes between three types of immigrant workers: 'settled', 'precarious' and 'illegal'. 'Settled' immigrants are those who have achieved a 'stable' integration in the labour market where nationals typically work, and a certain degree of settlement in the Spanish society. 'Precarious' immigrants are those who live in Spain in a legal situation but who have not achieved a stable integration. Finally, 'illegal' immigrants are those whose situation is irregular with regard to their residence and/or work permits. At the end of 1993, it was estimated that the total number of non-EU foreign workers was of 190,000 to 265,000. Of these, between 59,000 and 42,000 were 'settled' immigrants; between 57,000 and 74,000 were 'precarious', and between 74,000 and 150,000 were 'illegal' (Cachón, 1994).

At the end of 1993, 75% of the 115,000 foreign workers in Spain with a valid work permit (not considering EU workers) were concentrated in six activity areas: domestic service (18%), catering (13%), construction (13%), retail trade (11%, mostly peddling), farming (10%) and services to companies (8%). However, these activities only represent 38% of total employment in Spain. This sectorial concentration coincides with specialisation depending on the immigrants' origin and the area of residence in Spain. In general, immigrants occupy low qualified positions.

1.4.15 SWEDEN

If "immigrants" are defined as all those born in another country, plus their children, Sweden has 1.6 million immigrants. Major changes have occurred in the composition of the immigrant population during the last 20 years. Throughout the 1970s immigration was still dominated by the Nordic countries, especially Finland, but there was a presence of immigrants from other European countries. During the 1980s, the picture changed. In 1986, the majority of new immigrants arrived from countries outside of Europe. Immigration was predominantly from Asia during the 1980s, and particularly from Iran in the latter half of the decade. In 1993 and 1994, European immigration increased dramatically with the arrival of refugees from what had been Yugoslavia.

Non-Nordic immigration to Sweden today consists mainly of refugee immigration. In 1994, this accounted for 62 per cent of all immigration. Another large category accounting for 36 per cent of total immigration is comprised of the close relatives of refugees and labour immigrants (SIV 1995/06). Of the little over 100,000 refuges Sweden received during the period 1988-1994, over a third were asylum seekers from former Yugoslavia, with the other largest groups from Iraq, Iran, African countries and Chile (SIV 1995/06).

The labour market

In 1994, the total number of Nordic citizens in the workforce, i.e. employed and unemployed in the age group 16-64, was 91,000, and non-Nordic citizens, 122,000. In the same year, the total number of foreign citizens in Sweden was 537,000. Around 374,000 were aged between 16 and 64, of whom 213,000 were part of the workforce. This is equivalent to 4.9 per cent of the entire workforce. Finnish citizens were the largest group, and comprised 25 per cent of the foreign workforce. Among the non-Nordic citizens, Yugoslavians were the largest group, accounting for around five per cent (SIV 1995/06).

The proportion of people employed in blue collar occupations is higher among those born abroad, especially in the category of unskilled workers. Compared with the native population, immigrants are employed to a much greater extent in manufacturing industries, restaurants and hotels, cleaning and maintenance. Immigrants are employed to a much lower extent than Swedes in agriculture, forestry and fisheries. There are, however, differences between national groups. Finnish citizens belonging to the category of labour migrants are strongly over-represented among employees in manufacturing industry, particularly men. However, these are relatively few in the retail trade, and in hotels and restaurants. Finnish men are also less likely to be employed in the public sector. Within the Turkish group, employment is concentrated in the retail trade, hotel and restaurant sector. Compared with the average male worker, almost three times as many Turkish men derive their income from this sector. The proportion of women employed in the public sector is also relatively higher for the Turkish group. A particularly high proportion of Iranian and Chilean citizens, as well as citizens of African countries, derive their income from the public sector.

Unemployment

In 1989 only 1.4% of the workforce were unemployed, and for foreign citizens the figure was 3.4%. Since then, increasing numbers of immigrants have fallen outside the labour market. Foreign citizens and Swedish citizens born abroad of non-Swedish parents have been hardest hit by the changes in the labour market. In 1992, unemployment had risen to 5% for Swedish citizens and 14.2% for foreign citizens. In 1994, foreign citizens comprised 13 per cent of the unemployed in Sweden. They have lower levels of employment and higher levels of unemployment than the rest of the population for all age groups and gender. The weakness of their position in the labour market is reflected not only in higher levels of unemployment, but also in their being in short-term employment to a greater extent than the general population. Unemployment among naturalised citizens is lower than among foreign citizens, and citizens from non-European countries have significantly higher unemployment rates than foreign citizens generally.

Self employment
The proportion of self-employed is especially high among Iranians and Turks, 25 per cent and 20 per cent respectively. Among Swedes the figure was 11 per cent in 1993. The increase in the number of self-employed since 1990 is most noticeable among Iranians.

1.4.16 THE UK

Britain has one of the largest populations of ethnic minority people in the EU. In contrast to all other European countries, the British Census collects information on the ethnic group of each individual in the population (though this practice only began in 1991). Minority ethnic groups comprise 5.5 per cent of the British population, in all just over 3 million people. Nearly half of all people in the minority ethnic groups are from three South Asian ethnic groups, Indian, Pakistani and Bangladeshi, the largest of which is the Indian ethnic group. While Afro-Caribbean people represent the bulk of the remainder, there are substantial numbers of people in the three remaining categories, with 290,000 people from various smaller ethnic groups (such as Arabs and Iranians) and of mixed parentage.

The labour market
Although in theory most post-war migrant workers hold the same rights as white British workers, in practice they have held a subordinate position in employment, and for many employers they were seen as a workforce of last resort (Brown 1992). Over time, they have remained in a relatively restricted spectrum of occupational areas, over-represented in low-paid and insecure jobs, working anti-social hours in unhealthy or dangerous environments (Lee and Wrench, 1980). Research has more recently confirmed that the descendants of these workers who were born and educated in the UK are still more likely than their equivalent white peers to be unemployed, or employed beneath their qualification level (Brown, 1984; Cross et al, 1990; Drew et al, 1992; Brown 1992).

For minority ethnic groups as a whole, the distribution of female employment is very similar to that of white women. However, men from minority ethnic groups are much more likely than white men to work in the textiles and clothing, distribution, transport and communications and public health and education industries, and much less likely to work in the primary sector and the construction industry. The 1991 Census shows that Black-Caribbean men are over-represented in transport and communications and engineering, with a relatively high per centage employed in distribution. Women are relatively under-represented in the main industries employing women, but over-represented in the public health and education services. Indian men are over-represented in the engineering, textiles and clothing, distribution, transport and communications and public health and education sectors. Women are also over-represented in the engineering and textiles and clothing industries, together with distribution. Pakistani men are over-represented in textiles and clothing, distribution and transport and communications. Women are over-represented in the same three industrial sectors. Bangladeshi men are largely found in the textiles and clothing and distribution industries, the latter containing two-thirds of all men in work. Women are concentrated into the textiles and clothing, distribution, public health and education and public administration industrial sectors.

Unemployment

Minority ethnic groups suffer much higher rates of unemployment than do people from the white ethnic group. For males, the average unemployment rate is nearly twice that for whites, while the differential is even greater for females. Amongst all men aged 16-64, unemployment rates are highest for the Bangladeshi, Black-African and Pakistani ethnic groups, reaching a maximum of 30.8 per cent, nearly three times the white unemployment rate. The unemployment rate for Indian men is about 25 to 30 per cent higher than that for white men. The pattern of unemployment rates amongst women aged 16-59 displays marked differences. The Pakistani and Bangladeshi ethnic groups again display the highest unemployment rates, and are higher than the corresponding male unemployment rates, despite the fact that female unemployment rates are generally markedly lower than those for men. A quarter of Black-African women are unemployed, an unemployment rate well above those of the other Black ethnic groups. Chinese women display the lowest unemployment rate, but in contrast to men, this is higher than the rate for whites group. Indian women again display the next lowest unemployment rates, very similar to those of men in the same ethnic groups, and just lower than the unemployment rates for Black-Caribbean women.

Self-employment

The share of ethnic minorities in the total of self-employed people is slightly higher than their share of the population as a whole. However, within this aggregate pattern, Black groups are substantially under-represented while South Asians, particularly Indians, are relatively more prominent among the self-employed.

2. THE LABOUR MARKET, INEQUALITY AND DISCRIMINATION

There are good reasons for seeing employment as the key sector when considering those factors which aid or hinder the successful social integration of migrants and minorities.

> The vicious circle of discrimination and disadvantage in various social fields can probably more effectively and certainly more directly be broken by opening up the labor market and providing minority groups with some economic power than by intervening in the world of schooling and housing (Bovenkerk, 1992).

In 1990 the International Labour Office published a review of evidence of discrimination against migrant workers in six Western European countries: Belgium, France, the then Federal Republic of Germany, the Netherlands, Switzerland and the United Kingdom (Zegers de Beijl, 1990). The conclusion of the report was that discrimination in the employment of migrant workers is pervasive and widespread, although it is neither openly admitted nor easy to detect. Discrimination across Western Europe is "so widespread, systematic and irrefutable that national and international policy-makers are called upon to reflect on ways and means of combating this discrimination". Yet employers, officials and politicians continue to deny that discrimination exists. This is particularly true in countries where there is no tradition of research investigation on this subject, and/or no formal anti-discrimination legislation which could generate cases for public review. Sometimes the absence of legal cases relating to discrimination is itself taken as "proof" of the absence of discrimination (Banton, 1991).

2.1 FACTORS INFLUENCING INEQUALITY

This section of the report selects examples of statistics, research and individual cases to demonstrate evidence of discrimination in the labour market in different European countries. It is important to make the point that the operation of discrimination is often subtle and hidden, and some aspects are only discovered through specific investigations. The concealed nature of many of these processes leads to the danger of underestimating the extent of labour market racism at any one time.

However, this is not to say that the persistence of inequality in the labour market for migrants and ethnic minorities is simply a result of racial discrimination. Even in countries where most post-war migrants have citizenship and civic rights and face no legal barriers to employment opportunity, there are a whole range of forces which could still conceivably lead to the perpetuation of inequality amongst migrant groups and ethnic minorities long after the first generations have become settled and consolidated. These could be factors such as the persistence of language and cultural differences, the educational attainment of the descendants of migrants, the geographical areas they settled in, the particular occupational and industrial sectors the first migrants originally found work in, and their own aspirations, preferences and choices.

The factors which produce and maintain inequality in employment and a high rate of unemployment among migrants and ethnic minorities in the EU can be broadly categorised under four headings:

- Developments in the economy and the labour market.
- Characteristics of the migrants/ethnic minorities themselves
- Discrimination in national and EU policies
- Processes of direct and indirect discrimination

2.1.1 Developments in the economy and the labour market.

There are a range of broader developments in the economy, labour market and organisation of work which could have a direct effect on the employment prospects of migrants and ethnic minorities. These might include the decline in manufacturing employment and the old industries which have traditionally employed migrants, the increasing need for fewer but higher-skilled employees, and the relocation of employment away from the urban areas and old industrial conurbations where migrants settled, to new greenfield sites and areas where migrants are few. For example, in the UK there has been shown to be a clear relationship between unemployment and the industrial specialisation and location of an ethnic group. Pakistanis have tended to be concentrated in major urban areas of the Midlands and northern England and to be employed in manufacturing industries and manual occupations. The severe employment contraction of these areas and sectors has led to particularly high unemployment amongst this ethnic group (Owen and Green, 1992). Cyclical patterns of unemployment have affected some social groups more than others. Particularly hard hit have been young people, especially school leavers, and migrants tend to be a 'young' population.

There is also the increase in 'atypical' work, the trend towards casualisation of work, deregulation and 'flexibility, increasing part-time work, and sub-contracting, which can all have potential implications for the employment of migrants and ethnic minorities. In many countries, budget deficits have led to cutbacks in the public sector, in areas such as health and social services, which have traditionally been important sources of employment for migrant and ethnic minority women.

2.1.2 Characteristics of migrants and ethnic minorities themselves

Factors which could be relevant under this heading include the countries of origin and ethnic group, human capital skills such as educational achievements, cultural factors, traditional preferences and motivations.

One of the most important factors here is education. Across Europe the demand for technical qualifications has increased, and many foreign nationals face barriers of insufficient general and technical education. In the labour market, a higher level of education appears to be accompanied by a higher degree of participation, and the probability of being made redundant is greatest for semi- or unskilled workers.

Generally, migrants across Europe have a lower level of education than the indigenous population. In many European countries young people of migrant communities are more likely to leave school without adequate qualifications, giving them a poor start in the labour market. Added to this is an inadequate command of the host country language for some migrant groups.

However, it should also be stressed here that this is not always the case. Many people within migrant populations are well-educated, but take jobs below their level of qualification. In some countries the EU migrant populations have produced second and third generations who speak the host language as a first language, are ambitious, do well in school and achieve high qualifications. When this is the case, the reasons for higher unemployment need to be sought elsewhere, and this leads to consideration of the factors of discrimination.

2.1.3 Discrimination in national and EU policies

Although discrimination is generally though of as an individual act, it is also possible to categorise certain laws, or national or EU policies, as discriminatory. There may be policies and practices of individual member states which hinder the integration into the labour market of migrants, including citizenship policies, or legal barriers to certain occupations or sectors. The fact that legally resident denizens who have lived for 15 or more years in a member state, raised children and paid taxes, are still excluded from full membership of and participation in the country by restrictive citizenship laws can be seen as a form of discrimination.

Certain aspects of European integration, such as the single market, may cause a reduction in employment chances for migrants. The inclusion of European citizenship in the Treaty of Maastricht gave the right to reside and move freely within and between member states. However, nationals of non-member countries are excluded from these rights. The process of constructing the European Union has in itself instituted discrimination by creating different categories of people: citizens, denizens from EU countries, denizens from non-EU countries, and foreigners.

The principles of free movement laid down in the Schengen agreement ignore third country nationals, who may be established, legally-resident workers of long standing. An example of the effect of this can be seen with the closure of old industries which employed large numbers of migrants. After redundancy, EU denizens are able to look for new work in neighbouring countries, whereas non-EU denizens do not have that option. The way to gain the European citizenship freedoms set out in the Treaty of Maastricht, such as the freedom to move and reside freely within the territory of the Community, is to become naturalised: however, access to citizenship via naturalisation is not easy in many countries.

The processes of tightening the EU borders has helped to increase the number of people with insecure employment status, including undocumented workers and asylum seekers, and in some member states the laws against migrants and asylum seekers have forced more workers into the clandestine labour market. In these circumstances anti-discrimination law has severe limitations. Thus we can see that measures taken at a national European level can have an impact on both illegal working and the further labour market exclusion of settled migrants in Europe.

2.1.4 Processes of direct and indirect discrimination

Discrimination can occur in the recruitment policies and practices of organisations and gatekeepers in the labour market. Employers, trade unions, and employment agencies can all be a party to this. Sometimes directly racist practices are encountered; at other times, institutional practices might have the unintended consequences of excluding or deterring ethnic minority applicants. There may also be problematic practices within the workplace, such as differential treatment of migrant and minority employees on access to training and promotion which may render them more insecure in their employment, leading to periodic unemployment. They may be unfairly selected for redundancy. There might be problems of racial harassment, abuse, insults and violence at the workplace, whether from workmates or supervisors. One reason why migrant and ethnic minority communities may be deterred from moving to areas of new employment opportunity may be the insecurity generated by discrimination and the fear of racist experiences in new areas (Wrench et al, 1993).

A mixture of causal factors
Different politicians and social commentators often emphasise one rather than another of these four factors as the main issue in debates on the social inclusion or exclusion of ethnic minorities and migrants, and this will have implications for the related social policies which are recommended (Wrench and Solomos, 1993). For example, if structural changes in the economy are responsible for a worsening position of the migrant descended population of Europe, then broader economic policies, rather than 'race' or ethnicity specific polices are implied. If the problem is seen primarily to lie within the character and behaviour of the excluded groups themselves, then polices aimed at improving their stock of human capital or changing their behaviour are relevant. If existing national or EU policies are seen to be a major factor, then there will be pressure to modify these policies. And if discrimination is seen as the major factor, then anti-discrimination measures are important.

In reality, all of these factors have a part to play. However, the aim of this report is not to examine equally all these various factors which contribute to the social and employment exclusion of migrants and ethnic minorities in Europe. This report focuses on the last two factors, covering the 'group' discrimination resulting from unfair legal or administrative acts, and the more individual 'racial discrimination' experienced in their daily lives by migrants and visible minorities in Europe.

Whilst recognising that racial discrimination is just one factor which operates amongst many, there are good reasons for paying particular attention to it. For one thing, the factor of discrimination is often neglected in discussions on issues such as the high unemployment rate of young people of migrant descent. Whilst factors such as educational and language problems, regional disparities in employment, and structural decline in old industries are recognised and accepted as playing their part in social exclusion, there is still a tendency to underplay the routine processes of exclusion of migrants and ethnic minorities through acts of discrimination in daily life. Furthermore, it remains a fact that policies to counter exclusion at all the other levels - education and re-training policies, regional policies, language initiatives - will come to no avail and all prove to be wastes of resources if the factor of discrimination is not simultaneously addressed.

There is now a body of experience in several countries of different anti-discrimination measures which are able to be critically examined, evaluated, and made available to others. These will be considered in Chapter 3, 4 and 5. The current chapter now looks at evidence for discrimination in different member states. First it considers the legal and administrative discrimination which contributes to the reduction in employment opportunities of whole categories of people. Secondly it considers the problem of the more individualised racial discrimination in employment.

2.2 LEGAL AND ADMINISTRATIVE DISCRIMINATION

There are, of course, legal barriers to entering an EU country to find work. All member states except Portugal require migrants from third countries to have a residence and work permit, and in most member states this process has become very restrictive. Official policy within a member state might be to issue permits only in cases where there is no citizen or EU national to do the work. After a certain minimum period of legal residence and work, it is possible for migrants to obtain a less restricted work permit, or remain without a permit at all. However, in some countries there are barriers of law and of administrative practice which effectively discriminate against the employment of legally resident non-EU nationals. There are even barriers in some member states which discriminate against other EU nationals too, despite the inclusion of the concept of "European Citizenship" in the Treaty of Maastricht.

2.2.1 Legal discrimination against non-EU nationals

Discrimination on grounds of nationality is not considered unlawful in international law, provided it does not deny "a minimum of civilised treatment" which the State is required to extend to non-nationals and there is no infringement of the provisions set out in an international convention. At all events, it is generally accepted that non-nationals need not necessarily enjoy the political rights accorded to nationals and that certain of their rights may be suspended when permission is granted for them to stay in the country (Lochak, 1990). Citizens of EU countries have the right to reside, work and move freely within and between member states. Nationals of non-member countries are excluded from these rights. There are two main ways in which their rights are restricted with regard to employment. Firstly, they are restricted in their freedom to find work in other member states. Secondly, they are excluded from certain categories of jobs within the member state in which they live.

The way to gain the citizenship freedoms set out in the Treaty of Maastricht is to become naturalised; however, access to citizenship via naturalisation is not easy in many countries. For denizens who are not EU nationals there are legal barriers which add to the general insecurity of the migrant's employment position. This insecurity is a source of institutionalised discrimination in itself, and adds to the insecurity produced by other forms of labour market discrimination for migrants.

Although the above restrictions are found in all member states, they are obviously of far greater significance in those countries where naturalisation is not easy. For example, in **Germany**, some rights are explicitly restricted to Germans (see Kalpaka et al, 1992). For instance, they do not have the same freedoms of assembly or of association. Migrants can in theory be expelled if they have committed a crime or if they have to live on social security. Although such expulsions do not often occur, they produce insecurity amongst the migrant population, along with feelings of anger at being treated as a "second class" category of people. In Germany the general law setting out the limitations of foreigner status is the "Ausländergesetz" (Foreigners law). More specifically, with regard to employment there is legislation which in theory prioritises Germans and EU nationals over other employees (paragraph 19 of the 'Arbeitsförderungsgesetz' - the law concerning the promotion of labour). The "Allgemeine Arbeitserlaubnis" (general work permit) is only issued to a migrant if an employer cannot find employees amongst these prioritised groups (with Turks being prioritised among non-EU members). Exceptions are only possible under certain conditions, e.g. if language knowledge is necessary. The stipulation that no German or EU citizen should be available does not apply if within the last eight years the foreigner has been working in Germany for five years without a break. In this case s/he gets a "special work permit" - (Besondere Arbeitserlaubnis). However, if, for example, the migrant takes a six month break to go abroad in the middle of the five year period, this invalidates it. This permit can also be given to certain groups of foreigners such as family members of Germans (Beauftragte der Bundesregierung für die Belange der Ausländer, 1994). One problem with this is that young foreigners who were born in Germany still need this work permit for their first job, and even if in practice this is unlikely to be withheld, some critics see this as a symbolic form of exclusion.

In Germany since 1991 it has become easier for certain groups to obtain citizenship. Citizenship is more easily available for young people between 16 and 23 who have been living in Germany for at least eight years, and have attended school for at least six. However, dual citizenship is still in theory not available. Generally speaking, the condition for taking German citizenship is that you give up your own, except in those cases where your original country makes it impossible for you to give up their citizenship. Although in practice many in Germany do hold dual citizenship, a high proportion of those who retained their original citizenship at naturalisation are those of German ethnic origin. In general, in any country where dual citizenship is difficult to attain, the per centage of naturalisation will remain low. In some countries this means that the migrant population remains excluded by the legislation which prioritises the employment of EU nationals.

Austria is a country where the legal discrimination operating against migrant workers through national policy is so comprehensive that it overshadows any discrimination which might operate at the informal level. An array of legal instruments establishes substantial legal inequality between foreign nationals and Austrians in the labour market. As described in Section 1.4.1, foreign nationals, in order to be an active part of the labour force, require a residence permit and a labour market permit. There are four different kinds of labour market permits, none of them permanent. Access to the labour market is tightly controlled, and the law, currently, sets the foreign labour force at an absolute ceiling of nine per cent of the total labour force. As the ceiling is approached, very few new entries into the labour market are allowed, even of persons legally residing in Austria.

Amongst other things, this leads to unemployment patterns unlike those for migrant workers in other European countries, with foreign nationals in Austria exhibiting *lower* unemployment rates than Austrian wage earners, and with the unemployment rate *increasing* for those with less restrictive work permits. These patterns can be explained by looking at the effects of the legal restrictions in operation. If a third-country national becomes unemployed, he or she will not be entitled to unemployment benefit for the same period of time as for Austrian citizens. Unemployment benefits are cut short, with the most common duration of benefits for third-country nationals being only 30 weeks. Once benefits run out, and no new employment has been found, or if a new Employment Permit has not been granted, and if there are no other sources of income, destitution results. This, by Austrian law, leads to the loss of the right to reside in the country, followed by an order to leave which in turn is enforceable by deportation unless social ties are held to be stronger than the public interest in deportation. The crucial aspect here is that even if deportation is stayed, the right to remain in the country has already been lost. Further residence may be tolerated for the time being but it will be based on a visa that does not permit access to the labour market. There will be no access to legal employment or any kind of legal income.

These two elements of the law, the shortened duration of insurance benefits and the exclusion from legal income it leads to, put serious pressure on foreign nationals. In the first instance they put a time constraint on the unemployed. Regardless of the kind of permit they hold, they are under pressure to find new employment quickly in order to escape the threat of becoming 'illegal'. Thus they have to accept whatever conditions are offered in order not to remain unemployed for too long. The result is the absence of long-term unemployment observed in the statistics, but also a systematic allocation of foreign workers to the worst occupations.

The effects of this legal inequality are compounded by a further legal restriction. Foreign nationals, although not excluded from voting in works council elections, are ineligible to be elected to them. This deprives them of the opportunity to bargain over issues such as wages, working hours, and working conditions. Since foreign and Austrian workers do not often work side by side but tend to be concentrated in different occupations within one plant which are either spatially or hierarchically segregated, there are sections and strata of the workforce that tend not to be represented.

All this has the effect that foreign workers are not only under pressure to accept jobs with poor working conditions, arbitrary hours and low pay, but they also have to remain compliant within them. Foreign nationals therefore are very attractive to employers as a relatively powerless and highly flexible workforce. Consequently, foreign nationals are a preferred category of employees for unskilled and semi-skilled occupations without customer contact.

Therefore, Austria contrasts with many other European countries mentioned in this report where the continued over-representation of migrant workers in inferior employment is explained by the operation of informal practices of direct and indirect discrimination. In Austria it is the formal and legal discrimination which is so clearly predominant, and which explains why foreign nationals are systematically overrepresented in the jobs offering the worst conditions (Wimmer, 1986).

In **Belgium** citizenship is very restricted, and despite the long established existence of settled ethnic minority groups, there is no automatic right to citizenship for second and third generation Belgian-born children (Forbes and Mead, 1992). Foreign workers do not have free access to the labour market. Both the employer who wishes to take on a foreigner and the foreign worker who wishes to work in Belgium must be authorised - the former to employ foreign workers and the latter to undertake paid work in Belgium (Nys et al, 1992). Work permits are necessary for all foreign workers who wish to undertake paid work and to their employers, with the exception of EU nationals and various categories of people who do not need a work permit because of their country of origin or the nature of their work (Nys and Beauchesne, 1992).

The issues described above are particularly problematic for those third country nationals whose freedom is constrained by the need for a fixed-term work permit. However, there are also problems for those non-EU denizens who have full rights to work and residency in a member state, in that they can be denied equal access to some public sector jobs. In **France** a large number of jobs - approximately a third of all paid employment - were, until recent constitutional changes took effect, restricted to French nationals. Until 1991, access to civil service jobs was barred to all foreigners. These jobs are now open to EU nationals, except for the police, the armed forces, the judiciary and national administrations exercising sovereign powers of state. Public sector enterprises, such as the gas and electricity utilities (Gaz de France, Electricité de France), the state railways (Société Nationale des Chemins de Fer Français - SNCF), the Paris transport undertaking (Régie Autonome des Transports Parisiens - RATP) etc., also apply the rule of excluding foreigners other than EU nationals. Three and half million national and local government jobs and two and a half million jobs in nationalised or similar undertakings are thus closed to foreigners other than EU nationals. The great majority of these jobs do not involve the exercise of any real powers of state. In practice, many foreigners from outside the EU are employed in public service activities - though without enjoying the corresponding status - either under contract (which is the case, for example, of foreign doctors and assistant teachers) or under arrangements with employment associations (particularly in the social services).

Foreigners are also excluded from a variety of independent professions: they may not direct the publication of a periodical or operate an audio-visual communications service, a public place of entertainment or a private detective agency. They may not run an outlet for the sale of alcoholic beverages or tobacco or run a gambling club or casino. They may not engage in security or surveillance activities or supply services for the transport of valuables. They are excluded from a whole range of occupations connected with transport, insurance, the stock market, fire-arms and munitions.

Foreign nationals may vote in elections to the Conseils de Prud'hommes (industrial tribunals) but may not serve on them. They are also barred from the commercial tribunals and consultative bodies (chambers of commerce and industry, chamber of agriculture, chamber of trades) and from serving as a mediator or conciliator. Nor may they serve on Comités techniques regionaux et nationaux de prévention des accidents du travail (Regional or National Industrial Safety Committees). The French report makes the point that in view of the fact that, statistically, non-nationals tend to be employed in jobs in which the accident risk is high, it is hard to understand the reasons for continuing to exclude them, under provisions dating from 1946 and still in force today.

In the **Netherlands** public sector employers are allowed to discriminate against non-nationals in a limited number of cases: Dutch nationality is explicitly required for high ranking posts in the judiciary, the military, the police and the diplomatic service, and in positions involving state security (Zegers de Beijl, 1995). In **Greece** the public sector is not open to foreigners; even in the teaching profession very few foreigners are employed in the state schools. Consequently, almost all of the roughly 26,000 foreigners with work permits are employed in the private sector of the economy. Non-Greek citizens cannot be chairmen of any trade union, federation or labour centre. In **Portugal** foreign nationals are prohibited from taking public office except on the authorisation of the Minister responsible for the sector. In theory the Constitution allows that foreign nationals may exercise public service actions of a predominantly technical nature, i.e. which do not involve the exercise of powers of authority. In reality this only allows EU nationals and others who enjoy equal status such as Brazilians. Foreign nationals remain excluded from competing for entry to the public service, although, in the opinion of some commentators, this is constitutionally dubious. There is also a restriction on the employment of foreign nationals in another way: a company with more than five employees can only employ foreign nationals as long as the level of their Portuguese employees remains at 90%. Since foreign workers tend to be concentrated in certain limited sectors, this provision has encouraged the development of illegal work. The 10% ceiling can be exceeded if justified by reasons of 'public interest'.

Examples of other, lower level, legal or administrative barriers can be found in Spain, Luxembourg and Italy. In **Spain** the clearest evidence of discrimination is evident regarding unemployment benefits. In order to be eligible for unemployment benefits from the Social Security, the law requires the worker to prove his willingness and readiness to work. But if an immigrant worker is dismissed and his work permit expires, he becomes ineligible for unemployment benefits, because he does not have a valid work permit and thus isn't "available and ready" to work. The Social Court of the High Court of Justice in September 1992 recognised this contradiction:

> That the person who has worked and has had a work permit is not eligible to unemployment benefits whenever he is dismissed is contradictory. Since the worker and the employer have paid the corresponding contributions to those benefits, to be excluded from those social benefits is discriminatory. If the worker, in order to obtain a new work permit, needs a new work contract, he will obviously never be eligible to unemployment benefits. We therefore recommend to follow the case law adopted by the Central Labour Court and to

allow the foreign residents' eligibility to social benefits through the sole requirement of the residence permit (...)

Despite this declaration, many courts still follow a stricter line of interpretation, which does not recognise the eligibility for unemployment benefits for those foreign workers who do not have a valid work permit, even if they fulfil other legal requirements. Something similar was reported in the **Luxembourg** report. One individual who had been legally working in Luxembourg for 14 years was dismissed in February 1994, his work permit expiring in March of the same year. As it was up to his employer to apply for his permit's renewal, and he no longer had an employer to do this for him, the Employment Department refused to pay him unemployment benefit from March onwards as he was no longer permitted to work in Luxembourg.

Another example can be found in **Italy**. Many immigrants undertake illegal street selling. To become 'legal' they must obtain a trading licence. In theory immigrants can obtain this type of licence if they take the courses and examinations offered by Chambers of Commerce, who will then give them a certificate of aptitude for commercial activity. Yet immigrants rarely meet the necessary conditions of a certain level of education and skills, which they must be able to prove to Chambers of Commerce, and often, Chambers of Commerce show themselves to be unwilling to consider the special circumstances of immigrants. This may or may not reflect institutional racism but at least it demonstrates a rigidity that objectively perpetuates a form of discrimination.

2.2.2 Discrimination against EU nationals

Despite the rights given to citizens of the EU, in some countries some positions remain effectively closed even to nationals of other EU countries. In **Luxembourg** public sector jobs are barred to EU citizens One case which recently came to public attention was that of a Spanish national who was refused permission to sit a competitive examination organised by the National Museum of History and Art. Accordingly, the European Commission instituted an action against the Luxembourg Government on the grounds that it has not fulfilled its obligations. It made the following pronouncement:

> The Commission of the European Union does not accept this practice, and has therefore instituted an action against the Grand Duchy of Luxembourg. The purpose of this action is to establish that, by making nationality a condition for workers who are nationals of other Member States and are seeking employment as civil servants or as public sector employees in research, teaching, health, land transport, postal services and telecommunications, and water, gas and electricity distribution, the Grand Duchy has reneged on its obligations under the Treaty of Rome.

Similarly in **Greece**, by law, the overwhelming majority of public sector jobs are reserved for Greek nationals, with no more than a few dozen nationals of other EU countries employed in the broader public sector. In other EU member states such as Belgium and France, exclusion operates at an informal rather than a formal level, so that although in theory EU denizens have equal access to public sector jobs such as teaching, in practice this is rare.

2.3 EVIDENCE FOR INDIVIDUAL RACIAL DISCRIMINATION

The above section considered the exclusion of whole categories of people by legal or administrative devices. This section considers the sort of exclusion which is more difficult to recognise - acts of discrimination which operate at an individual level and which collectively build up to ensure that the opportunities of groups of people are severely undermined. Sometimes these are open acts of racism which are recognised by those who experience it, but may be difficult to demonstrate to others. More commonly, they operate quietly and are not even recognised by the victims. There are a number of different ways that such acts and their effects come to notice.

2.3.1 Statistical evidence

Sometimes data in statistical form can show patterns which suggest the operation of discrimination. Such data might be those which exist in company records, those created by academic research, or official data at a national level. For example, in 1991 the British Census for the first time began to collect information on the ethnic group of each individual, showing at a national level the unequal patterns of employment of minority ethnic groups in the UK. The UK and the Netherlands are two countries which have a large amount of statistical evidence and where there has been a tradition of research into the employment circumstances of ethnic minorities, including large scale survey research. In the **Netherlands** the operation of discrimination has been deduced from an analysis of statistical data. After holding constant other variables, such as education, age, sex, occupational level, and region, several researchers have still found a discrepancy in large data sets between the unemployment figures of native Dutch, and those of ethnic minorities (Veenman, 1990; Kloek, 1992; Speller and Willems, 1990). They conclude that only a small part of this unemployment discrepancy can be accounted for by the level of education and other characteristics. Therefore, they assume that discrimination plays a substantial part in the difference between the unemployment figures of native Dutch and those of ethnic minorities. A similar example from the **UK** comes from research published in 1992, using data from the second and third Youth Cohort Studies (Drew et al, 1992). A nationally-representative sample of 28,000 young people who were first eligible to leave school in 1985 and 1986 had their subsequent progress tracked. Even after taking account of factors such as attainment and local labour market conditions, young people from ethnic minorities were found to be more likely to experience both higher rates and longer spells of unemployment. These findings strongly suggest, therefore, that racial discrimination is still a factor which operates in the labour market.

In **Sweden** statistical patterns point to discrimination on the basis of country of origin affecting the success of refugees finding work. After other things are held constant, refugees from Eastern Europe and Latin America are found to do better than refugees from Iran, Iraq, Africa, the Far East and the Middle East. Smaller scale investigations can give statistical indications of unequal treatment. In the **Netherlands**, Verweij (1991) investigated employees leaving 107 companies and discovered that those with an ethnic minority background had been victims of compulsory redundancy more often than native employees. The **French** report describes how at a company level, when statistics exist, they show instances of differences in the treatment of foreign and French workers: discrepancies in pay, in chances of promotion, in access to vocational training, and in bonuses paid.

Nevertheless, it has to be recognised that evidence of this sort, whether at national or company level, is not *proof* that discrimination lies behind labour market inequality. Such statistics can at best suggest that there is a problem worth investigating. The evidence is a starting point: complementary and more direct evidence comes from a variety of other sources. One of these is "discrimination testing".

2.3.2 Discrimination testing

The method of discrimination testing seems to have used first in the UK, and has been adopted by researchers in many other countries. In the Netherlands it is known as "situation testing".

In the **UK** the results of testing carried out in the 1960s influenced public policy and paved the way for the strengthening of the Race Relations Act (Daniel, 1968). The method utilises two or more testers, one belonging to a majority group and the others to minority ethnic groups, all of whom apply for the same jobs. The testers are matched for all the criteria which should be normally taken into account by an employer, such as age, qualifications, experience and schooling. If over a period of repeated testing the applicant from the majority background is systematically preferred to the others, then this points to the operation of discrimination according to ethnic background (see Bovenkerk, 1992). One example of such testing was commissioned by the CRE to test labour market discrimination in those jobs for which for 'second generation' young ethnic minority people would be reasonably expected to apply. In the late 1970s researchers acting in the guise of young applicants from ethnic minority backgrounds 'applied' by letter to non-manual jobs advertised in the local paper of one English city (Hubbuck and Carter, 1980). To each vacancy was sent a letter of application from three test candidates, one native white, one Afro-Caribbean and one Asian. Each 'applicant' was matched in terms of qualifications, previous job experience, age and sex. Standard letters were used to control for content and handwriting, so that the only 'variable' was the ethnic origin of the applicant, which was made clear to the reader in different ways within the letters. This enabled the researchers to test whether there were ethnic differences in the success rates of being offered an interview. A total of 103 jobs were tested across all sectors of industry and commerce. Where all three candidates were called for an interview, this was seen by the researchers to be 'non-discrimination'. In fact in 48 per cent of the cases the Afro-Caribbean or Asian 'applicant' was refused interview whilst the white applicant was called for interview, whereas in only 6 per cent of the cases did the reverse happen. The researchers concluded that this represented clear evidence of systematic rejection on racial grounds, and that the fact that there was no difference in the success rates between the Afro-Caribbean and Asian candidates supported the view that racial discrimination was based on a general colour prejudice. This clearly demonstrated the existence of racial discrimination in employment recruitment.

Fourteen years later the CRE commissioned a repeat of the study in the same town to see if things had changed (Simpson and Stevenson, 1994). One difference from the previous study was that, after a decade of mass unemployment, job prospects were bleak for all the applicants, and in some of the job categories tested, the very low success rate for *any* candidate created methodological problems. Nevertheless, the test found that, as before, the white applicant's chances of getting an interview were twice as high as those of either the Asian or Afro-Caribbean applicant.

A final example from the UK focuses on occupations at the higher professional level. In 1993 two doctors who used a method of controlled discrimination testing were able to demonstrate quite clearly the operation of routine racial discrimination in the medical profession. An account of their research was published in the *British Medical Journal* (Esmail and Everington 1993). The researchers developed a curriculum vitae for each of six equivalent applicants, three with Asian names and three with English names. All the "applicants" were male, the same age, and educated and trained in Britain, with a similar length of experience of work in hospitals. All were applying for their first senior house officer post, and each CV was tailored to the particular post by including a short paragraph on why the candidate was applying for the job. The comparability of the CVs was confirmed by two consultants who were unaware of the purpose of the research and who were asked to rate the CVs after the names had been removed. Matched pairs of applications were sent for each post to see who would be called for interview, and when applicants were short listed the researchers immediately cancelled any interviews. A total of 46 applications were sent to 23 advertised posts. The researchers found that hospitals were twice as likely to shortlist candidates for medical jobs if they had Anglo-Saxon rather than Asian names. (The Asian candidate was never short listed unless the English-named candidate was also short listed.)

In the **Netherlands** in the late 1970s, Bovenkerk and Breunig-van Leeuwen demonstrated, using this method, that employers and personnel managers, in their selection of personnel, discriminated on the basis of ethnic origin (Bovenkerk and Breunig-van Leeuwen, 1978). They had two, equally qualified, applicants respond to the same vacancy. The only difference between the two applicants was their ethnic background; one would be, for example, a Surinamese boy, called Romeo Pengel, and the other was a native Dutch boy, called Piet Doesburg. In over 20% of the applications, the employers gave preference to the native Dutch person. Skilled, as well as unskilled manual work was covered in this experiment. Recently, this research was repeated, on the authority of the International Labour Organisation (ILO) as part of the ILO's ongoing programme "Combating discrimination against (im)migrant workers and ethnic minorities in the world of work". Discrimination was tested against Moroccan and Surinamese applicants, when applying for semi-skilled jobs and when applying for jobs requiring a college education (Bovenkerk et al, 1994). At the lower job level, discrimination was encountered by both ethnic groups, by males as well as females, in one out of three applications. At higher levels, the outcome was less pronounced: in one out of five applications, preference was given to the native Dutch men. No discrimination could be demonstrated against college-educated non-native women. In the private sector, discrimination occurred twice as often as it did in the public sector.

The method of discrimination testing is one of the most important and effective means of demonstrating the existence of the problem area in the face of those who deny that discrimination occurs. In the UK and the Netherlands it has been shown to have great effect in raising consciousness and changing public policy. Unfortunately, although the method has been used in countries such as Canada and the US, it has still not been widely applied in other EU countries. In some countries - Sweden, for example - the method has been deemed to be in breach of rules guiding research ethics. However, under the ILO programme, similar research is underway in a number of other EU countries.

Although discrimination testing is effective in demonstrating discrimination at the first stages of the recruitment process, it merely measures the results of the selection process, and offers few clues as to the specific motives and processes behind this rejection. Further research has been able to provide qualitative insights into processes of labour market exclusion.

2.3.3 Research into the actions of employers

Qualitative research can give an insight into what lies behind the direct labour market exclusion revealed in discrimination testing. Sometimes such research can discover open prejudice, directly expressed. In the **Netherlands**, interviews with employers, in which they are questioned about their views concerning ethnic minorities, have been a common research method, demonstrating the fact that prejudices against foreign employees do exist. Despite the fact that employers and personnel managers are unlikely to be completely candid and open to researchers about their actions, this method has regularly revealed a massive preference for native Dutch people. Research by Hooghiemstra (1991), demonstrated that 37% of personnel managers say that, in case of equal qualification, native Dutch are preferred. Van Beek (1993) reported that as many as 80% of personnel managers interviewed gave preference to an applicant with a Dutch background, in the case of equally qualified applicants. Twenty per cent of the interviewees thought a person from an ethnic minority would be completely unacceptable.

The **Swedish** report described a study of personnel responsible for recruitment in over a hundred companies in the Göteborg region, who saw immigrants in terms of negative stereotypes, with clearly discriminatory consequences. In this study, the main problem was seen to lie with foremen and work group leaders and lower level managers, rather than with staff in the upper echelons of personnel departments. Another Swedish study (Andersson, 1992) shows how ethnic background is an important barrier to employment, with employers' practices appearing to be guided by not objective criteria but by prejudice. A comprehensive study of a car plant near Göteborg (Schierup and Paulson, 1994) examined the workings of an internal labour market, recruitment and promotion, access to training, job levels, education, work related injuries and health, and the position of women. The results indicated that immigrants are systematically disadvantaged in virtually all aspects of working life in the plant.

In a recent study in **Norway**, 160 managers representing the 400 largest Norwegian firms were interviewed (Økonomisk rapport 1995). Almost eight out of ten managers thought that managers in Norway do discriminate against immigrants in the recruitment process. They were asked what they thought were the three main reasons for this. The answers indicate that 'difference in culture' was regarded as the most important reason (60 per cent). But also 'not having a knowledge of the language' (59 per cent), 'uncertainty about their formal qualifications' (35 per cent), 'xenophobia' (26 per cent) and 'racism and negative attitudes towards foreigners' (22.4 per cent), all featured as reasons. With respect to the 'language' explanation, the writers of another Norwegian study found that immigrants who speak Norwegian fluently were nevertheless found to face the same barriers as others (Berg and Vedi, 1995).

The actions and statements of employers can reveal evidence of direct discrimination. For example, respondents interviewed for the **French** report described efforts openly made by some employers not to recruit persons from North Africa and Africa generally. For some employers, refusal is systematic, whatever the type of job, with no justification offered other than, for example, "I already have one black on my site; I don't want two, because then they get difficult to handle." Some employers interviewed in the **UK** made plain their prejudices and stereotyped perceptions: for example, they labelled West Indians as 'lethargic', or having a "laissez-faire approach", or "not very mechanical"; Pakistani boys had "a lack of technical language ... a lack of mechanical curiosity"; Asians were "weak in mechanical design". One engineering manager said " The West Indians fit in better. The Asians have funny food. We don't want the whites disturbed by funny practices" (Lee and Wrench, 1983).

More often employers will admit that their actions are determined not by their own prejudices but by the prejudices of others. The **Danish** report describes an interview with the owner of a company doing plumbing work. He argued that he was not a racist at a personal level. He had nothing against immigrants and refugees - in fact he had coloured friends - however, he would not employ immigrants and refugees. He knew that some of his employees would not like to work with immigrants and refugees as long as there were unemployed Danes who could do the work. The main reason was that some of his customers would object to having a tradesman of foreign origin coming into their house and doing maintenance or other types of work on behalf of his firm. He was convinced he would lose customers if he took on immigrants and refugees, and he might not be able to afford to lose customers. He felt that in his trade, very few firms would take on foreigners, even as apprentices.

Research done by the author of the **UK** report similarly described employers who would argue that it was not they themselves who were prejudiced, but that they had to take account of the prejudices of others, such as their workforce or their customers. Employers recruiting young people for apprenticeship training described 'No go areas' in their firms, where white workers would refuse to work with a black trainee: these tended to be skilled areas of work, such as craft, toolroom, sheet metal working, maintenance and supervision. A respondent from an Engineering Training Group said

"Some firms can't take one - the skilled workers won't have it. The management wants them, but they know they can't force a black in. Never. This is because they can't afford to upset a good toolmaker - this would cost the firm money" (Lee and Wrench 1983). Officials who assisted school leavers to find work encountered employers who said they didn't want Asian girls for shop assistants because "It's not right for our customers", or that they were a high class store and "It may affect the selling" (Cross et al, 1990).

The **French** report also described employers who justify their unwillingness to take on applicants by claiming that the other employees at the plant will not work with foreigners or "coloured" people. Sometimes, employers excuse their actions by the idea that employment of immigrants "would detract from the firm's image". One of the main justifications put forward is that "coloured" persons or those whose foreign origin is "visible" cannot be employed in situations where they have to be in contact with the public. A number of those interviewed for the French report confirmed the existence of practices for eliminating categories of candidates for vacancies, such as psychological tests, statements that the applicant is "over-qualified" for the job in question, and requests for photographs to be supplied where the candidate's name raises doubts about his or her origin.

Informal criteria in recruitment
Sometimes the prejudices of employers are not expressed directly, but can be teased out from certain statements and practices which are expressed in more socially acceptable ways. Many of these fall under the heading of informal criteria in recruitment and selection decisions. Jenkins (1986), in his UK study of employers' recruitment practices, contrasted the "suitability" of applicants - their educational and technical qualifications, with their "acceptability" - the more informal and subjectively judged characteristics on which recruiters form judgements as to whether someone will 'fit in' to the organisation. Good "equal opportunities" practice emphasises criteria of suitability rather than acceptability, and this principle forms part of the "Code of Practice for the Elimination of Discrimination and the Promotion of Equal Opportunity in Employment" in the UK.

In a 1989 study of equal opportunities practises in **UK** companies Jewson and Mason (1991) found that technical qualifications would be regarded as first screening devices, with much importance given to "acceptability" criteria in making the final selections. It is precisely the criteria of "acceptability" where negative racial and ethnic stereotypes come in to play. More recently two UK researchers carried out an extensive survey on company recruiters on what they look for when recruiting graduates (Brown and Scase, 1994). They found that during the present oversupply of graduates, employers emphasise "transferable skills" which in practice turned out to be the subjective characteristics already found amongst privileged graduates from the old prestigious universities. Employers are now applying the criteria to all graduates which used only to be applied to "high flyers" who were being recruited for executive material and leadership. This means that working class and ethnic minority students who have managed, often in adverse circumstances, to gain entry to higher education, and whose academic qualifications would once have been sufficient to get them a professional job, are now denied a place on the career ladder.

There have been some similar research projects carried out in the **Netherlands**. The Dutch report revealed the subjectivity of the criteria used by many employers. Socially normative criteria, such as the motivation and reliability of the applicant and 'fitting into the team', appear to be more important factors in the selection of personnel, than technically instrumental criteria, such as education and work experience (Verweij, 1991). Over 90% of personnel managers interviewed, indicated that 'motivation' is the decisive criterion in the decision about an applicant (Hooghiemstra, 1991). The stress on socially normative criteria appears to work to the ethnic minorities' disadvantage (Veenman, 1991), as a consequence of the difficulty of objectively judging matters like 'motivation' and 'reliability'. With this form of judgement, prejudices creep in more easily than with judgements on the basis of objective criteria, such as education and work experience.

Something similar is described in the **French** report, which found evidence of the removal of 'occupational content' from recruitment procedures. It seems that recruitment procedures in France have evolved in the direction of placing more and more emphasis on personal interviews, at the expense of written tests. Employers now take it upon themselves to examine the "personality" of job applicants, their personal opinions and aspects of their lives which have increasingly little to do with their vocational aptitudes (Lyon-Caen, 1992). This change is particularly marked in the civil service, which used to take pride in recruiting staff on the basis of anonymous, "competitive" written examinations. Anonymity is increasingly less assured.

In one case in **Denmark** the increasing use of 'social' criteria in recruitment was related to the introduction of new technology. A housing construction company reorganised its production and invested in new technology, which reduced the demand for qualifications and made the work more simple. In order to reduce costs, most foremen were laid off. Because of the new technology, the need for individual supervision was no longer so important, and employees were able to work on their own. However, they now had to train new employees. Training of new employees had formerly been the responsibility of the foremen, who had even had time to instruct those who did not speak Danish. The new system increased the demand for new workers to be able to 'get on' with existing employees, and speak and understand Danish. The personnel manager said that they no longer used the Labour Exchange to find new workers; instead they simply asked their employees if they could find people. This had been successful and ensured that only persons whom the employees regarded as people they could work with were taken on.

Similar developments were noted in the **Swedish** report, which described the expansion of new types of job which require communication skills, especially a good command of Swedish, and a high level of education, as well as 'social competence'. They also involve the delegation of responsibility, a stress upon individual initiative and a greater reliance on teamwork. However, some authorities saw this as an understandable justification for not employing immigrants. The Swedish Immigrant Policy Committee Report (SOU 1995) stated that:

> 'All special treatment on the basis of cultural difference need not be discrimination. In today's companies the demand for social competence is increasing, i.e. the demand that employees, regardless of whether they are

Swedes or immigrants, fit into the work culture, function in a team, etc. Knowledge of and familiarity with functioning in a Swedish environment can be assumed to be an important part of such competence. This means that an employer can take account of certain factors when employing [someone] which disqualify cultural difference. It is obvious that the dividing line between justifiable demands for social competence and what is discrimination can be difficult to establish.

The authors of the Swedish report find fault with this line of argument, pointing out that similar arguments were employed in earlier years to block the entry of women to male-dominated working places. Today, the Swedish Law on Equal Opportunity does not allow this kind of "cultural argument" to be used as a barrier to women's participation on the same terms as men, and such arguments should be similarly unjustifiable for immigrants.

Furthermore, other examples can be found to show that new production pressures for this sort of "social competence" do not have to lead to the exclusion of migrants. At a German-owned manufacturing plant in **Austria**, the introduction of "lean production" necessitated the ability of employees to communicate quickly and reliably. Of the 2,000 employees, 15 per cent were of foreign nationality and about 180 were identified as lacking sufficient skills in German to function appropriately in the plan's new structure. However, the management decided not to fire the 180 but to offer them and others language training, seeking the financial assistance of Vienna's Municipal Integration Fund. Groups of around eight participants were formed and received job-related German language training in the plant. After three months, 76 out of the first batch of 78 trainees received their certificates (Wiener Intergrationsfonds 1995).

Misconceptions
A study by Andersson (1992) showed that **Swedish** employers often regarded refugees as unqualified, when in reality they were often over-qualified for the positions they held or were offered. Researchers in **Germany** interviewed employers and found that they too had certain misconceptions and stereotypes about young migrants. For example, managers, and clerks in employment bureaux often argued in interviews that migrants and their offspring are not interested in learning a trade or profession, because they want to earn money quickly. However, the few empirical studies that exist do not support this view. In a study of Greek, Italian and Portuguese young people for the national employment bureau, for instance, (Boos-Nünning et al, 1990) the authors find that a majority of them and their parents emphasise the importance of gaining a good education, either learning a trade in industry, or (and this is true especially for Greek parents) studying for an academic profession. Another study in Hamburg (Haugg, 1994) found that young migrants in secondary education had the same ambitions concerning their future professions as their indigenous counterparts. They wanted to become artists or engineers, or do 'something with languages'. In any event they wanted their work to be interesting and demanding. Their parents had even greater ambitions: most of them wanted their children to go to high-school and to go on to study.

A similar study in the **UK** interviewed managers about apprenticeship recruitment in the West Midlands (Lee and Wrench, 1983). Employers explained the absence of ethnic minority apprentices by saying "they don't apply" or "they don't get the qualifications". In fact the research showed that ethnic minority young people were applying, and they were just as well qualified as their white peers. Nevertheless, of all those applying from four Birmingham schools, 44% of the whites were successful, compared to only 15% for Afro-Caribbeans and 13% for Asians. Most of the reasons for this were found to lie in processes of indirect discrimination.

2.3.4 Indirect discrimination

Indirect discrimination in employment exists with job requirements or recruitment practices which, although applied equally to all, in practice treat members of one ethnic group more favourably than another. The exclusion resulting from indirect discrimination can be either accidental or intentional. In some countries, as social norms become stronger against open prejudice and racist rejection, discrimination in recruitment becomes more sophisticated and "coded".

Examples of indirect discrimination revealed in the **UK** apprenticeship study were as follows:

- Many firms relied for recruitment in significant part on the family members of existing employees, and trade unions would often support this policy. Thus, in a largely white workforce, this excluded ethnic minorities.
- Many firms didn't advertise their vacancies for apprenticeships. They relied on word-of-mouth recruitment, with the result that ethnic minorities would be less likely to hear of vacancies than white school leavers who had contacts within a firm.
- Many employers restricted their recruitment to a local catchment area when faced with a large number of applicants. As the largest employers were located in white outer suburbs of cities this excluded ethnic minority applicants from the beginning.

Examples of all these three factors were found in other reports. The selective use of 'white' geographical areas for recruitment is a process of indirect discrimination which is also reported in **France**: Job applicants are rejected by banks and insurance companies because of their place of residence, particularly when their homes are in areas with a poor reputation. The municipality of St Denis, as part of an urban regeneration programme, changed a number of address indications in order to remove the stigmatising effect of certain estate names.

As in the UK apprenticeship study, internal recruitment, and recruitment through the family and friends of the company's own personnel, was seen to also lead to indirect discrimination in the **Netherlands** (Veenman, 1985; Becker and Kempen, 1982; Abell et al., 1985; Bovenkerk, 1986). In **Portugal** it was noted that white apprentices are often relatives of skilled workers, which helps them to find work, whilst ethnic minorities have no such support. In **Denmark**, many companies where employers used to recruit new employees through the Labour Exchange now mainly recruit new workers by asking their employees to find someone. The reason is said to be that it has become more important to get employees who are 'able to co-operate'. This makes it very difficult for immigrants without social contacts with employees in expanding companies to find employment. In **Germany** 70 companies in Nordhrhein Westfalen were asked about their recruitment strategies (Schaub, 1993) and it was found that one reason for the under-representation of migrant young people in the modern sectors of industry was the practice of recruiting the children of employees. The recruitment methods most commonly used in **Finland** are said to be network, informal and internal recruitment. One estimate is that employment agencies in Finland are informed about less than 30 per cent of vacancies. Such practices pre-select ethnic minorities out of the recruitment pool at the beginning of the process. In **Sweden**, the use of family ties, friends and acquaintances accounts for filling 70 per cent of vacancies according to a study by AMS (AMS, 1991; Paulson, 1991). Thus, newly arrived immigrants are at clear disadvantage if their only means of finding work is through the employment services.

The **French** report describes the approach adopted by certain nationalised enterprises, where the State is the employer but the activities are economic, rather than purely administrative (e.g. transport). Even where there is no nationality clause, these organisations use a variety of methods to give preference to French nationals in allocating jobs, one of the most effective of which is to give priority to the children of employees already working in the enterprise. Thus, in the major public services, job vacancies are first circulated among staff and are already occupied by their relatives by the time they are advertised externally. One of informants for the French report stated that 80% of contracts offered by a public transport enterprise in the Paris region under the Emploi Solidarité scheme had been placed in this way. These practices, discreetly referred to as "informal recruitment networks" (Bouvier, 1989; Giraud and Marie, 1990), and particularly common in the public services, are an obstacle to the recruitment of staff who, though themselves French nationals, have no access to the internal information channels, since their parents, as non-nationals, could not obtain employment there before them. Preference for the "children of staff" is an unwritten law in France, widely subscribed to and often encouraged by the trade unions. The resulting picture thus differs considerably as between firms that employed large numbers of immigrants 15 or 20 years ago and those that did not. Firms that used to employ a lot of immigrants (those in the motor industry and in building and civil engineering, for example) are in recession and are taking on very few new people.

Another example of indirect discrimination, described in the **Netherlands,** concerns the minimum height demand for entry to some occupations (e.g. the armed forces, and the police). Those who are indirectly harmed by these demands are those ethnic minority groups who are, on average, smaller in height than the indigenous population.

With indirect discrimination it is not easy to come to a judgement as to whether its effects are truly inadvertent, or whether the exclusion is intentional. This no doubt varies. With a long-established criterion such as minimum height, the exclusion effect is likely to be unintentional. The demand for minimum language skills is a genuine criterion for many occupations; however, where apparently unnecessary language skills are required for many unskilled jobs, one is more likely to be suspicious. The discriminatory effects of a decision to restrict recruitment to a particular region or catchment area which excludes migrants and ethnic minorities is likely to be quite obvious to a recruiter, and this is far less likely to be 'accidental' in its effects.

2.3.5 Employment agencies

When studying recruitment, it is important to consider not only employers and personnel managers but also those agencies which assist employers to find staff, such as official job centres and private employment agencies. In the **UK** in the early 1990s public notice was drawn to a number of cases of discrimination by external agencies used as a filter between people seeking work and employers looking for staff. By quietly making their requirements known to a third party doing the recruiting, racist employers can appear to 'keep their hands clean'. Evidence of this was demonstrated in a television documentary in 1990 which revealed how some private employment agencies were uncritically co-operating with instructions from employers not to send them ethnic minority staff. A recently published study of direct and indirect discrimination in the **Danish** labour market by Schierup described how officials of the Labour Exchange informed him 'off the record' that they take notice of the wishes of employers when they specifically ask not to be sent immigrants and refugees. The **French** report describes the use of coded messages written into job offers placed with temporary employment agencies which signify "no foreigners". One is the "BBR" code - these letters stand for 'Bleu, Blanc, Rouge' (Blue, White, Red), using the colours of the flag of the Republic to signify that a particular employer is looking for a white candidate, preferably of French stock.

A similar agency to a job centre in the **UK** is the local authority Careers Service, where careers officers give vocational advice to school leavers and put them in touch with suitable local employers or training schemes. The Careers Service functions as an important and influential bridge between school and work in Britain, being both a provider of vocational guidance in schools and a labour market placement agency, involved in most of the recruitment to training schemes. By interviewing people who provide a service to employers a researcher can sometimes discover things that employers are doing and saying which could not be discovered in interviews with employers themselves. In a programme of qualitative interviews with careers officers (Cross et al, 1990), the respondents were able to recount many examples of overt racial discrimination by employers, encountered when they were trying to place young people in training schemes or jobs. Officers told of stories of employers who provided work experience for training schemes refusing to interview Asian youngsters on hearing their name, and of supervisors on schemes collaborating with such employers who specified 'We want a white youngster'. A clothing company manager refused to recruit Asians because "If we trained Asians they would go off and start their own business. I couldn't work with them - they make me sick". An engineering employer told a careers officer "We don't like West Indians. We find them lazy" and a waste paper company stated "We don't want any Asians ... they don't work". More often, a careers officer would find that an ethnic minority young person would be told by an employer that the vacancy had gone, whilst a white youngster would later be told that it was still available. The research also revealed that, instead of confronting racist employers, many careers officers would engage in 'protective channelling', directing ethnic minority young people away from firms and schemes where they suspect they will be rejected. For example, it would become apparent which training schemes were willing to take on ethnic minorities, and the young people would be sent to these in the knowledge that they would be accepted. However, these were less likely to include the most 'desirable' training schemes and occupations. The careers officers' stated aim was to protect the young person from negative and disappointing experiences. Therefore, practices such as protective channelling, together with the anticipatory avoidance by young people of unsympathetic employers and hostile parts of the city, show how racial exclusion and inequality can be perpetuated without the occurrence of a specific racist act of rejection.

2.3.6 Evidence from migrants and ethnic minorities

Research into the experiences of migrants with discrimination and racism provides an added source of evidence of discrimination. It is significant, because it demonstrates whether individuals or groups are experiencing the behaviour of others as discriminatory or racist. Of course, this type of evidence is not always reliable. A 'victim' may perceive discrimination where it doesn't exist; on the other hand, research has demonstrated that migrants can underestimate discrimination (Smith, 1977).

It is very difficult for any one individual to know that they have been unfairly discriminated against when rejected for a job. Interviews with migrants are more likely to reveal a more generalised disillusion. For example, the unemployed son of Algerian migrants to France told a journalist "The French make you feel like a foreigner, especially when you try to find work. They have ways of letting you know you are well down the list." (*Observer* 17 September 1995). Interviews with ethnic minorities in a **UK** new town recorded exasperation on the part of visible minorities that they were constantly turned town for jobs for which they thought they had a good chance (Wrench et al, 1993). Only occasionally did they find real evidence for their suspicions: "My son applied for a job at [local supermarket] twice and was told the jobs had gone ... When a white friend of his applied, he was given the job". A black woman who was looking for Saturday employment told the interviewer that a large retailer phoned her up and told her they were desperate for Saturday workers and asked her to start the same day. "So I struggled in - pouring with rain - and all of a sudden they didn't want me".

Whilst suspicions of unfair discrimination in recruitment are difficult for an individual to justify, differential treatment *within* the workplace is more visible and tangible for the victim. It is still, however, difficult to prove. The **Danish** report describes how some foreigners have expressed the feeling that they are not given the same opportunities as their Danish colleagues. Very often supervisors and others overlook them, and do not instruct or train them as well as they do Danish employees. Young people of foreign origin who have grown up in Denmark have complained that they have greater difficulty in making a successful career within a firm than their Danish colleagues, and are more likely to remain at the bottom of the ladder. Sometimes specific research can demonstrate the problem. In the **Netherlands**, experiences of migrants with discrimination are described in Bouw and Nelissen (1988), Essed

(1984), Biegel and Tjoen-Tak-Sen (1986), and Biegel et al (1987). These researchers demonstrated that discrimination is experienced with promotion and in employment and working conditions. Research by Brassé and Sikking (1988) demonstrated that migrants experience discrimination on the shop floor over the distribution of duties.

In **Sweden** the Ombudsman for Employment Discrimination receives many telephone calls about harassment at work, something which for the victim is tangible and quite unambiguous. However, less tangible are the processes of exclusion from opportunities of employment or promotion. Although the Ombudsman receives many complaints from people who feel they have been excluded from the sorts of jobs which require a high level of education or professional skills, these rarely go forward to become official complaints as they are so difficult to prove. A survey commissioned by the Ombudsman was carried out among approximately 1,000 Africans, Arabs, Latin Americans and Poles to ascertain their subjective experiences of ethnic discrimination in different social spheres, including work. Twenty five per cent of Latin Americans and Poles and 34% of Africans believed that they had been discriminated against on account of their ethnic background when applying for work for which they were qualified during the last five years (Lange, 1995). Commenting on the survey in a press release, the Ombudsman stated:

> 'Even if [the results] deal with [subjective] experience of discrimination and not actual [verifiable] discrimination I think that these figures ought to give those who contend that ethnic discrimination in the labour market is a marginal problem something to think about. Stronger legislation is needed but also other measures, not least greater awareness of the competence a workforce with another background can provide a company' (Press Release 1995).

In research in **Germany**, migrant workers complained about company recruitment policies, promotion policies, distribution of apartments owned by the company, and discriminatory attitudes of supervisors (Kühne, 1991). Other research discovered complaints by migrant workers of verbal harassment, contempt from colleagues and supervisors, additional work given by supervisors, and the denial of training and promotion opportunities (Räthzel and Sarica, 1994). Discrimination at the workplace can also be exercised by shop stewards themselves. West (1994) gives some examples for this: in a large enterprise, indigenous shop stewards paid more attention to German workers than their migrant colleagues; rather than listening to their questions they referred them immediately to migrant shop stewards; they also gave preference to indigenous workers when it came to things such as the distribution of easier jobs for older workers. In a survey among Turkish women in companies in Berlin, Toksöz (1990) found out that when the women complained to shop stewards about discriminatory treatment - for instance having to clean their workplace during their break, which the indigenous workers were not required to do - nothing happened.

However, such subjective feelings are often difficult to justify with evidence. The **French** report describes how, as things stand, it is difficult to obtain proof of discriminatory behaviour directed at individuals or groups in such matters as working conditions, pay, grading, promotion and dismissal. The confidentiality of personal data, duly protected by law, in effect makes it impossible to obtain evidence of unequal treatment of individuals or groups. Even if they wished or were able to do so, research workers and labour inspectors would have a job on their hands in overcoming the in-built obstacles to compiling comparative case-histories. It is therefore understandable that the majority of people interviewed, whatever their position (trade unionists, labour inspectors, officers of antiracist organisations) had little information to offer on what actually happens at the workplace. Meanwhile, interviews with carried out for the French report described a workplace culture of racist remarks, jokes in dubious taste and the routine use of stereotypes by employers, supervisory staff and workmates.

2.3.7 Individual cases

Individual cases of direct racial discrimination in employment occasionally come to public attention through the campaigns of pressure groups and activists, or through the attention of the media. The factors which assist or inhibit the bringing of cases into public notice vary in different countries. In the UK the existence of the Race Relations Act for nearly 20 years and the corresponding media attention paid to industrial tribunal discrimination cases and the formal investigations of the CRE have presented to aggrieved employees models and precedents for action. In the Netherlands, however, it seems that it is research which has brought cases to the surface, rather than legal action. In France, court cases in matters involving discrimination in recruitment or employment are rare and do not provide a viable source. Instances of discrimination prohibited by law arising during employment and in dismissal procedures are usually impossible to verify and impossible to prove in individual cases; hence they very seldom come to court. Instead, cases reported in the media are more likely to be those collected by anti-racist or immigrant associations.

In the **UK,** confirmation of processes of racism and discrimination in the labour market and employment comes from the work of industrial tribunals and the regular formal investigation reports by the CRE. In the first year of operation of the 1976 Race Relations Act, in July 1977, a black Birmingham-born man applied for a job at British Leyland's Castle Bromwich plant as a machine tool fitter, a job for which he was well qualified. Some of the toolroom maintenance fitters asked the union (AUEW) shop steward to arrange a meeting, and a motion was passed that they would not accept a coloured fitter. Consequently Mr Jones, the black applicant, was rejected for the job. The case came to light after a white employee informed the CRE some nine months after the event, and a formal investigation by the CRE found that BL Cars Ltd and the two AUEW shop stewards had contravened the Race Relations Act. Since then, many cases have made the news each year. A tribunal case in 1989 ruled that a Kent Health Authority was guilty of discrimination because they had left a nurse in an "anomalous and humiliating" job for eight years because she was Asian; London Underground was found to have overlooked 90% of its ethnic minority middle managers in a promotions exercise in 1990; in 1991 a supervisor at a Birmingham firm was found to have told clerical workers who were taking phone enquiries about vacancies to tell any Pakistanis who rang that the job was gone; in 1993 Yorkshire textile mills were found to be discriminating against Asian workers in new holiday arrangements and working practices. Over 20 years, many cases have been recorded, and a large proportion of them would not have come to public attention if it were not for the existence of the CRE and the opportunities of legal measures of redress for victims of discrimination.

In **France,** in contrast to the UK, publicity from legal proceedings on issues of racism and discrimination in employment is not so common. Whenever inequities give rise to legal proceedings, they are usually dealt with as industrial disputes, and the racist or xenophobic aspect is taken up either as a secondary issue or not at all. Similarly, the trade unions often prefer to rely on arguments which have been tried and tested in disputes between employers and workers, rather than risk getting bogged down in a case where the validity of the evidence of discrimination could be challenged. Recourse to industrial tribunals, the usual procedure adopted, places limits on a plea of discrimination, since discrimination as such tends to be seen as a matter of criminal law (although, pursuant to the Labour Code, it seems possible that the remit of the industrial tribunals might be extended in this respect) (GISTI, 1994). According to the French report it is well known that foreigners, French nationals of foreign origin and non-white French persons run greater risks in their trade-union activities or in exercising the right to strike than persons seen to be "of French stock". Here too, it is often difficult to make a charge of discrimination stick. Any action taken tends to be based on other legal irregularities, referring only secondarily, or not at all, to the discriminatory nature of the acts complained about.

One problem is that in countries where there is no effective legal machinery, or no history of activism by anti-racist organisations, or no tradition of research into the area, then cases are less likely to come to notice. The **Irish** report makes the point that it is widely acknowledged that Travellers, Ireland's indigenous ethnic minority, have suffered endemic levels of discrimination in numerous areas of their lives for many years, yet no comprehensive research has been conducted to date on the incidence of racial discrimination in the workplace. Similarly in **Luxembourg** very few cases are known; although on an anecdotal level Cape Verdeans have spoken of problems, there are no known cases of discrimination caused by the attitudes of employers towards their employees, and no research being done on this.

2.4 DISCRIMINATION AND THE INFORMAL ECONOMY

In Southern EU member states the relative newness of their status as countries of immigration means that they have qualitatively different experiences of discrimination. As past countries of emigration there is a legacy of sympathy for migrants and the racist intolerance they experience in new countries. Nevertheless, new migrants within these countries are now also experiencing racism and discrimination in employment. However, unlike in some countries with longer experience of the issues, there is no established tradition of using legislation and other specific anti-discrimination measures to tackle discrimination at work. Immigration in these countries is characterised by a significant proportion of undocumented workers, and/or participation in an illegal labour market. The issue of discrimination in this context is different from how the problem is seen in Northern countries. It concerns the super-exploitation of large numbers of migrants, whether undocumented or not, in poor or illegal work, suffering conditions which would not be tolerated by native workers, but which they are not in a position to reject. The concerns in many

Northern European countries - the direct and indirect discrimination which excludes established migrant communities and their children from the employment opportunities they desire - are less relevant. As the Greek report says, it is not easy in these conditions to make the necessary distinction between 'racism' and employers' exploitation.

In **Greece**, given that large and medium-sized manufacturing firms are under the close supervision of both the Ministry of Labour and the Social Insurance organisations, few undocumented foreigners are employed by these firms directly. Some, however, do work indirectly, employed by sub-contractors who undertake various manufacturing jobs. Many more are employed by smaller firms which are mostly family undertakings and can avoid labour inspections and social insurance contributions. Immigrants take up jobs which the locals avoid. The construction industry is subject to intense seasonal fluctuations which cause high unemployment during the seasonal troughs in winter, alternating with labour shortages during the summer months. A large proportion of building workers are undocumented foreigners. About one third of the Poles and the Albanians, the two most numerous groups of economic immigrants, find seasonal and casual jobs in it. Undocumented foreigners of all nationalities work during the seasonal peaks of activity in picking fruit and doing other seasonal jobs on the land. There is evidence that increasing numbers of undocumented immigrants are also employed in more regular jobs in greenhouses and in animal husbandry. Many poultry, sheep and cattle farms, fisheries and the like depend now on foreign labour. Finally, economic immigrants without work permits are employed in practically all kinds of relatively low-status services, especially in catering, tourism, transport, trade and domestic work. Among those without permits, unemployment is high with frequent periods of inactivity between one job and another.

The informal economy is put at about 30 per cent of the total economic activity. It is larger than that in the more developed European countries, but only marginally above that in Italy and Spain. The undocumented economic immigrants are estimated at over 350,000, about eight to nine per cent of the registered labour force of 4.1m. They work in all productive sectors in unskilled or low-skilled manual jobs, they are not covered by social insurance, and their pay is about half of the market rate in Greece. The Greek report describes them as an 'underclass'; they are threatened by deportation and they often face racism at the workplace. However, information on what happens at work is limited. In Greece there is a general absence of adequate statistical or other information on racism at the workplace. An indication of its low priority as a social issue is the fact that, as well as not having conducted any research on those issues, the Labour Institute of the General Confederation of Greek Labour (GCGL) has not published any paper or even an editorial article on discrimination at the workplace in its bulletin. Neither have the employers' research institutes conducted any relevant research or published information on racism at the workplace. Although other research institutes have carried out research on political aspects of ethnic minorities, nothing has been done on discrimination at the workplace, and relatively little has been published on the problems faced by the large number of undocumented economic migrants.

In **Spain**, in those sectors where there is a higher concentration of immigrant workers, there are a number of facts which suggest the existence of discrimination. Discriminatory practices are frequent with legal immigrant workers, but are obviously worse with unregistered, illegal immigrants, who were estimated to represent 40 to 60% of all immigrant (non-EU) workers in Spain at the end of 1993. Illegal immigrants work with no contract or social security benefits and often suffer exploitative working conditions in terms of wages, quality, intensity or duration of their work, practices which violate regulations and Union agreements. Employers hiring this type of labour force have the advantage of holding absolute power over their employees, since illegal immigrants cannot make formal complaints or take legal actions. In certain sectors employers prefer to employ immigrants because of the low cost, pliability and vulnerability of this type of labour force.

Immigrants occupy low-qualified positions where employers find it difficult to hire national a labour force. Most work in five sectors: domestic service, catering, construction, retail trade and farming. All five branches of activity have in common the relative precariousness of the working conditions; however, this precariousness does not necessarily mean irregularity: in fact, the legal situation of these workers varies greatly depending on the sector, the geographical area, the origin and the time of immigration.

Immigrants in domestic service - women mostly - are concentrated in Madrid and Barcelona. Most of them live in the houses where they work, but the number of women who work by the hour is increasing. The largest groups are Filipinos, Dominicans, Moroccans and Portuguese. A survey (Marrodán, 1991) carried out with 424 immigrant workers of this sector in Madrid and Barcelona in 1990 showed that only 10% had a stable work contract, 10% had a temporary work contract, and 80% did not have any contract at all. Often the immigrants have to pay for their Social Security themselves, as if they were self-employed paid by the hour. The most frequent complaints concern the agreed hours of working, which are often not respected (normally from 8 a.m. to 11 p.m.), the delay in monthly pay, and dismissal without pay (Colectivo IOE, 1991). In this sector, it is difficult to document employers' abuses or cases of over-exploitation, because of the vulnerability of these workers: on the one hand, they need to keep the job in order to have a work permit, and on the other, there are no witnesses to their employers' abuses except for other members of the family.

Immigrants who work in the construction sector in Madrid are for the most part Moroccans, and also Polish, though in a smaller proportion. The working conditions of these immigrants are very bad, with high risks of injury, no contract or Social Security benefits, below minimum wages, and arbitrary dismissal, sometimes without wages. Some live in temporary accommodation on site and have money for this deducted from their wages. Immigrant workers who work in farming usually do seasonal jobs such as collecting fruit (strawberries in Huelva, tomatoes in Badajoz, and fruit in Catalonia and Aragon), or other agricultural products, except in some areas in the South where the activity is more intense throughout the year, as for example in the plastic greenhouses of Almeria. The CCOO Union describes the situation of the immigrants who went to Huelva's 1994 strawberry harvest: "there are constant cases of exploitation of foreign workers by strawberry farmers, who use immigrants as cheap labour force and take advantage of their vulnerability and illegal situation. They work with no contracts or insurance, and live in huts with no light or running water". In extreme cases, the situation of some irregular immigrants is close to the characteristics of "slavery". The police defined as a "semi-slavery system" the living and working conditions of Chinese immigrants found in Madrid, Bilbao and other towns where around 700 people worked in 20 clandestine clothing factories in 1993 and 1994. These immigrants were forced to sell their freedom of movement to those who facilitated the trip from China to Spain Once in Spain, the gangs take their documents away and force them to live in unhealthy conditions and to work crowded together for endless working days, only receiving food and lodging in return (Diario *El Pais*, 1994).

The circumstances of legal immigrants from underdeveloped countries vary a great deal. Some of them work for companies in regular work similar to that of Spanish nationals. But even if the immigrants are "regular", they are always conditioned by the annual five-year renewal of their work permit. That is to say, they are in an institutionalised situation of temporary employment and residence. Many legal immigrants in Spain are subjected to similar conditions to those of illegal immigrants: they work with no contract or social security benefits, with lower wages and/or longer working days than allowed by union agreements in that sector. However, they are not as vulnerable as illegal immigrants because they can take legal action and make formal complaints, even if in practice this is not always easy to carry out.

In Spain there is no general information available on any discriminatory practices that immigrants may be subjected to within the workplace and it is difficult to portray accurately the conditions of over-exploitation that immigrant workers are subjected to. Although the over-exploitation of immigrant workers is well-known, immigrants themselves rarely report discriminatory practices, particularly when they have no documents. Under these circumstances, it is not surprising that they should even avoid organisations which are trying to help them, such as the unions and other NGOs.

In **Italy** there are legal rigidities which force many immigrants to work illegally. Officially, current regulations do not provide for the possibility of transferring from one type of residence permit to another, even in the event of a change in "status". For example, a worker with a residence permit that entitles him to undertake employed work cannot apply for one that entitles him to undertake self-employed work, and vice versa, until the existing permit expires. And even when the current permit does expire, transfer is not automatic. Employers may not take on immigrants who have a "family", "study" or "self-employment" permit. Trade unions oppose this inflexibility, which leads to discrimination between workers and, therefore, goes against the principle of "equality of treatment" or "equality of opportunities" (laid down by Law No 943). In the case of over-work and the violation of rights, workers have no opportunity to protect themselves, precisely because of their illegal (or, at least, "semi-legal") position. The current policy of restrictions with regard to immigrants who are already resident in Italy and the difficulties they have in securing the legalisation of their position are thus perpetuating and reinforcing these conditions of marginalisation.

The "informal economy" - namely that relating to the violation of trade union and legal rights - affects both workers who are legal, in that they have a residence and work permit, and workers who are illegal. It is this latter group that forms the largest reserve of labour for undeclared employment, especially in sectors such as agriculture. The data collected by the Ispettorato del Lavoro reveal differences between North and South in the various economic sectors. In Central and Northern Italy, the industrial sector and the hotel and catering trade have the most illegal workers, whereas in Southern Italy and the islands, there is more undeclared employment in the agricultural sector. Agriculture is the sector in which undeclared employment is the most common, even for indigenous workers, and where, consequently, immigrants are at risk of suffering discrimination. Because of their mobility, immigrants are this sector's preferred labour force, especially for certain phases of the production cycle (fruit-picking and other seasonal jobs). In the agricultural sector, particularly in the South, employed work is insecure, temporary and/or seasonal and is rarely covered by trade union protection as regards pay and working conditions. Although at a formal level the sector is covered by the trade unions and there are agreed national and local work contracts, it is difficult for the trade unions to guarantee effective application of these contracts, not only for immigrants but also for indigenous workers. This means that, in practice, pay is much lower than contractually agreed and is paid directly to workers, in cash, often each day.

In **Portugal** foreign workers are mainly concentrated in industry, construction and transport, and in service sectors such the cleaning department of the municipal council of Greater Lisbon, and in domestic service. Some of the immigrants from Portuguese-speaking parts of Africa have Portuguese citizenship; many do not, and those who work in unskilled work for below average pay without a contract or social security coverage are unable to challenge their employers over poor working conditions, or to seek work elsewhere. About 50% of ethnic minority workers have no employment contract, with no legal protection, welfare rights, or protection against abuses of safety or working hours. Work accidents are highest in those sectors which employ migrants. Added to this is the racism they encounter which further reduces their opportunities. The Portuguese report states that complaints from the immigrants about racism are rare, although in these circumstances it is not easy to see what is happening. In general, the report concludes, 'racism' in Portugal is demonstrated in the sense of the concentration of ethnic minorities in poor working conditions, but is less manifest in working relations between ethnic minorities and white workers at the workplace.

It is clear, then, that the perception of the problem of discrimination in the labour market of countries of Southern Europe is different from that which pre-occupies observers in the North. In countries of Northern Europe, where migrants are longer established and issues of the 'second generation' are important, the concern is with the unjustified exclusion on 'racial' or ethnic grounds of migrants and ethnic minorities from employment opportunities, and the related phenomenon of the over-representation of migrants and ethnic minorities in unemployment. In countries of Southern Europe, in contrast, immigrants are actively preferred and recruited because they are cheaper, more vulnerable, and more pliable - they are less able to resist over-exploitation in terms of work intensity or working hours. They experience a perverse kind of "positive discrimination" in the selection process and then in work suffer the "negative" discrimination of conditions which indigenous workers would not tolerate. Immigrants themselves are often reluctant to bring to public attention their conditions; sometimes trade unions work to expose abuses in the media, but there has been relatively little academic investigation of racist and discriminatory practices within the workplace.

3. NATIONAL POLICIES AGAINST RACISM AND DISCRIMINATION

The policies considered in this chapter are those which are specifically directed against racism and discrimination in the sphere of employment. We are less concerned here with those broader social policies concerned to enhance the social integration of migrants. Integration policies may consist of, for example, those measures directed at migrants themselves, to improve their language or occupational skills, or ability to operate successfully with the institutional structure of the new society. Although in some cases reference will be made to this type of provision, which can be very important in facilitating the successful integration of migrants, the main emphasis of this chapter is those anti-discrimination measures which by their nature are generally directed not at migrant populations but at the gatekeepers, officials and institutions of society. It is important to note that as migrant populations become settled ethnic minority communities over the passage of time, integration policies diminish in importance, whereas anti-discrimination policies continue to be necessary.

It is not the intention of this chapter to set out a comparison of all the legislative and administrative measures against racism and discrimination in different member states in all their legal and technical detail. This is best done by people with legal expertise. Furthermore this would duplicate effort already carried out elsewhere: for example, this exercise was carried out for two recent reports "Measure for Measure: A Comparative Analysis of Measures to Combat Racial Discrimination in Member State Countries of the European Community" (Forbes and Mead, 1992), and "Legal Instruments to Combat Racism and Xenophobia: Comparative assessment of the legal instruments implemented in the various Member States to combat all forms of discrimination, racism and xenophobia and incitement to hatred and racial violence" (Commission of the European Communities 1992). Similar comparative work is also being carried out as part of the ongoing International Labour Office programme "Combating discrimination against (im)migrant workers and ethnic minorities in the world of work" (See Zegers de Beijl, 1991, 1995).

This chapter draws in particular on the work of Forbes and Mead (1992), whilst adding material from countries that were not covered in their report, and new developments which have arisen since their report was completed. Three member states are considered to be the "front-runners" in the development of measures against racism and discrimination: the UK, the Netherlands and Sweden (Zegers de Beijl, 1991). Therefore these countries will be considered first, and in more detail than others.

3.1 THE UK

Legislation
The UK has ratified the International Convention on the Elimination of All Forms of Racial Discrimination (ICERD), but not the International Labour Organisation Convention 111 (ILO 111). The Race Relations Act 1976 came into force in June 1977 and applies to the whole of Great Britain (i.e. this excludes Northern Ireland).

The Act replaces the two previous Race Relations Acts and extends the scope of the law against discrimination to employment, training and education, housing and the provision of goods, facilities, services and planning. The Act further renders unlawful "pressure to discriminate", i.e. inducing another person to perform an act of unlawful discrimination, and forbids any advertisement which indicates that an employer is intending to discriminate on the grounds of 'race'. It gives individual victims a right of direct access to the civil courts and industrial tribunals for legal remedies against unlawful discrimination. It amended the Public Order Act 1936 to make incitement to racial hatred a criminal offence, although prosecution before criminal courts may be instituted only with the consent of the Attorney General.

When the Act refers to discrimination on 'racial grounds' it means grounds of colour, race, nationality, or ethnic or national origins, and a 'racial group' similarly means a group of persons defined by colour, race, nationality, or ethnic or national origins. The Act does not permit 'reverse discrimination' or 'positive discrimination', and therefore it is unlawful to discriminate in favour of a person of a minority racial or ethnic group in recruitment or promotion.

An important feature of the Race Relations 1976 is that it outlaws both *direct* and *indirect* discrimination on racial grounds. Although the Act does not use the words 'direct discrimination', this is now common shorthand for the type of discrimination covered by section 1(1)(a). A person carries out this type of discrimination if on racial grounds he treats that person less favourably than he treats or would treat other persons. Similarly, the words "indirect discrimination" are not used in the legislation but have become the standard way of defining this type. It occurs in employment with a job requirement or condition which, although applied equally to all, in practice treat one race less favourably than another, and have the effect of excluding a higher proportion of members of certain racial groups than members of other racial groups. Section 2 of the legislation covers *victimisation*: it grants protection to individuals who are treated less favourably than other persons by reason of their bringing a complaint under the Act, giving information in proceedings brought by another person, or alleging that there has been discrimination contrary to the Act.

Tribunals
Under the Race Relations Act 1976, aggrieved individuals have direct access to industrial tribunals in employment, training and related cases. Industrial tribunals are composed of a legally qualified chairman and two lay members who are generally recruited from workers' and employers' organisations. Individuals who lodge a complaint with an industrial tribunal may get preliminary legal assistance from a solicitor at little or no cost, provided their income is within a certain limits, under the Legal Aid Act. The legal aid scheme, however does not extend to the tribunal proceedings itself (Zegers de Beijl, 1991).

Copies of complaints under the Race Relations Act are sent to the local office of the Advisory, Conciliation and Arbitration Service (ACAS). This will first try to facilitate a conciliation settlement; if the complaint is not resolved by conciliation or withdrawn for any other reason, it will then proceed to a tribunal hearing. At the hearing complainants and respondents (the people complained against) may put their case in person or be represented by someone such as a solicitor, a representative of a trade union or employers' organisation or by the Commission for Racial Equality (Zegers de Beijl, 1991).

If a tribunal decides in favour of the complainant it may require the respondent to pay compensation to the complainant. A tribunal may also recommend that the respondent take a particular course of action within a specified period of time in order to reduce or eliminate any adverse effects of discrimination on the complainant. The tribunal has the power to recommend, for example, reinstatement or promotion of the complainant (Forbes and Mead, 1992).

In 1989, out of the total number of requests to the CRE for legal assistance, complaints about employment related discrimination were by far the most important. The majority concerned unfair dismissal and detriment, with complaints relating to refusal to offer employment and refused promotion coming in second and third place respectively. Taken together, these complaints made up over 90 per cent of all employment related complaints (Zegers de Beijl, 1991).

Agency
The Race Relations Act 1976 established an independent Commission for Racial Equality (CRE) which replaced both the Race Relations Board and the Community Relations Commission. The CRE exists independently of government, although it is funded by government. The CRE is a statutory body comprised of 15 Commissioners who are selected and appointed by the Home Secretary. Under section 43 of the Act its statutory duties are:

- to work towards the elimination of racial discrimination
- to promote equality of opportunity and good relations between persons of different racial backgrounds; and
- to keep the operation of the Act under review and to make such recommendations for amending it, as may be appropriate, to the Secretary of State

The Commission for Racial Equality is vested with wide powers and has a major law enforcement function. It can conduct formal investigations where it is believed that discrimination is or has been occurring, issue non-discrimination notices, institute legal proceedings in cases of persistent discrimination, take proceedings in respect of discriminatory practices, advertisements and in respect of instructions or pressure to discriminate, and assist individual complainants.

Positive action
The above described legal interventions through the Race Relations Act could be described as "protective", involving the creation of rights, which the weaker party can assert through litigation. The other type of legal intervention could be called "facilitative" when a group (of employers, perhaps) is enabled to act in a particular way not previously permissible (Lustgarten, 1987). The Race Relations Act also has provisions which could be labelled "facilitative", such as those on positive action.

Sections of the Race Relations Act enable employers, training bodies or others to take a range of positive action measures to help members of racial groups who are under-represented in particular work to compete for that work on a more equal footing with the others in the labour market. This may be necessary because previous discrimination and other causes of disadvantage have prevented certain groups of employees from achieving their full potential. Positive action does not seek to remove competition for jobs but to provide for fairer competition, and selection must remain on the basis of merit, not race.

The Act allows employers and training bodies to restrict access to facilities for education, training, or welfare to members of a particular racial group when it meets the special needs of that group. An example is a course of English for speakers of another language. The Act allows employers and training bodies to train members of a particular racial group for particular work in which their racial group is under-represented; it also allows employers to encourage members of a particular racial group to apply for jobs in which they are under represented, or to provide training for their existing employees from a particular racial group who are under-represented in particular work. Again, there must be no guarantee of a job for successful trainees.

Positive action covers measures designed to overcome disadvantage over and above what is required to prevent actual discrimination against ethnic minorities. However, as this definition would also include positive discrimination, positive action needs to be more precisely differentiated. The Act does not allow for 'reverse' or 'positive' discrimination or 'quotas', as used in the United States. Unlike positive discrimination, positive action stops at giving ethnic minorities more favourable treatment in competition for jobs. Positive action in employment is the promotion of ethnic minority interests and chances *within existing procedures* for distributing and allocating jobs and training. Positive discrimination on the other hand involves *overriding* existing allocation practices by, for example, appointing minority group members to jobs over the top of the meritocratic competitive system (Edwards, 1988).

Contract compliance
Section 71 of the Race Relations Act imposes a duty on local authorities to ensure that their functions are carried out with due regard to the need to eliminate unlawful racial discrimination and to promote equality of opportunity, as well as good relations between persons of different racial groups. This provision makes it possible for local authorities to pursue a policy of 'contract compliance'; this is when local authorities encourage companies to which they give contracts to supply goods or services to comply with minimum requirements on employment practices, including on equal opportunities.

Since the 1980s a number of local authorities have used "contract compliance" as a means of sifting private companies which tender for local government contracts. Many authorities have a special contract compliance unit, and in one 1990 survey the majority of London councils said that these policies had produced measurable benefits in terms of improved equal opportunities amongst locally based companies (*IRS Employment Trends* 462; 19 April 1990). A report by the Inner London Education Authority (ILEA) contract compliance unit stated that the use of contract compliance policies over a period of seven years had suggested that they can lead to greatly improved equal opportunities practices in the companies involved. In its own evaluation study of the operation of its contract compliance policy covering 152 companies, it found that while only 18% operated an equal opportunities policy before the intervention of the contract compliance unit, 75% did so afterwards. In addition, whereas only 2% originally mentioned equal opportunities in job advertisements, 80% did so after review by the unit (*IRS Employment Trends* 462; 19 April 1990).

Codes of practice
Under section 47 of the Race Relations Act the CRE is empowered to issue codes of practice in the field of employment. The Commission's 1984 "Code of Practice for the Elimination of Racial Discrimination and the Promotion of Equal Opportunity in Employment" was drawn up in consultation with employers' and workers' organisations. The Code's primary aim is to give guidance to help employers and others to understand the law. It gives recommendations on policies which can be implemented to help to eliminate racial discrimination and enhance equality of opportunity on the workfloor (Zegers de Beijl, 1991).

The Code gives practical guidance designed to explain the implications of the Race Relations Act in the context of employment. It broadly allocates "responsibilities" designed to achieve these purposes to employers, individual employees, trade unions and staff associations, and employment agencies. It also recommends a series of measures to reduce the possibility of unlawful behaviour occurring, including recommendations about training, ethnic record keeping and monitoring, and the use of 'positive action' measures. The Code itself does not impose legal obligations. It only has advisory status but failure to observe its recommendations could result in breaches of the law. Also, evidence about the performance of the Code's recommendations can be taken into account by industrial tribunals in deciding whether an act of unlawful discrimination has occurred and assessing the degree of liability by employers for any such acts (Gribbin, 1994).

3.2 THE NETHERLANDS

Integration policy
For some years, the Netherlands has operated a special integration policy for newcomers. This policy, by which migrants are counselled in seeking or applying for jobs, is considered necessary because the relatively low level of education of ethnic minorities and poor command of the Dutch language diminishes their opportunities on the labour market (Tesser, 1993). Since 1990, a number of institutions have been set up specifically to facilitate integration projects for newcomers, when needed. The integration programme may consist of language courses, courses in becoming acquainted with Dutch society, social support, education and vocational orientation, and an introduction to the labour market. Recently, two professors, Entzinger and Van der Zwan, published a report, commissioned by the Ministry of the Interior, which recommended a new emphasis in integration policies. In order to achieve greater participation of minorities on the labour market, they argued for a naturalisation programme for all newcomers, which will take approximately three years, and will consist of Dutch language lessons, lessons in social skills, general education, vocational education, and/or application courses for participants who already have certificates of proficiency. During this period, they will receive a salary below the legal minimum. The complete programme will be compulsory. Sanctions

may be imposed upon persons who do not finish the programme successfully, or who terminate the programme halfway through. In the worst cases, these people may be compelled to leave the country. When the programme is concluded successfully, the migrant will get the prospect of a full-time position, and companies which create job opportunities for minorities will receive a concession from the government.

Entzinger and Van der Zwan's plan was criticised by, among others, the National Bureau for Combating Discrimination (Landelijk Bureau Racismebestrijding, LBR) (Overdijk-Francis, 1993) who opposed the compulsory nature of the programme, and who were concerned that the proposal to pay migrants below minimum wages might lead to misuse of migrant labour. The Bureau's view was that Entzinger and Van der Zwan ignored in their report the phenomenon of discrimination, which is one of the causes of high unemployment among ethnic minorities. In this sense Entzinger and Van der Zwan's plan should be seen as an integration measure directed at migrants themselves rather than an anti-discrimination measure which aims to change the behaviour of gatekeepers.

Legislation
As well as integration programmes, there are extensive anti-discrimination measures in the Netherlands. The Netherlands has ratified both the International Convention on the Elimination of All Forms of Racial Discrimination (ICERD) and the International Labour Organisation Convention 111 (ILO 111). The first article of the Constitution states "All persons in the Netherlands shall be treated equally in equal circumstances. Discrimination on the grounds of religion, belief, political opinion, race, sex or any other ground whatsoever shall not be permitted". Dutch law does include a number of general and specific regulations, in order to prevent discrimination on the labour market (see Kartaram, 1992 and Zegers de Beijl, 1991). Articles in the Criminal Code prohibit and penalise racial discrimination in the recruitment of new employees and in the treatment of existing employees in regard to conditions of work, promotion and dismissal. Case law has established that both direct and indirect discrimination is covered. Individuals who believe themselves to be discriminated against in employment may complain to the police, although discrimination is difficult to prove, sanctions are limited, and most complaints never reach the stage of criminal proceedings. Some complainants are discouraged from going to the police through fear that their complaint will not treated sympathetically.

However, there is also the possibility of gaining compensation at the same time under Civil Law, and where someone is assessed by a District Judge as having engaged in unlawful behaviour, they may be obliged to pay appropriate damages. "The relatively open norm for this type of behaviour has proved to be effective in obtaining financial remedies in discrimination cases" (Zegers de Beijl, 1995). There is also provision in labour law prohibiting racial discrimination in the context of collective agreements. However, a serious gap in the legislation is the lack of protection against victimisation of those who bring a complaint of discrimination (Forbes and Mead, 1992).

Recently, statutory provisions and the possibility of gaining redress improved considerably (Zegers de Beijl, 1995). Faced with the low number of cases appearing before the courts and the continued problems in proving discrimination, the Dutch Parliament instituted a new Act on Equal Treatment, which came into operation in

1995, a comprehensive law prohibiting direct and indirect discrimination on wide ranging grounds. With regard to employment, it covers recruitment procedures, the employment relationship, terms and conditions, and access to training and promotion. Positive action for women, migrants and ethnic minorities is explicitly allowed (Zegers de Beijl, 1995).

Agency
In 1985, the National Bureau for Combating Discrimination (Landelijk Bureau Racismebestrijding, LBR) was established in Utrecht. Its main aim is to prevent and to fight racial discrimination in the Netherlands. It does so mainly by uncovering forms of racial discrimination by means of research, and combating these phenomena through legal action, by training legal aid workers, by supporting anti-discrimination agencies, by supporting the victims of discrimination, and by setting up and preserving a national network of legal aid workers, and by formulating codes of practice. The National Bureau for Combating Discrimination is subsidised by the government. However, the bureau does not have any legal power, and accordingly, it does not have a legal enforcement function.

Codes of practice
As well as legislative measures there are those which could be called facilitative or administrative, such as positive action and codes of practice. Anti-discrimination codes specify, within the legal framework of what is allowable and not allowable, good practice for a company or institution. In the Netherlands, a number of codes of practice have been established, as a consequence of complaints concerning racial discrimination.

In 1987, the code of practice for employment agencies was established, as a result of complaints regarding racial discrimination within the employment agency business, as well as the research by den Uyl et al (1986) in which the occurrence of discrimination in employment agencies was explored, and a motion in the Lower Chamber about the subject. Its aim is to prevent both direct and indirect discrimination; all job-seekers are to be treated equally and ethnic characteristics of job-seekers are not to be registered. People working for employment agencies receive guidelines about how to act and react in certain situations. Services should be refused to employers who put forward discriminatory requirements. Employment agencies are encouraged to make an effort to accept more persons from minority groups into their personnel files.

In 1987, the Ministry for Social Affairs and Employment, drafted an anti-discrimination leaflet for the Labour Exchange offices. Labour Exchange offices are no longer allowed to register vacancies with employers who make, either directly, or indirectly, discriminatory job demands. Furthermore, they can take measures whenever they think that an employer has discriminated against a job-seeker, and are entitled to refuse all services to this employer. The leaflet also give instructions about how to notify the Public Prosecutor in case of discrimination by an employer (Pattipawae, 1992).

In July, 1994, the code of practice against racial discrimination by the Ministry of the Interior was formulated. It contains guidelines for the functioning of employees within the Ministry, with regard to the daily contact with each other. The code also contains guidelines regarding personnel policy. This part covers non-discrimination stipulations, as well as positive action measures. In the case of equal qualification, preference should be given to an applicant from an ethnic minority background, and in the event of collective dismissals, ethnic minorities should not represent a disproportionately large share of the exodus. Furthermore, employers are not allowed to apply any recruitment methods which predominantly exclude applicants of non-native descent, and non-recognised foreign qualifications should, in conformance with the advice of the appropriate body, also be considered when making judgements about suitable criteria for vacancies. Furthermore, organisations which provide services to the Ministry, and organisations which give training and education to the Ministry's employees, are requested to subscribe to this code. Finally, the code makes it possible to lodge a complaint with a grievance committee, especially set up for this purpose.

Positive action
A report by the Minorities Research and Advisory Commission (Bovenkerk 1986) argued for positive action measures. These measures include, for example, preferential treatment of minority persons in case of equal qualification, or in case of sufficient qualification; reserving a certain amount of available vacancies for ethnic minorities only ("quotas"); publicly advertising vacancies, and refraining from exclusively recruiting internally; organising targeted recruitment and promotion campaigns; screening and adjusting all procedures of appointment, promotion and dismissal, including psychological tests for discriminatory items, and, when necessary, abandoning the 'last in first out' rule in the case of collective dismissals. Positive action has nothing to do with requiring lower standards or quality. For example, if a non-native applicant who is insufficiently qualified for the vacancy is selected instead of a well qualified native applicant, this is "positive discrimination" not "positive action". Positive discrimination is explicitly discouraged in the ACOM report. The ACOM report also advised the government to switch over to contract compliance, allowing authorities, in granting subsidies or contracts to companies, to make demands with regard to the personnel policies of these companies (Bovenkerk, 1986). In answer to the recommendations formulated in the report, the government drafted two Positive Action programmes for its own personnel policy; one to provide a thousand jobs for unemployed Moluccans, and one to strive for a proportional representation of ethnic minorities in public sector jobs (Werkgelegenheid voor etnische minderheden bij de Rijksoverheid, EMO plan) (see Kosten, 1994).

In 1989, the government requested advice from the Scientific Council for Government Policy (WRR), regarding the minorities policy in general. The report, released in 1989, mainly dealt with the minorities' poor labour market position and emphasised integration measures such as improving education, training, and work experience for ethnic minorities. However, the Council also pleaded in favour of some positive action measures, namely an Act for the Promotion of Labour Opportunities, based upon the Canadian Employment Equity Act. This act, which had already been in effect in Canada for two years, commits companies to employ as many minorities as is needed to bring about a proportional representation of the country's population. In order to achieve this, employers should, in consultation with employees' organisations, formulate public policy plans with goals and timetables. However, no sanctions are imposed if a company does not succeed in this. The act also imposes a legal obligation for employers to release public reports annually, in which they have to notify the proportion of minorities in their work force. The idea of making the figures public is to allow social pressure to be exerted on a company to improve its employment of minorities. This measure is legally sanctioned; when a company does not make its annual report it will be fined. As an additional sanction, the government will be able to use 'contract compliance' to cancel orders to a company that is not seen to be striving for a more proportional representation (Kosten, 1994)

Although the cabinet was enthusiastic about most aspects of this plan, employers were less keen. In 1990, employers and employees' organisations came to an agreement which was incorporated in the document 'More jobs for minorities'. By this, employers and employees organisations agreed to work towards at least 60,000 jobs for minorities, over a period of five years. This plan would need to be worked out regionally, sectorally and by each company individually. This agreement made the cabinet decide that an Act for the Promotion of Labour Opportunities was, for the time being, not necessary, and that neither was there a reason to apply contract compliance. However, one year after the implementation of this agreement, the outcomes appeared to be disappointing (LTD, 1992). An evaluation of the agreement demonstrated that only 23% of employers knew what the agreement was about, and no more than 3% had actually done something as a result of it.

Thus in 1994 an Act for the Promotion of Proportional Labour Participation of Non-Natives (Wet Bevordering Evenredige Arbeidsdeelname Allochtonen, WBEAA), was passed, based upon the earlier described Canadian Employment Equity Act. The Act commits companies with more than 35 employees to strive for a proportional representation of non-natives in their work force, and to formulate a plan about the way they intend to achieve this. Furthermore, they must release an annual public report on the proportion of ethnic minorities in their work force. Only the last commitment has legal sanction behind it.

Zegers de Beijl (1995) concludes that the adoption of the 1994 Act on Equal Treatment has improved anti-discrimination measures in the Netherlands considerably. Until then, "anti-discrimination provisions were patchy and scattered over the statute books, rendering them highly inaccessible to victims as well as to the judiciary". Now, the Act provides a clearly codified norm of equal treatment as well as a redress mechanism with wide investigative powers, elaborating in a straightforward way the Constitutional norm of non-discrimination. When combined with the new Act for the Promotion of Proportional Labour Participation of Non-Natives, the potential for effective anti-discrimination activities has been considerably enhanced.

3.3 SWEDEN

Sweden has ratified ILO Convention 111 and the International Convention on the Elimination of all Forms of Racial Discrimination (ICERD). The basic rules which protect against ethnic discrimination are found in the constitutional law (Grundlagen) which forbids discriminatory legislation and discrimination by the authorities on the grounds that all people are equal and should be treated equally. The right of ethnic, linguistic and religious groups to retain and develop their own culture should be encouraged. Legislation may not be passed which discriminates against a citizen on the basis of race, skin colour, ethnic origin, or membership of a minority, and this applies to both foreign and Swedish citizens. The regulations also allow positive special treatment of ethnic minorities or similar groups. In addition to these basic rules there are also criminal laws which directly or indirectly deal with actions or utterances which are racist or discriminatory in some way. Of central importance here is the law forbidding 'hets mot folkgrupp' - persecution or agitation against a national or ethnic group - which prohibits public displays of threat or insult on the basis of race, skin colour, nationality, origin or religious faith.

As early as 1968, it was recognised by a government inquiry that ethnic discrimination was not covered by the current legislation, but it was also concluded that insufficient evidence of ethnic discrimination existed to justify legislation. In addition, there was a reluctance to interfere in the relationship between the labour market partners. Instead, the government argued that the labour market partners should come to mutual agreement on the matter (SOU 1983.18; Reg. Prop. 1993/94:101). However, in 1983, the Parliamentary Commission on Discrimination found that the UN Convention on Racial Discrimination obliged Sweden to legislate against ethnic discrimination in working life: "The inquiry found that a widespread ethnic discrimination occurs in the Swedish labour market" (Reg. Prop. 1993/94:101). A proposal was made which would have criminalised ethnic discrimination in the labour market, but it was felt by the government that this was premature. Instead, in 1986, the General Law on Discrimination was passed with special reference to the labour market. The law condemned ethnic discrimination but did not forbid it. The law also set up the office of the Ombudsman for Ethnic Discrimination (DO). Sweden did not therefore have a specific law against ethnic discrimination in the labour market until July 1994. The reason was that measures against ethnic discrimination were seen as the concern of the labour market partners, in keeping with the Swedish Model, rather than a matter for direct state intervention in the form of legislation (SOU 1983:18).

In 1989, the Commission against Racism and Xenophobia expressed the opinion that Sweden needed further measures, even after the DO had been established, as immigrants felt that they were discriminated against in the labour market. The Commission was also of the opinion that the DO's job would be made easier if effective legal measures were placed at its disposal. However, an evaluation of the DO, commissioned by the government in 1989, did not consider stronger legal regulation to be necessary and concluded that the legal means currently available for the DO were sufficient (Reg.Prop. 1993/94:101).

The absence of a law against ethnic discrimination in the labour market gave rise to a request from the international committee with responsibility for overseeing the implementation of the ILO Convention 111 that the Swedish government make public the measures it had taken or intended to take to fulfil the terms of the Convention (SOU 1992:96). The Government Inquiry of 1992 into ethnic discrimination was asked by the government to look at the need for new legislation. The committee concluded that while there was no obligation to legislate it would be in accordance with the spirit of the conventions. The inquiry also concluded that the current legislation gave insufficient protection. While unable to determine the actual extent of ethnic discrimination, the inquiry was convinced of its existence and expressed worries about its future development (SOU 1992:96).

The 1994 Law Against Ethnic Discrimination in Working Life

The 1994 law against ethnic discrimination, which came into force on July 1 1994, forbids discrimination in working life. The law consists mainly of two parts. The first is comprised of the previous 1986 law against ethnic discrimination - the 'DO law'. The other part consists of the law governing employment and the sanctions against unjustified negative special treatment of both employees and job applicants. An employer who discriminates can be forced to pay compensation to those who have been discriminated against. The new law is part of Civil Law, which is in keeping with the existing regulation of the labour market.

The law shall, according to the Government White Paper, provide protection against 'such cases of ethnic discrimination in working life which are directly offensive to public conceptions of justice, and where the element of discrimination plays an obvious part' (Reg. Prop. 1993/94:101). By discrimination is meant unjust treatment or an insult to personal integrity on the basis of race, skin colour, national or ethnic origins, or religious faith, the so called 'ethnic factor'. There must be a causal connection between the employer's actions or failure to act and the 'ethnic factor', i.e. that the employer would not have acted as he/she did, (by refusing to hire, paying lower wages etc.), if the applicant or employee had been of the same ethnic background as other applicants or employees.

The new law applies both to those who are seeking employment and those who are already employed. According to paragraph 8 'An employer may not unfairly deal with an applicant by rejecting [him/her] on the basis of his or her race, skin colour, national or ethnic origin or religious conviction.' Paragraph 9 states that 'An employer may not unfairly deal with an employee on the basis of his or her race, skin colour, national or ethnic origin, or religious conviction by:

- applying disadvantageous employment or other conditions,
- managing or assigning work in a way which is obviously disadvantageous for the employee, or
- giving notice, or dismissing, making redundant, or taking any other comparable action against the employee.

The protection the law affords covers all those employed by both public and private employers. However, it does not apply to discrimination by work colleagues and customers. Neither does the new law cover all stages of recruitment. It is confined to the actual decision to employee or not too employ an applicant. Critics have argued that the legislation should also include cases where a suitable applicant is not even called to an interview or any other circumstances where an applicant has clearly not received fair treatment. It was, however, felt by the government that a process of recording all forms of contact between an employer and prospective employee would be too complex to implement. For this reason, it is only possible to benefit from the law once an actual decision to employ someone has been made which the complainant feels is discriminatory.

Because the prohibition against ethnic discrimination is a matter of civil law this means that an employer who breaks the law can be liable to pay compensation to the discriminated party. An employer cannot, however, be sentenced to pay a fine or to a term of imprisonment as is the case in, for example, refusing entry to a restaurant or refusing to rent accommodation on the basis of ethnicity. A job applicant who has been discriminated against has the right to so called 'general compensation'. This entitles the complainant to receive compensation for the violation of personal integrity which discrimination has caused but not for economic loss. An employee who has been discriminated against can receive both general compensation and economic compensation. This means that an employer is liable to compensate the employee for economic losses as a result of discrimination, such as loss of income after dismissal. If discrimination is suspected, then the offended party can turn directly to the Ombudsman for Ethnic Discrimination (DO). Alternatively, he or she can contact the trade union representative first, who can then contact the DO.

According to the government, it is the long-term impact of the new law on public opinion and practice which is of greatest importance. The existence of the law alone should bring about the desired effect on employers. For this reason the law has to be clear and concrete. Ease of comprehension is therefore to be preferred over width of application (Reg Prop. 1993/94:101). One of the practical consequences of this is that the DO, according to Paragraph 17, prosecutes cases which are likely to have significant consequences for developing legal praxis or cases which are significant for other special reasons. In all other cases, the goal is an agreement between the two sides in the dispute. The government was of the opinion that the question was of such complexity that detailed regulation was an impossibility because of the risk of a miscarriage of justice and ' because of the risk that irritation would be created which could adversely affect those to be protected.' (Reg. Prop. 1993/4:101)

Enforcement Mechanisms
In 1986 the special office of the Ombudsman for Ethnic Discrimination, (DO), was established. The activities of the new office were first regulated by the 1986 law against ethnic discrimination and are presently regulated by the 1994 law. The Ombudsman has responsibility for all areas of society with the exception of private life. The role of the Ombudsman is to:

- Ensure that discrimination does not occur in working life or in any other area in society.
- Provide advice and in other ways, ensure that those who are subjected to ethnic discrimination can make use of their rights.
- Provide information and take the initiative [in developing] measures against ethnic discrimination.
- Promote good relations between different ethnic groups in society.
- Express an opinion in disputes over unjustified negative treatment

The current legislation against ethnic discrimination means that the DO has responsibility for overseeing and investigating the extent of ethnic discrimination and also for informing public opinion. It is in the area of public opinion and consultation that the DO is expected to play a prominent role. The DO is to work to eliminate ethnic discrimination in both individual cases and to prevent discrimination generally.

In cases of discrimination, the DO is to play the role of arbitrator as a first step. If this fails, then the DO is to have the case tried in a work tribunal.

The First Year with the New Law
The application of the new legislation in individual cases has been discussed in the DO's report of August 1995. The DO received 75 written complaints from individual members of the public about suspected ethnic discrimination during the first year the law was in force. That is almost double the number received in the previous year. In addition, the DO office dealt with numerous telephone calls on the subject of ethnic discrimination. The complaints and questions involved both job applicants and employees, and public and private employers. Two employers also contacted DO with inquiries about setting up a plan for ethnic equality.

A number of the cases were dropped after the initial examination, on the grounds that there was not sufficient evidence available to support a charge of ethnic discrimination. In other cases, in accordance with the law's recommendations, the DO arranged contacts between the complainant and his/her union and subsequently followed the actions of the union and acted as advisor to the union representatives. In some cases with the help of the DO the complainant and the employer were able to reach an agreement after which the matter was closed. During the first year with the new law, neither the DO nor an employee organisation were able to use the law to press charges and have a case tried in a work tribunal (Arbetsdomstol).

3.4 AUSTRIA

Austria has ratified the ICERD. There are criminal sanctions for actively propagating Nazi sentiments, and incitement to hatred on religious or racial grounds is a criminal offence. Article 7 of the constitution affirms the principle of non-discrimination, whilst allowing that there may be discrimination between citizens and foreigners on 'factual' grounds. This would not permit discrimination on the grounds of race, colour, descent, or national or ethnic origin.

There is, however, no extra anti-discrimination legislation, nor any specialised agency or enforcement mechanism for discrimination issues. The problems of direct or indirect discrimination in employment - in the sense of those practices which are targeted by the anti-discrimination legislation which exists in other European countries - is simply not an issue in Austria. Indeed, the legal restrictions governing immigrants in relation to residence, employment and works councils are so severe that it might be argued that legislation against 'informal' discrimination would be of little value until the system of legal discrimination had been dismantled. Foreign workers are legally pressured to accept jobs with poor working conditions, and remain compliant within them. In the words of the Austrian report, "the legal regime in Austria produces racism instead of combating it".

3.5 BELGIUM

Legislation
To the limited extent that the Belgian constitution provides protection against racial discrimination in employment it is for the protection of Belgian citizens alone, and as Belgian citizenship is very restricted, the number of non-white citizens covered by this is quite insignificant (Forbes and Mead, 1992). Belgium has just one legislative act on racism and xenophobia, which dates back to 30 July 1981. In theory this covers crimes inspired by racism and xenophobia but in practice has been very rarely implemented and did not cover employment discrimination. It was amended on 12 April 1994 by the insertion of Article 2a (discrimination in matters of employment), covering discrimination on the grounds of race, colour, descent, national or ethnic origins, and nationality. This comes under Criminal Law and is based on the International Convention on the Elimination of All Forms of Racial Discrimination. The act covers discrimination in regard to employment, vocational training, job vacancies, recruitment, execution of the contract of employment and the dismissal of workers. Trade unions or employers' associations are allowed to assist plaintiffs or defendants in legal proceedings. It is difficult to make any sort of overall evaluation of the effectiveness of the law concerning employment discrimination because of the fact that it has only been in operation since April 1994.

Agency
The Centre pour l'Egalité des Chances et la Lutte contre le Racisme (Centre for Equal Opportunities and the Prevention of Racism), was set up within the Prime Minister's Office in 1993 to promote equal opportunities and prevent all forms of distinction, exclusion, restriction or preference based on race, colour, descent, origin or nationality. Amongst other things, it is responsible for :

- conducting all the necessary studies and research to achieve its aims;
- providing the public authorities with opinions and recommendations, with a view to improving enforcement of Article 2 of this law;
- providing the public authorities and private individuals and institutions with recommendations based on the findings of the studies and research mentioned above;
- assisting anybody requesting information on their rights and obligations.
- producing and distributing all kinds of information and useful documentation, within the framework of its responsibilities.

Furthermore, Article 7 empowers the Centre pour l'Egalité des Chances et la Lutte contre le Racisme to be a party to legal proceedings in any disputes that may arise as a result of application of the Law of 30 July 1981 against racism.

The Centre pour l'Egalité des Chances et la Lutte contre le Racisme is virtually the sole example of the establishment of a real public service responsible for preventing racism, and endeavours to collaborate with all public authorities and private initiatives. It has sought to place the emphasis on preventing racist practices, particularly by setting up a complaints office, whilst continuing to make suggestions and recommendations to the public authorities, with a view to promoting better integration of foreign population groups. Discrimination in the world of work is, in quantitative terms, the most important cause of complaints received by the legal department. Complaints concern both discrimination in the private sector and, to a lesser extent, the problem of access to civil service posts for foreign nationals. The monitoring the legal service conducts in this sphere usually comprises a consultation with the person being discriminated against and, possibly, contact with the employer concerned. Since the integration of labour relations in the law against racism (Law of 12 April 1994), the means of legal action open to the Centre pour l'Egalité des Chances et la Lutte contre le Racisme have been increased considerably.

Proposals for other measures
The Final Report of the Commissariat Royal à la Politique des Immigrés (Royal Commission on Policy concerning Immigrants, February 1993) produced a number of recommendations concerning employment and vocational training services, including the training of public employees responsible for the employment of unemployed immigrants, a guarantee for immigrants that they will be offered a fair share in programmes to combat unemployment, and effective application of the regulatory obligation to advertise vacant posts. Proposals have been made for positive action measures, the setting up of equal opportunities programmes for immigrants, and contract compliance. At the moment no measures have been taken to include incentives for the recruitment of immigrants in employment policy.

The Belgian report argues that there is an urgent need for a legal framework for an equal opportunities policy for immigrants. The first step could be a law prohibiting discrimination between workers on the grounds of race, colour, descent or national or ethnic origin with regard to working conditions and access to work, vocational training and promotion, and with regard to access to self-employment. Positive features of policies in Belgium are two collective labour agreements (Nos.9a and 38a), which give workers' delegates some control over practices that may give rise to discrimination at enterprise level, and the law which covers discrimination in the recruitment and dismissal of workers, although it does not cover all stages of working life. However, it is argued that the law is only a first step in the formulation of a non-discrimination policy, which will have to be supplemented by other positive-action measures. In 1992 and 1993, six positive-action schemes were set up (with the collaboration of the Fondation Roi Baudouin), with the specific objective of encouraging employers and the social partners to adopt an equal-opportunities policy in favour of immigrants (see Chapter 4). The results of these schemes should be used to develop a more general policy.

A positive action scheme's chances of success are greater when it is the product of collaboration between employers and trade unions. However, the Belgian report argues that it may be difficult to persuade employers to implement measures when the authorities themselves are not taking any initiative in this respect or when nothing is done to support employers' efforts in this direction. It concludes that there is a need to highlight and publicise the problem of discrimination on the grounds of ethnic origin at the recruitment stage and throughout a person's working life. This could also be achieved through the use of complaints offices. In this way, some complaints would lead to the implementation of positive action (or, for example, codes of good practice). The Centre pour l'Egalité des Chances et la Lutte contre le Racisme could take as its examples the Dutch "Landelijk Bureau Racismebestrijding" and the British

Commission for Racial Equality, which have used surveys and projects to raise the awareness both of the public and of decision-makers.

3.6 DENMARK

Legislation
Danish anti-discrimination legislation is limited. The Constitution has no general provision protecting against discrimination, racism or xenophobia. One Section protects against deprivation of civil or political rights based on religion or origin, and another Section prohibits confinement on the grounds of political or religious conviction or origin. Denmark has ratified the CERD and ILO 111 but has no specific law against racist discrimination at the workplace. There is a rule that workplace collective bargaining cannot unfairly distinguish between employees on the grounds of 'race' but this protection does not cover recruitment (Forbes and Mead 1992). Denmark has no official institutionalised inspection of the workplace dealing with ethnic or racial discrimination. There is an industrial tribunal system, but there are no specific rules regarding racism at the workplace, and no cases dealing with racism at the workplace have ever been before the court. Since the middle of the 1970s the Danish institution of the Ombudsman has dealt with a number of cases of discrimination against immigrants and refugees, although not in cases concerned with racial discrimination of immigrants and refugees in the workplace. Recently the Ombudsman considered a complaint against the Minister of Labour with the result that the rules on placement activities were made more precise in relation to the staff of the public employment service.

Agency
In 1993 a Board of Ethnic Equality was established. It is an advisory board and its aims are to ensure that racial equality forms as integral a part of the life of the community as possible and that any discrimination between persons of Danish origin and persons of other ethnic origin is brought to light and discouraged. It is also the task of the Board to combat all types of discrimination and to help ensure that all ethnic groups in the community, regardless of differences in background, are able to exercise their activities on an equal footing. The Board is not empowered to investigate individual cases.

There are no codes of practice in existence, and there are no specific provisions in domestic legislation to encourage positive actions preventing racial discrimination at the workplace in Denmark. Public funds have, however, been allocated to information campaigns to promote understanding, tolerance and openness towards immigrants and refugees, and recently the Danish Minister of Labour started a two year action programme to improve education in Danish, vocational training and guidance.

On May 1994 the Minister of Labour published a plan of action to break down the barriers preventing the employment of immigrants and refugees, to be implemented over a period of 2 years. The plan contains proposals for more classes in Danish, special courses in vocational training and better guidance. Employees of the Labour Exchanges will receive special training on guidance for immigrants and refugees.

Special funds are provided. The Minister of Labour has now tabled a bill prohibiting labour market discrimination.

3.7 FINLAND

Finland has ratified the major international conventions such as ICERD. The Penal Code provides for fines or prison for "statements where a certain race or national or ethnic or religious group is threatened, slandered or insulted", but it has been weakly interpreted. In 1995 Parliament passed an amendment to the Constitution Act of Finland. According to Article 5, all persons shall be equal before the law. No distinction shall be made without acceptable reason on the basis of sex, age, origin, language, religion, conviction, opinion health or disability. The Finnish report states that at the moment it is unclear how this new act will affect the position of minorities.

There are a number special employment and training projects directed at immigrants, aiming to counter their exclusion from the labour market. However, there are as yet no affirmative or positive action programmes concerning migrants and ethnic minorities (with the exception of those language measures for the Swedish speaking minority). There is an Ombusdsman for Aliens whose remit is the protection of foreigners in Finland. Foreigners usually turn to this office for advice on matters of residence and work permits, deportation issues, and social security matters. However, relatively few of these are concerned with issues of employment.

Generally speaking, there is little public debate on issues of racism and discrimination in employment. In 1995 the Advisory Board for Refugee and Migration Affairs initiated an action plan "Towards a Tolerant Finland", recommending measures to be taken by authorities and organisations. One of the objectives of this campaign is to organise a systematic monitoring of racist violence and discrimination. A proposition also recently came from this Board that the post of an Ombudsman for Discrimination should be established.

The Finnish report concludes that because the number of immigrants in Finland is relatively small, problems relating to immigrants' unemployment or racism within the workplace have been looked upon as marginal in the realm of national politics. Immigrants' own organisations and pressure groups are still relatively small and weak, so they have as yet had little success in bringing these issues to public discussion.

3.8 FRANCE

Legislation
France has ratified the two major international conventions, ICERD and ILO 111. A relatively wide array of legal resources is available and is constantly being added to, particularly by way of international treaties and conventions to which France is a party and which sometimes lead to changes in national law. A few major texts govern the general principle of equality and explicitly forbid discrimination based on race, colour, sex, language, religion, political opinion, country of origin, social origin, birth and personal wealth. Key documents are the Declaration of the Rights of Man of

1789, the Universal Declaration of Human Rights of 1948, the Preamble to the 1946 Constitution and Article 2 of the Constitution of 1958. It is particularly since the 1970s that France has shown concern to enshrine in its legislation not only the principles but also the means for combating racism and discrimination. Some of these legal measures stem from the adoption of international treaties and conventions on human rights in particular. This has led to the enactment of two laws against racism (1972 and 1990, the second complementing the first), to changes in the Penal Code and the Labour Code, to the adoption of the Law on data processing, records and rights (Informatique, fichiers et libertés) of 1978.

The prohibition of discriminatory job offers and sanctions in respect of them apply both to employers and to intermediaries (the press, employment bureaux etc.). A number of judgements handed down in recent years have at last allowed the application of long-standing provisions of the Penal Code and the 1972 law against racism, which provide penalties to act as a deterrent. Legislation covers both public and private employers under Criminal Law in respect of both refusal to recruit, and dismissal on the grounds of 'race'. However, it seems that indirect discrimination is not covered by the legislation. Most of the cases are brought or supported by organisations dedicated to fighting racism. These associations offer specialist advice and are entitled to exercise the right accorded to civil parties in criminal proceedings provided that they have been lawfully registered for five years (Forbes and Mead 1992).

The main barrier to successful claims under the Acts is the difficulty of producing evidence. Under the Criminal Code an employer is not required to record the reasons for a choice between applicants. The fact that the Penal Code does not foresee remedies such as reinstatement or financial compensation for the victims of unlawful discrimination means that there is a considerable disincentive for victims to institute proceedings (Zegers de Beijl, 1995). The Labour Code provides for equal treatment during employment only for punishment or dismissal by an employer, but not for more general equal treatment and opportunity during employment (Zegers de Beijl, 1995).

Forbes and Mead (1992) conclude that in France the reasonable access to the law is offset by the lack of convictions. One problem is the 'invisibility' of groups under the law. Even though the law recognises that a group of people may be discriminated against on the basis of their ethnic origin, race, or religion, no direct jurisprudence arises from that recognition in respect of the group. Thus each case has to be fought individually, making it more difficult to prove harm against ethnic groups as such. Furthermore the possibility of positive action in theory is undermined by the restrictions on the collection of ethnic and colour-sensitive statistics. In general, French law has no texts incorporating measures for the protection of or attribution of particular rights to ethnic or "racial" groups falling victim to historical or contemporary prejudice. In its adherence to basic human rights and the principles of equality and individual freedom, France accords no legal status to the concept of "minority".

3.9 GERMANY

Legislation

Germany has ratified both ICERD and ILO 111. There is no special anti-discrimination legislation in Germany. As legislation and politics are based on the principle of 'equality' (Gleichstellung) the official opinion of the government is that special legislation against discrimination is not necessary. The Basic Law prohibits discrimination against individuals on grounds of 'gender, race, language, homeland or origin, faith, religious or political opinions' (Art.3. Abs.3 GG) However Article 3 binds only the legislature, the executive, and the judiciary as directly enforceable law. Thus, Article 3 itself does not prohibit racist discrimination by private persons or companies.

With regard to employment in the private sector, the Works Constitution Act ('Betriebsverfassungsgesetz') is the only legislation that explicitly outlaws discrimination against individuals according to their race, origin or nationality. This industrial relations law describes the integration of migrant workers as one of the tasks of shop stewards. In Para 75 of the Betriebsverfassungsgesetz, employers and works council have to ensure that all employees are treated justly and equally, and that they are not discriminated against on the grounds of 'origin, religion, nationality, political or trade union activities, gender or opinions'. But it is lawful to treat individuals differently according to their different characteristics: for instance, knowledge of language of the host country.

Forbes and Mead conclude that access to the works council offers the most straightforward and immediate resolution to discrimination for those in employment, and has the potential for improving recruiting standards. Generally speaking, trade unions, rather than bringing court actions over discrimination, will be more likely to put pressure on employers. However, this is more feasible with large employers where there is strong union representation, rather than with small employers (Forbes and Mead, 1992).

Major weaknesses in the above provisions are that *indirect* discrimination is not covered, and discrimination in *access* to employment is not outlawed by the industrial relations law. Recourse to civil remedies for discrimination is hampered by the difficulty of proving discriminatory intent, and the financial risk involved in the legal process (Zegers de Beijl, 1995). There is no other civil legislation explicitly prohibiting discrimination on the grounds of gender, 'race', origin, etc. However, some laws prohibit discrimination as regards the provision of certain services indirectly (e.g. private transport companies are under an obligation to transport everybody fulfilling certain minimum requirements). As there is no established body of anti-discrimination law there are no enforcement and implementation mechanisms. Neither are there any control mechanisms evaluating the efficiency of the few laws that do exist against discrimination.

Integration policies

Rather than anti-discrimination legislation, the Federal Republic of Germany has developed some integration measures aimed at the migrant population. Policies of integration exist on three levels: counselling, language courses and courses to obtain a qualification. About 1100 social workers are employed by charity organisations like 'Arbeiterwohlfahrt', 'Deutscher Caritasverbandï' and 'Diakonisches Werk' to help migrants with legal problems, concerned mainly with work and housing. But personal problems and school problems are also dealt with. This work is subsidised by the state - for instance, by 38 million DM in 1991 (The migrant population was then about five and a half million). Language courses are also financed by a state-based organisation. These courses are specifically for migrant workers from the countries of recruitment. In addition, there are special courses for 'ethnic Germans'. Asylum-seekers are not allowed into these courses. The government argues they would then develop links with Germany and it would be more difficult to expel them where necessary.

3.10 GREECE

Greece has ratified the two main conventions ICERD and ILO 111. However, there is no comprehensive legislation dealing with racial discrimination in employment. The Constitution has a provision which confers a right of all employees to equal pay for equal work, with no discrimination on grounds of sex or any other distinction, which is therefore assumed to cover race and colour. However, there are no specific provisions dealing with discrimination at the stages of recruitment and selection, and no evidence that international conventions have in practice been drawn upon to fill this gap. Liability for breach of employment laws on discrimination is covered by civil law (Forbes and Mead, 1992). There is very little information on the number of cases that have been attempted or brought before the courts, and a general lack of awareness of the existing provisions. Forbes and Mead conclude that racial discrimination has yet to receive serious attention from the Greek government.

3.11 IRELAND

Legislation
Ireland has not ratified ICERD or ILO 111. There are no statutory provisions prohibiting racial discrimination in relation to access to, or conditions of employment in Ireland. The only forms of discrimination currently illegal in these areas of employment are those outlined under the Employment Equality Act (1977) which makes it unlawful to discriminate on grounds of sex or marital status in relation to access to employment. One aspect of employment law which does cover the specific issue of racial discrimination is in the area of employment termination. Under section 6(2)(e) of the Unfair Dismissal Acts 1977 to 1993, a dismissal resulting wholly or mainly from "race or colour of the employee" is unfair. However, there are significant limitations; while amendments to the Act have now extended protection to part-time workers (the Act now covers employees normally expected to work eight hours or more each week) it does not cover those with less than a year's continuous service. Another weakness is that redress available under the Act is quite limited given that in the majority of cases, employees have obtained relatively low levels of monetary compensation rather than reinstatement in their old jobs. The Act also does not cover a significant body of workers in the State including: members of the defence forces and the Gardai; persons undergoing full-time training or apprenticeships in FAS (State Training Agency) establishments; state employees' other than certain

industrial categories and officers of local authorities, health boards (other than temporary officers) and vocational education committees.

To date the only protection for Travellers who experience discrimination in areas of employment is the Unfair Dismissals Act (1977), which was amended in 1993 to include Travellers. This act deems a dismissal resulting wholly or mainly from a person's membership of the Travelling Community to be automatically unfair. However, this protection provides only limited benefits to the Travelling Community who are significantly under-represented in the labour force, most being either dependent on social welfare or engaged in forms of economic activity based on the extended family, which remains the main unit of organisation in the Travelling Community. In effect, Travellers are not protected from discrimination in those areas where it is most likely to arise: access to waged employment, and when trying to develop their own traditional forms of economic activity.

The Republic of Ireland also has a written constitution which, among other things, allows an aggrieved employee to seek redress under the Constitution, in addition to any relevant statutory or common law rights. Racial discrimination in employment could be found to infringe on the prospective employee's constitutional rights, but this is an issue yet to be decided. While no protection is provided against racial discrimination under the Employment Equality Act, some protection is provided under European law for EU nationals. Article 48.2 of the Treaty of Rome provides that free movement of workers shall entail the abolition of any discrimination based on nationality between workers of the member States as regards employment, remuneration and other conditions of work and employment. However, despite the possible redress available under either the Constitution or European law, the protection provided only covers Irish citizens with regard to the Constitution and EU nationals in relation to European law. This has serious implications for those working in Ireland who fall into neither category - for example, registered aliens The assistance available for taking cases is also severely restricted.

Proposals for change
The Irish Government has committed itself to bringing forward comprehensive change in the whole area of legislative protection against discrimination. The Department of Equality and Law Reform is preparing two major pieces of anti-discrimination legislation which will include protection against discrimination on the grounds of race, colour, nationality or national or ethnic origins. The two pieces of legislation are:

1. Revised Employment Equality Legislation. The proposals here would re-enact, with improvements, the existing equal pay and employment equality laws which are primarily gender based. These would also extend the scope of the new law to cover other forms of discrimination including those based on race and membership of the Travelling Community.

2. Equal Status Legislation. The proposals here would extend anti-discrimination law beyond non-employment areas. As outlined in the Programme for Government, the proposals here would declare unlawful many forms of

discrimination, including those related to race and membership of the Travelling Community.

It is likely that employment related discrimination on the grounds of race or ethnic background will cover both direct and indirect forms of discrimination as currently applies in the case of discrimination on the basis of sex or marital status in relation to access to and conditions of employment.

3.12 ITALY

Italy has ratified the two major conventions on racial discrimination, ICERD and ILO 111. The Constitution guarantees a right to 'equal social status' and 'equality before the law' regardless of race and language, and legal opinion is that this provision probably now places obligations upon private as well as public bodies. With regard to employment, legislation in 1977 declares null and void all acts and agreements on hiring, dismissals, transfers and promotions grounded upon the race, colour, ethnic or national origin of the employee or applicant. While the concept of indirect discrimination has recently been introduced in the area of sex discrimination, it is yet undeveloped in racial discrimination (Forbes and Mead, 1992).

Forbes and Mead conclude that implementation of laws and policies to combat discrimination is patchy in Italy. Complaints of discrimination are dealt with by the Labour Inspectorate. However, the Inspectorate has no special training in this field and there are no codes of practice to offer guidance. Trade unions have reacted positively to issues of migration and discrimination and will seek to negotiate directly with an employer over a complaint of discrimination. If this is not successful the trade union can assist the complainant to go to court. However, at the level of the courts, the chances of a complaint being proven are limited. Statistical evidence is not accepted in court, and courts will only consider objective evidence that a person has been unfairly disadvantaged and will not consider subjective evidence on the intention to discriminate.

There is some legislation at the regional level which provides for positive action, or even positive discrimination, to deal with racial discrimination. For example, in the Trentino-Alto Adige region there is the right to be hired in public posts in proportion to numbers in each area (Forbes and Mead, 1992). More common are local measures of integration: for example, the laws of Piedmont and Lazio provide for courses in Italian and Italian culture to be made available to adult immigrants by granting subsidies to bodies and associations. Another commitment is to develop longer-term activities by setting up schemes whose purpose is to train Italian school pupils in "multi-culturalism" or "inter-culturalism".

3.13 LUXEMBOURG

The Constitution contains no anti-discriminatory clauses. Luxembourg law contains only one anti-discriminatory provision: this is the International Convention on the Elimination of all Forms of Racial Discrimination, which was incorporated into the

Law of 9 August 1980. This legislation is relatively ineffective; it is unclear whether private employers are bound by it, and it has never been invoked.

Some improvement came with Chapter 2 of the Law of 27 July 1993 on the integration of foreigners into Luxembourg, entitled, "Measures in support of stronger action against all forms of racial, ethnic and religious discrimination". This new law includes discrimination against a person, group of persons or a community based on the race, colour, ancestry, or ethnic or national origin of that person. This therefore is seen to cover discrimination in employment. However, it is not backed up by any major penal sanctions.

In September, four anti-racist organisations (ASTI, CLAE, LICRA and SOS Racisme) drew up proposals for strengthening anti-racist legislation. They argued that there are instances of racism and discriminatory behaviour in the field of employment. Although to prove that they are discriminatory is very difficult, it is nonetheless important that Luxembourg legislation should incorporate the notion of discrimination in the recruitment and dismissal of employees, and that there should be sanctions to deal with it. "Legislation must contain provisions that act as deterrents and which, at the very least, offer protection." A Draft Law of 20 November 1991 was tabled in the Chamber of Deputies. This sought to add an extra paragraph to Article 454 of the Penal Code to cover "anyone who refuses to recruit, or who dismisses, a person by reason of his/her race, colour, ancestry or ethnic or national origin." These provisions have not yet become law.

Following the Corfu European Council, which set out to reinforce anti-racist legal provisions, the new Luxembourg Government stated in a declaration of general policy on 22 July 1994: "Given the upsurge of racism and xenophobia, this is an appropriate time to review, or add to, existing laws (as the case may be) in order to establish the kind of legislation needed to repress effectively the racist and xenophobic acts that are so prejudicial to efforts of integrating the non-Luxembourg population."

Given the inadequacy of legal and regulatory arguments in the struggle against discrimination, it is hardly surprising that the mechanisms for applying the above measures have been put to little use. A survey carried out by Labour Inspectorate officials shows that not one case of racial discrimination in the workplace has resulted in a complaint to them. Nor is there any case law that uses discriminatory arguments relating to employment.

3.14 NORWAY

The UN convention on the elimination of racial discrimination was ratified in Norway and came into force in 1969. The Penal Code section 135a concerning racial discrimination was amended in 1969 to be in line with the UN convention (Haagensen et al, 1990). Section 135a of the Norwegian Penal Code states that it is a criminal offence to spread discriminatory written or spoken information and that people are to be treated equally regardless of religious belief, race, skin colour, nationality or ethnic origin. It is against the law to discriminate on any of these grounds in daily life or work. Section 349a states that it is an offence to deny a person goods or equal services on the grounds of that person's religious beliefs, race, skin colour, nationality or ethnic origin. However, this section does not apply to a situation where an immigrant is rejected for a job for one of the reasons stated above (religious beliefs, race, skin colour, nationality or ethnic origin). The Norwegian Penal code is general, and consequently there is no special law against discrimination at the workplace.

Norway has no special enforcement mechanisms (such as inspectorate, industrial tribunals, police, ombudsmen) for dealing with ethnic discrimination. The job of the ombudsman for public administration is to try to ensure that the system does not treat any person differently from another. People who consider themselves to be discriminated against can appeal to the ombudsman.

3.15 PORTUGAL

Portugal has ratified the two main conventions ICERD and ILO 111. As these are seen to be directly applicable with the Portuguese legal system, the government has made no attempt to create domestic legislation addressing the problem of racial discrimination in employment. Some constitutional provisions lay down specific rights within the employment context. The constitution makes express provision for the obligation not to discriminate to be imposed on *all* employers, and not simply on public employers. Forbes and Mead argue that while the right to equal treatment at the stage of application is not covered by the particular provision relating to employment, such a right can probably be derived from a more general provision at the beginning of the Constitution. The Constitution also expressly stipulates that dismissals without 'good cause' are unlawful (Forbes and Mead, 1992).

However, Forbes and Mead conclude that the there is something of a gap between theory and practice, and that the operation of the law in this area is relatively ineffective. In general, the information made available to immigrants is limited, and it is reasonable to assume that knowledge of constitutional law and the procedures and remedies for addressing acts of discrimination are not widely understood or readily available An aggrieved individual can take a case before an employment tribunal and the national court, or eventually to the European Court of Human Rights Committee. An ombudsman may also hear complaints and make representations. However, there are no specific codes of practice governing employment practices relating to discrimination, or positive action policies relating to the needs of the visible minority within Portugal. There is little recognition of the problem at government level (Forbes and Mead 1992).

3.16 SPAIN

Spain has ratified the two main conventions ICERD and ILO 111. Legislation on racial discrimination in employment complies with the requirements of these directives. Equality provisions in the Constitution seem to place obligations only on public bodies and authorities. The act to promulgate a Worker's Charter of 1980 confers on all employees who are not public servants a right to freedom from discrimination on grounds of race when seeking employment or after having found employment. The act further provides that regulations and collective agreements must not discriminate on grounds of race or origin, although it is unclear whether the provision covers indirect discrimination. The act does allow for positive action by the government to help groups of unemployed workers who have difficulty finding work (Forbes and Mead, 1992).

Access to the law for complainants of discrimination is through the Labour Inspectorate, constitutional court and the People's Advocate. A body of good practice has developed in respect of the travelling community, but very little is related to employment. There is no developed case law concerning racial discrimination in employment, and no codes of practice. Positive action programmes are allowed and some have been implemented in the case of gypsies, suggesting that they could also be applied more widely to visible minorities.

Forbes and Mead conclude that in general, measures are not uniformly or consistently implemented by the authorities responsible for devising and administering policies, partly because there is considerable variety in the attitudes and practices between the seventeen autonomous regions and municipal authorities in Spain (Forbes and Mead, 1992).

4. COMPANY POLICIES AGAINST RACISM AND DISCRIMINATION

The preceding chapter of the report looked at the legal or administrative machinery to counter discrimination at a national level. This chapter examines measures introduced by private sector companies and public sector organisations to remove barriers to the employment of ethnic minorities and migrants and to further equal opportunities at the workplace. Most initiatives covered in this section are 'voluntary', in that they go beyond legal minimum requirements.

There may be a number of reasons why an individual employer might decide to introduce specific measures to counter discrimination and to further equal opportunities at the workplace. In countries where there is legislation against discrimination, their introduction may be motivated by a desire to reduce the likelihood of unlawful behaviour occurring within the organisation. There may be a calculation of commercial advantage by making the company more attractive to ethnic minority clients, or improving the company image. It may form part of an internal labour market policy to maximise the potential of existing valued employees. Or it may be motivated by broader moral and social concerns over the divisions in the social fabric which may result from unwarranted exclusion from opportunities of one section of the community (see also Section 7.2.6).

Although national anti-discrimination legislation is an important first step in bringing about change, legislation alone will not bring about more equal treatment in the labour market. Alongside this must operate at a company level other measures such as positive action and codes of good practice. Of the twelve national reports, the **UK** report contains most evidence of such policies at company level. Despite the continuing ignorance by some UK employers about the nature of equal opportunities policies, (Wrench et al, 1993) it remains true that many parts of private sector employment in the UK do exhibit an acceptance of equal opportunity measures, with some even positively enthusiastic about them, particularly in the retail sector. The kinds of measures operated by employers in the UK are those recommended by the UK Department of Employment's Race Relations Employment Advisory Service (RREAS). This provides advice and guidance to employers and others on the promotion of equal opportunity and other issues relating to a multi-racial workforce. Amongst other things employers are encouraged to develop an equal opportunities policy embracing recruitment, promotion and training, to review recruitment, selection, promotion and training procedures regularly, to draw up clear and justifiable job criteria, to set an action plan including targets, to provide training for all to help people throughout the organisation understand the importance of equal opportunities, and to provide additional training for staff who recruit, select and train. Employers are also encouraged to develop the organisation's image within the community, and develop links with local community groups, organisations and schools.

Code of practice
As stated in the preceding chapter, the UK Commission for Racial Equality introduced in 1984 the "Code of Practice for the Elimination of Racial Discrimination and the Promotion of Equal Opportunity in Employment" which gives guidance and

recommendations on policies which can be implemented to help to eliminate racial discrimination and enhance equality of opportunity in the workplace. A nation-wide survey into the effectiveness of the Code of Practice was carried out by the Commission for Racial Equality (CRE, 1989). This found that only a minority of employers were fully implementing the recommendations of the Code. The proportion was significantly higher among large employers, public sector employers and employers with a substantial ethnic minority workforce. There was, however a high level of basic awareness of the Code: two thirds of the employers surveyed had heard of it, rising to 95% amongst large employers. Twenty five per cent of employers had read the Code, and these were interviewed. Of these employers, two thirds had formal (written) equal opportunities policies, but fewer than four per cent had comprehensive policies with adequate systems for monitoring their effectiveness. Over half of the employers interviewed said that they had checked their recruitment practices and ten per cent found evidence of racial discrimination. Over one third of the employers said that as a direct result of the Code of Practice they had drawn up or revised their equal opportunities policy, had reviewed their recruitment methods and selection criteria and had taken some form of action to encourage ethnic minority applicants. Twelve per cent of the employers interviewed also said that they had recruited more ethnic minority employees as a result of action taken to implement equal opportunity programmes These research findings suggest that the code can be effective in reducing racial discrimination in employment, but there is little incentive for employers to implement its recommendations voluntarily (Zegers de Beijl, 1991).

The Code of Practice recommends that employers should not use recruitment methods that can give rise to indirect discrimination; for example, word-of-mouth recruitment through the recommendations of existing employees where the workforce concerned is predominantly white or black or where only members of a particular racial group would come forward. The CRE survey found that while substantial proportions of employers used formal methods such as press advertising, job centres and careers offices in recruiting for all types of workers, nearly a fifth of employers (19%) reported using personal recommendations from existing staff to fill unskilled and semi-skilled manual job vacancies, and nearly a third (31%) used unsolicited applications (CRE 1989: 9). Previous research has shown that such informal recruitment methods can be major sources of indirect discrimination (Lee and Wrench, 1983).

In autumn 1992 a UK publication, *Equal Opportunities Review*, (EOR) carried out a survey of its subscribers to identify which initiatives are being undertaken by employers to promote equal opportunities for ethnic minorities. The most popular initiatives were the provision of guidance on race equality to recruiters and selectors, and recruitment initiatives to encourage ethnic minority applicants. In contrast only a minority of respondents had introduced positive action training schemes or had set equality targets for ethnic minority recruitment or ethnic minority representation in management positions.

Equality targets
Equality targets consist of a figure of ethnic minority employees which employers would aim to reach by a specific date, through both positive action and through measures to eliminate direct and indirect discrimination. They may be defined in

relation to the per centage of ethnic minority population in the relevant area or labour market, but they are not quotas and must not be reached by discriminatory selection decisions.

The Employment Department's "Equal opportunities 10-point plan for employers" suggests that equality targets should:

- relate to numbers or proportions of under represented groups in, or recruited to, particular jobs or grades
- cover jobs which require higher-grade skills, carry additional responsibility, or provide essential experience for longer-term career development
- be expressed, where appropriate, in terms of composition of the workforce as a whole

Employers should encourage the interest of those they are trying to attract, and take other positive steps, but should then select candidates solely on the basis of their suitability for that job. This is different from a quota. Setting a quota for people from ethnic minorities would almost certainly involve selection on the basis of race rather than on merit alone, which would be unlawful (*Equal Opportunities Review* No.48, March/April 1993)

In the UK, equality targets do not have the force that goals and timetables have in the USA, and they are less common amongst UK employers. They are more likely to be found amongst local authorities, such as Birmingham and some London Boroughs. The EOR survey asked respondents whether they had set any numerical targets for the recruitment of ethnic minorities and if so what these targets were, how they were determined, and how the respondents proposed to meet them. Forty-eight organisations (28.9%) stated that they had set recruitment targets. In the majority of cases the local labour market was the basis for setting targets. However, where an organisation is recruiting graduates for professional jobs, the national labour market is used as the basis for setting targets (*Equal Opportunities Review* No.48, March/April 1993).

Positive action
Positive action is a voluntary measure, made permissible, not obligatory, by the Race Relations Act. In September 1991 the Confederation of British Industry (CBI) urged employers to introduce positive action programmes for the employment and promotion of women and ethnic minorities. The CBI felt that companies would have to give higher priority to recruiting and promoting women and people from minority groups because of significant shifts under way in the composition of the national workforce. The CBI's own 1991 publication "Discriminate on Ability: Practical steps to add value to your workforce" provides examples of companies that have provided extra incentives, training and promotion opportunities to women and members of ethnic minority communities. For example, Asda, the supermarket chain, and TSB, the high street bank, advertise in the ethnic minority press in different languages to promote themselves to potential applicants from minority communities. The Ford Motor Company, Littlewoods in Liverpool and the "Ten Company Group" in the West Midlands are other well-known examples of companies operating positive action for

ethnic minorities. The Ten Company Group - whose members included the Rover Group, J.Sainsbury and the Trustee Savings Bank - increased the average proportion of recruits from ethnic minorities from four per cent to over ten per cent after adopting equal opportunity and positive action measures.

The UK Employment Department more recently commissioned its own survey of the use of positive action measures in employment (Welsh et al 1994). The main findings were as follows:

> 1. Most of the employers taking positive action were large organisations with 90% employing more than one thousand people. Some 88% of employers reported that the decision to introduce positive action was taken at board level or by the managing director or chief executive.
>
> 2. The most commonly cited reasons for introducing positive action were to demonstrate a commitment to social justice and to make better use of human resources. However, organisations also sought a variety of other benefits, including:
>
> - increased volume of trade with ethnic minority groups;
> - access to contracts where fair employment practices are a condition of tendering;
> - improved staff retention;
> - more effective service delivery to all sections of the community.
>
> 3. All of the employers surveyed had taken positive action in the context of an equal opportunities policy. Some 45 per cent of employers surveyed had targets and timetables for improved ethnic minority representation.

A number of outside bodies also influenced decisions to introduce positive action. The CRE, and its Code of Practice was the most common influence on employers and training bodies. Employers were also likely to be influenced by the RREAS, and training bodies by their funders. There was evidence that such external bodies, and publications, were of most help in raising the profile of the issue within the organisation.

The experience of positive action
A general conclusion of the research was that employers had made patchy use of the various types of positive action available under the Race Relations Act and that its overall impact is probably limited. Measures to encourage more ethnic minority applications were more widely undertaken than positive action training. Messages designed to solicit more ethnic minority applications had been included in advertisements by 82% of employers. Around four-fifths of the employers surveyed had advertised in the ethnic minority press and a similar proportion had sought to target job centres, schools and careers offices in ethnic minority areas. In contrast only 44% of employers studied organised pre-entry training and 33% provided in-service training. Where employers had organised positive action training (either for their own staff or for non-employees) the throughput on many schemes had been relatively small. Of the employers who had conducted training, about a half had

trained fewer than 50 trainees in the previous 3 years (and a third had trained fewer than 10 trainees). The implication of this is that the most widespread forms of positive action have been least effective, whilst those which appear more effective have been less widely undertaken, and conducted on a relatively small scale.

It is therefore likely that the positive action measures taken to date have had a relatively limited impact in terms of the overall numbers of ethnic minority individuals entering employment. Whilst the British evidence show that positive action when properly applied can produce results, the evidence also shows that the number of employers using positive action measures is still rather small.

After the UK, the **Netherlands** has the most experience of company equal opportunity measures. As stated in the preceding chapter, in the Netherlands a number of different codes of practice have been established for different sectors: for employment agencies, for labour exchanges and for the Ministry of the Interior. In 1991, research into the functioning of the code of practice for employment agencies was carried out, under the authority of the Ministry for Social Affairs and Employment. This demonstrated that the code is not yet functioning properly in all respects (Meloen, 1991). In only eight per cent of cases intermediaries were found to be conforming with the 1987 code. In many cases, agency staff still co-operated with discriminatory requests by employers ("no foreigners"). However, most employees of employment agencies did feel that the code of practice should be maintained. In 1993, the Confederation of Employment Agencies (ABU) and the National Bureau for Combating Discrimination (LBR) signed a covenant, in order to improve observance of the code. An evaluation of the functioning of the code for Labour Exchange offices found general approval with the guidelines but a need for extra staff training. In general, despite the good intentions behind the codes of practice, it seems that they are not meticulously observed and have been relatively insignificant in their effects, either because there is some resistance to the measures, or because employees are still not properly acquainted with them.

Positive action
As well as the national government, a number of local authorities turned to positive action. Research by the Association of Dutch Municipalities (Vereniging Nederlandse Gemeenten) (Mulder, 1991), demonstrated that of all (672) municipalities in the Netherlands, 116 of them were taking positive action measures for non-natives (20.7%). Two thirds were pursuing this policy for non-natives in general, whereas a third were pursuing a policy for specific groups of non-natives, in particular Surinamese, Antilleans, Moluccans, Turks and Moroccans. Most of the 116 municipalities had been following this policy for up to three years, with a few for over five years. Over 80% of the municipalities that were taking positive action measures operated a preference policy in the selection of employees. For 61% of them, this implied a preference for a non-native in the case of equal qualification, and for 27% in the case of sufficient qualification. Targets were being used by a quarter of the municipalities that were taking positive action measures. Over 40% of them found that the relative number of non-natives in their employment had increased. This increase was to be found mainly in the lowest salary scales. A number of municipalities have already included a stipulation that grants or licences to institutions or private persons will not be granted, or will be withdrawn, when this institution or

private person is guilty of racial discrimination. They are, however, still hesitant towards a contract compliance policy (Overdijk-Francis, 1993)

By 1991, Amsterdam and Rotterdam were municipalities which had already been taking positive action measures for more than five years. Amsterdam in 1988 adopted a policy to strive for a proportional representation of ethnic minorities in the municipal work force, related to the composition of the Amsterdam population (21%). In 1992 the total contribution of non-natives in the work force had risen to 10.1%, of which the larger part consisted of Surinamese. In 1985, the Rotterdam municipality started a positive action project for migrants (Smeets, 1993). The objective of this project was the same as in Amsterdam, although the Rotterdam target figure was lower, namely 15% (later, raised to 17.5%). The contribution of non-natives had increased from 5.5% in 1989 to 7.8% by the end of 1992, with some success in promoting the flow through to higher positions (Smeets, 1993).

The armed forces and the police have also started a positive action policy, with the aim of having the composition of their personnel reflect the Dutch population. The aim in the armed forces was to achieve a proportional inflow of non-natives over three years (1990-1993). The plan involved a temporary preference policy, giving, in the case of equal qualification, preference to the non-native applicant; training for newcomers who did not have sufficient command of the Dutch language or sufficient knowledge of Dutch society, and training for existing staff to reduce prejudice towards ethnic minorities, provide information on ethnic minority cultures, and inform them about the positive action policy (Pinto, 1993). By the end of the period, expectations were that about two-thirds of the target figure would be reached (Smeets, 1993).

After the Dutch government had set the example of a number of positive action measures for its own employees, it expected companies in the private sector to make an effort as well. As stated in the preceding section, the government discussed a number of different plans and options over many years with employers, with some resistance from employers over government pressure on them to introduce policies, a rejection of policies such as contract compliance, and objection to a proposed legal duty to make publicly available information on the composition of their workforce. An illustration of the limited effect of positive action is given in the research by Callender in 1989. Callender investigated 258 vacancies, in which it was claimed that, in case of equal qualification, preference would be given to the minority applicant. He concluded that in only 12 of these cases a person with an ethnic background had actually been appointed.

A rather more positive result of positive action policies was discovered through research by Bovenkerk and others (1995). They discovered that in vacancies in which preferential treatment was mentioned, the non-native applicant was not invited for interview any more often than the equally qualified native candidate. However, instead of preferential treatment for minority applicants, positive action programmes did at least seem to provide equal chances for all applicants. Although employers with such a programme did not favour Surinamese over Dutch applicants, the rate of net discrimination, as revealed in tests applied by the researchers, was reduced to zero.

Both the Dutch and UK reports agree that the principle of positive action is not flawed; the problem is seen to be the absence of a more general enthusiasm for adopting the measures. In the Netherlands there are many examples of schemes in the private sector, in company initiatives and collective labour agreements. The results are mixed: sometimes there are visible improvements in the inclusion of ethnic minorities; in other cases policies seem to be all words and no action. It will be interesting to observe the new Act for the Promotion of Proportional Labour Participation of Non-natives to see whether this will change the situation.

In **Sweden**, as in the Netherlands, examples of positive policies are found in the public sector. The health services have traditionally been a very large employer of immigrant labour, mainly in catering, cleaning duties, and auxiliary staff. Public transport has also been a major employer, especially in the large towns and cities. For this reason special attention is paid to Stockholm County Council, (SLL), which is the largest employer of immigrants in the country and has responsibility for both healthcare services in the Stockholm area and for public transport in the Stockholm region.

As part of its recruitment policy, SLL views bilingual employees as a positive resource. They can, for example, act as interpreters in the health service for patients who have difficulty expressing themselves in Swedish. SLL has repeatedly recommended that language skills ought to be considered an advantage when applying for jobs. SLL's policy is to ensure that immigrants have access to information and an introduction to work which is comparable to that provided for other employees. SLL regards immigrants as a 'neglected resource'. Therefore, there is a policy of noting whenever a highly educated immigrant is employed in a job for which he/she is over-qualified. Employment services should then be informed of the situation and routines for following up the situation be agreed upon.

There are almost 10,000 employees within the seven companies which make up Stockholm Public Transport (SL) of whom 2,810 (28.2 per cent) are immigrants who were not born in Sweden. Over 120 different nationalities are represented. The largest immigrant groups are from Finland, Iran, Yugoslavia, Ethiopia, Turkey and Chile. SL has been a major employer of immigrants to Sweden since the 1960s and has always received large number of applications from immigrants. Immigrants are therefore a part of the company landscape. For this reason, it has not been felt necessary to design recruitment drives which appeal directly to immigrants. However, most recruitment campaigns, such as newspaper advertisements, do include people who are noticeably 'immigrant' in appearance.

Immigrant workers are heavily concentrated in the bus division and underground railway division of SL's operations. Immigrants are considered to be a stable and loyal category of workers. During recent years they have begun to advance up SL's occupational ladder. An important reason for this is the use of internal recruitment. Work group leaders have always been recruited internally. External recruitment is only used if no suitable candidate can be found within SL. This is especially true of the unions which represent traffic, station management and drivers.

There have been no 'positive action' programmes implemented by SL. However, a recent reorganisation has resulted in a form of 'positive discrimination'. Large working groups have been broken up into smaller units each with their own work leader. On the underground lines which serve areas with large immigrant populations the composition of work groups and the work leader backgrounds reflect the ethnic composition of the areas. This has not resulted in any complaints from other employees.

As for the private sector, the question of possible ethnic discrimination is rarely taken up by Swedish employers. Those problems which do exists are more likely to be ascribed to characteristics of immigrants themselves: lack of cultural and language skills, insufficient education, dependency on welfare and lack of information about the possibilities which do exist to help start a business. In order to change what are seen as unfavourable attitudes among employers and the public and make immigrants more attractive as potential employees, several projects have been initiated. Perhaps most noteworthy is the project 'Sweden 2000' in which 23 top managers representing some of the best known and largest Swedish companies are involved. The aim of the project is to use personnel networks to make multicultural Sweden more visible. In particular, the project intends to help young people, among whom will be a representative proportion of young immigrants. However, the Swedish report concludes that on the whole the efforts of major employers and their organisations have been fairly modest. It has taken time for employers to react to the problems facing immigrants, and, for the most part, initiatives have been in the form of information and persuasion rather than practical measures.

Although the experiences of company policies in the UK and the Netherlands and Sweden have been mixed, there are at least policies which exist in these countries, and examples of successful initiatives which have produced measurable change. In many other countries it is difficult to find many examples of company policies on this topic. In **Denmark** employers are generally resistant to such policies, sometimes confusing 'positive action' with 'positive discrimination'. The Danish Employers Association does not believe the problems of the high rate of unemployment among immigrants and refugees can be solved by introducing 'positive discrimination' or 'quotas', on the grounds that there are so many other marginalised groups which would also need such arrangements. With regard to recruitment, it is felt that it is the employer's right to employ whoever is needed, and recruitment should be able to be carried out in any way chosen by the employer. Therefore, new staff may be found by advertising, through the Labour Exchange, through private consultants or by asking friends, neighbours or their own employees. It seems that specific anti-discrimination initiatives are unknown amongst individual companies in the private sector. Increasingly common are 'managing diversity' policies for dealing with a multi-cultural environment.

With regard to the public sector, there have been recent initiatives in the public employment service, with the introduction of pilot projects concerning the employment of ethnic minority staff. Placement officers have participated in courses on work with ethnic minorities, and an action plan to break down barriers has stimulated initiatives which include giving a higher priority to education and training for ethnic minorities. Some local municipalities - such as Århus - have introduced specific policies regarding the recruitment of ethnic minority staff.

As part of the **German** report, a small piece of research was carried out. Of the 30 companies questioned, none had an equal opportunity or positive action policy, none had any policy of recruiting migrant workers for higher-qualified jobs, and none had special training or qualification programmes or programmes for career development. Employers replied that an equal opportunity policy was unnecessary, because everybody already had equal opportunities - every worker was treated in the same way, everybody had the same access to training and qualifications. The majority of companies explained the lack of conflicts between migrant and indigenous employees as resulting from this policy of 'equal treatment'.

Far more likely among the companies was some kind of 'social' or education policy on combating racism in general, especially right extremism, by, for example, making public declarations against 'hostility towards foreigners' in advertisements in the most popular national newspapers. Companies expressed their rejection of any form of hatred against aliens and declared their solidarity with 'foreign colleagues', stressing their usefulness for the German economy. They would finance projects which worked for integration or seminars for their training staff on right extremism and the situation of migrants in Germany. Other initiatives provided by companies were language courses, rooms for prayers, printed information in different languages, and opportunities for workers to take unpaid days off on their respective religious holidays. Some companies supported migrant workers in their search for housing and in legal matters. In general, recent years in Germany have seen an abundance of "joint action weeks", "initiative days", declarations and information initiatives from the social partners against racial prejudice at all levels, from individual companies to regional associations up to national level with umbrella organisations such as DGB and BDA. Whilst all the above initiatives continue to be important, necessary and valuable, there is one aspect which remains neglected, and that is the area of company policies designed specifically to counter discrimination towards migrants within the workplace itself. Whilst cultural, educational and political initiatives are important, they are not a substitute for more specifically-directed anti-discrimination measures.

In **Ireland** employers do not operate anti-racism policies. IBEC is the largest employers' organisation in country and as one of the 'social partners', takes part in tripartite discussions with the trade unions and Government to negotiate national policies regarding pay and working conditions. IBEC state that anti-racism policies are not something they have looked at to date. At present the focus of their activities in relation to discrimination policies (which includes representation on the board of the Employment Equality agency) concerns sex, marital and family discrimination, because these are the areas specifically covered by equality legislation. However, if the scope of current equality legislation is expanded as proposed, they state that this could possibly lead to an amendment of their equality policy to include race discrimination.

In **Belgium** there are very few studies to give an indication of employers' reactions and opinions as regards the questions of racism, equal treatment and equal opportunities at work. One study conducted in 1992 in the Brussels region, covering

30 import/export companies, 20 banks and 20 insurance companies, (Van Roost and Buyse, 1992) revealed that these employers were quite hostile to the introduction of even basic equal opportunities measures. However, the climate is beginning to change in Belgium, with more public debate on these issues and a recognition by many that racism needs to be addressed. In 1992 and 1993, six positive action schemes were set up (with the collaboration of the Fondation Roi Baudouin), with the specific objective of encouraging employers and the social partners to adopt an equal opportunities policy for immigrants. The schemes concerned are:

1. *Educam or the Fondation pour la Formation Professionnelle dans le Secteur Automobile* [Foundation for Vocational Training in the Automotive Industry]: this is an organisation of workers and employers that conducts initiatives concerning training and employment for "risk groups".

2. *BRTN (Belgische Radio en TV-Nederlands)*: in this case, the positive action programme for immigrants is being developed in parallel with a positive action programme for women. It has two basic aims: to promote the employment of immigrants in radio and television, and to improve the portrayal of immigrants in radio and television programmes.

3. *Chambre du Commerce et de l'Industrie d'Anvers* [Antwerp Chamber of Trade and Industry]: this regional employers' organisation wishes to create a bridge between private training initiatives and individual employers in the region, with projects which include the part-time employment of young immigrant apprentices.

4. *Association Chrétienne des Dirigeants et Cadres/Verbond van Kristelijke Werkgevers en Kaderleden* [Christian associations of managers and management staff]: these multi-industry employers' organisations are organising "Gerer la Diversité" [Managing Diversity] schemes in the Brussels region, which include strategies for the employment of more immigrants.

5. *Nouveau Saint-Servais*: this is a non-profit-making association based in Namur which has employed 20 young people, with the help of employment incentives (resulting from the decision of the Interministerial Conference on Policy concerning Immigrants).

6. *Manifestations liégeoises*: the purpose of this forum for collaboration between Liège employers' representatives, individual employers, the Liège alderman responsible for economic affairs and a management bureau is to promote the employment of young immigrants.

The aim of these schemes is to trigger the broader acceptability of such projects, although there are still major problems of misconceptions by employers on the nature of positive action.

In 1994, two Christian-based employers' organisations (ADIC and VKW), with the support of the Centre pour l'Egalité des Chances et la Lutte contre le Racisme and the Fondation Roi Baudouin, adopted a charter on "managing diversity". This includes the acceptance of equal opportunities and the rejection of discrimination, and supports the punishment of discriminatory behaviour and suggestions. (The phrase on 'rejecting discrimination' only appears in the Flemish version.) This charter is the result of several years' work in raising awareness among employers in Belgium. However, it remains to be seen whether it will be taken up by the Fédération des Entreprises de Belgique (FEB) and the various employers' federations that are members of it. These institutions alone are recognised as being genuinely representative of employers.

In **France** there seems to be little of what could be called genuine anti-racist and anti-discrimination policies adopted by employers. A number of educational programmes have been devised for policemen, magistrates, teachers, social workers etc. with the general aim of instilling a professional awareness of the diversity of population groups and cultural origins represented among those they have to deal with. With the same aim in mind, specialised agencies have been set up, such as the Agence pour le Développement des Relations Interculturelles (Agency for the Promotion of Intercultural Relations). However, these would fall under the heading of multi-cultural activities for service-providers, rather than anti-discrimination activity for labour market gatekeepers.

The different nature of the problem area in Southern Europe leads to very different issues, and there is no tradition of 'equal opportunities' measures in areas such as recruitment. In **Italy** recruitment of foreign workers commonly takes place after the migrant has presented himself on the enterprise's doorstep, and they are employed on the basis of this personal contact. Interviews with employers reveal that they often did not have any conscious intention of employing foreigners rather than Italians. On the contrary, they first regarded this as a risky option, forced on them by a lack of alternative workers. However, most employers interviewed said they were relatively happy with these workers, in both professional and social terms. One study of 93 enterprises in Lombardy indicated the existence of "migratory chains" in recruitment. Where the first immigrant employees were successfully integrated and labour demand remained relatively high, the first-comers informed their employers of compatriots seeking work. Employers were thus able to save on their recruitment and selection costs by operating a mechanism of positive preference: if their initial experience of integrating immigrant workers in their workforce was good, they were happy to give others a try. Sometimes employers themselves approach associations responsible for assisting immigrants, or sometimes the associations (as well as trade unions) approach employers.

In **Portugal** the only company policy specifically against racism noted was the move by larger employers to de-segregate canteen and accommodation facilities for ethnic minority workers. In **Spain** there is no information available on management practices with regard to immigrant workers within companies, or with regard to any racist or discriminatory experiences in employment. Correspondingly there is no research to draw on which covers the area of company policies against racism in Spain. Similarly the **Greek** report could find no research on the issue of discrimination in Greek companies and the policies against it. Very few companies in Greece employ significant numbers of persons with a foreign passport, and the issue is not seen to be relevant. Employers who do employ significant numbers are those who employ them illegally, and are by definition not operators of anti-discrimination policies.

In **Finland**, in a climate where there are many job-seekers for few vacancies, companies have seen no need to formulate polices on the employment of migrants and minorities. There are no statistics available on the recruitment of employees of ethnic minority origin, and there have been few studies of migrants and employment in Finland to bring the issue to public notice. In **Norway** there is no official company policy on the recruitment and selection of immigrant workers. The rights and obligations of foreign nationals are regulated by the same laws as Norwegians. The only thing approaching a 'special' policy for 'immigrant' recruitment is for high status jobs for recruits from Western Europe or the USA. After interviewing the leaders of thirteen firms, Addal-Jeboah et al. (1991) stated that most of the immigrants who occupied high status jobs within these firms were from Western Europe, the USA or had been educated in these areas. Firms carried out a "closed" advertising policy. Consequently, most of the immigrants employed were recruited directly from institutions and firms abroad. In **Austria** there is no research available on company policies regarding immigrants, or on workplace hostility against them. Given the pervasive legal discrimination against foreign nationals, companies have had little scope, or little need, to draw up explicit policies regarding their immigrant workforce. On provincial and national levels employers are organised in Chambers of Employers with compulsory membership. The Chambers, for understandable reasons, have always advocated a liberal immigration policy (Matuschek 1985; Parnreiter 1992, 1994) but have not taken a stance or action on issues of integration or ethnic hostility.

5. TRADE UNION POLICIES AGAINST RACISM AND DISCRIMINATION

National policies and company policies against discrimination are potentially important in any country. The practical significance of trade union policies, however, depends on the importance of trade unions in a member state, as reflected by the level of union density, union power in collective bargaining, and union influence in the political system. There is a great deal of variety between EU member states in this: for example, in Belgium, highly organised trade union institutions are strongly legitimised by their members and solidly established in the workplace, particularly in large enterprises. With a union density of 55-70% (according to different sources), the trade unions occupy a powerful position as regards anything concerning working conditions. The Belgian report therefore stresses that success in the battle against racism in the workplace will depend heavily on the awareness these organisations have of the problem and on the support they offer. In France, in contrast, the rate of unionisation is relatively low - around 10% - and unions have much less power and political influence.

Trade unions and their confederations have been the main actors in the application of international and European agreements to protect migrant workers. However, as the Belgian report concludes, the issue of union policies and practices towards migrant workers divides the working classes more than it unites them. In the workplace, trade union representatives usually do not see this issue as being a major priority or of any great urgency. For them, maintaining and saving jobs and purchasing power remain the urgent issues.

It has been argued that trade union policies towards migrant and ethnic minority workers can be categorised by three dilemmas (Penninx and Roosblad, forthcoming). The first is whether to resist state immigration policies, or co-operate with them in order to influence their operation so as to minimise negative consequences for union members. The second dilemma arises when immigrants have arrived: should they be included in the union and accorded the full protection given to existing members. Although in theory the extension of membership to migrants, and the principle of equal treatment, are imperative in the fight to defend and improve working conditions, in practice this principle is often contended by workers already in employment (Martens, forthcoming). The third dilemma arises when immigrants are members: should special policies, services and facilities be established for immigrants and ethnic minorities within the workplace or within unions themselves.

Historically the first two dilemmas have already been transcended for most European union movements. With the inclusion of migrant workers into unions, and the transformation of migrant workers into minority ethnic workers, the third dilemma begins to take precedence over the previous two: that of equal versus special treatment. Should a trade union concern itself only with issues common to white and ethnic minority members or should it in addition operate special policies relating to the specific interests of the latter? If ethnic minority workers suffer disadvantages not experienced by white workers then "equal treatment" will allow these disadvantages to remain. However, if a union devotes extra resources to issues specifically concerning minority ethnic members, this may cause resentment and resistance on the part of white workers who see minority ethnic members as getting favourable treatment.

The issue of "equal versus special treatment" can itself be broken down into a number of sub-issues.

- **Policies concerned to better the integration of migrants into the union and into society.** In Spain and Italy, for example, unions have assisted with the setting up of special offices or worked with voluntary groups to help migrants with the regularisation of their status, or with finding housing or employment; they have also helped with initiatives to counter false information about migrants put out by the national media, or participated in anti-racist demonstrations. Special activities at this level seem to be the least controversial.

- **'Multi-cultural' activities at the workplace.** These are often slower to be implemented. They might include the provision of literature in foreign languages, or multi-cultural training and information provision for members.

- **Specific activities at work to counter racism and discrimination.** These are even slower to be implemented, perhaps because they are more likely to provoke resistance from some existing members. These policies might include providing support to victims of racist harassment from employer, supervisor or workmates, or giving financial or legal assistance who wish to take a case of discrimination to a tribunal.

- **Special activities which are internal to the union structure itself.** These measures encounter most resistance of all. Examples might be union disciplinary procedures against racism by union members, or the creation of special structures within the union to deal with migrant and ethnic minority issues.

In the **UK** (in contrast with many other European migrant-receiving countries) post-war migrant workers have had an above average propensity to join trade unions. For example, a Policy Studies Institute (PSI) survey showed that in 1982, 56% of Asian and West Indian employees were union members, compared with 47% of white employees (Brown, 1984). Although some of this difference is due to the fact that black workers are over-represented in those industrial sectors where trade union membership rates are higher for *all* workers, the PSI study reports that the greater inclination for black migrant workers to join unions holds true even when allowing for the differences in occupational concentration. The latest PSI study showed that employees from some ethnic groups still had higher rates of unionisation than white employees: Afro-Caribbean and Indian employees had 44 per cent and 38 per cent respectively, compared to 35 per cent of white employees. On the other hand, Pakistani and African Asian employees had slightly lower rates than whites (33 per cent and 28 per cent) and Bangladeshi employees significantly lower (14 per cent) (Jones, 1993).

With regard to the "third dilemma" there was initially a *de facto* consensus at all levels of the trade union movement in Britain that special policies were undesirable. Until the end of the 1960s the standard trade union position on this was exemplified by the Trades Union Council (TUC) view that to institute any special policies would be to discriminate against the white membership. As one TUC official put it in 1966: "There are no differences between an immigrant worker and an English worker. We believe that all workers should have the same rights and don't require any different or special consideration" (Radin 1966). In 1970, Vic Feather, TUC General Secretary, argued "The trade union movement is concerned with a man or woman as a worker. The colour of a man's skin has no relevance whatever to his work" (Wrench, 1987).

However, in the early 1970s the TUC began to adopt special policies against racism. This shift came about for a number of reasons. Firstly, there was the increasing organisation on the issue by black and white trade union activists; secondly, there were a number of industrial disputes in the late 1960s and early 1970s which had highlighted union racism towards striking black members, and thirdly, there was the growth of extreme right wing groups such as the National Front, who played on the divisions between black and white workers and gave open support to the white trade unionists in some of these disputes (Phizacklea and Miles, 1980). Thus the TUC, having first dropped its opposition to race relations legislation, now started active campaigns against racism in the movement.

In the late 1970s and early 1980s the TUC began to produce educational and training materials on equal opportunities for use in trade union education courses. In 1979 the TUC sent out a circular to all its affiliated unions recommending that they should adopt a policy on racists. In 1981 the TUC published "Black Workers: A TUC Charter for Equal Opportunity", encouraging unions be more active on the issue. The Charter's main points include:

- the production of union material in relevant ethnic minority languages when necessary;
- an emphasis on personnel procedures for recruitment and promotion being clearly laid down;
- the inclusion of equal opportunity clauses in collective agreements;
- the need for vigorous action on employment grievances concerning racial discrimination;
- a commitment to countering racialist propaganda;
- the need to remove barriers which prevent black workers from reaching union office.

Seven years later the TUC re-issued the Charter. The TUC also worked with the Commission for Racial Equality in the production of a "Code of Practice" for trade unions, and has encouraged unions to make use of this code. Increasingly in the UK, individual unions have set up separate committees or structures to deal with race relations and/or equal opportunities issues, and adopted equal opportunity policies and anti-racist statements. Many have created national officers to take responsibility for issues affecting black members, for encouraging the participation of black members and furthering equal opportunities. The TGWU, the largest manual union, has set up 'race advisory committees' for each of its eleven regions across the United Kingdom.

A 1993 survey of 21 unions, covering two-thirds of TUC affiliated membership, revealed "patchy progress" in the development of unions' internal policies (*Equal*

Opportunities Review September/October 1993). At a national level ten unions had a committee dealing specifically with race equality issues, and nine had some black full-time officials. Only one union, NALGO (a white collar union, now merged into UNISON) had a national officer dealing specifically with race equality. Nearly two-thirds of unions had taken positive action steps such as organising conferences for black members and producing literature in ethnic minority languages. However, only six undertook ethnic monitoring of new recruits and only one monitored existing members (Mason, 1994).

British unions operate in the context of more than 25 years of race relations legislation. Under the Race Relations Act individuals who feel that they have been the victims of racial discrimination may institute proceedings, and employment cases are heard by industrial tribunals. As shown earlier, the success rate of applications to industrial tribunals alleging unlawful discrimination is very small; experience shows, however, that the likelihood of success of an applicant increases if he or she is supported at the tribunal by their union. However, research published in 1992 showed that ethnic minority workers still have little faith in trade unions to take up grievances over discrimination and harassment. Instead, fearing a lack of sympathy from their own union, they prefer to seek the support of the Commission for Racial Equality (TUC 1991). Trade union officials have argued that they are reluctant to take racial discrimination cases to industrial tribunals because of the poor record of success in such cases. The Commission for Racial Equality is trying to encourage more unions to get involved with their members who have complaints in such cases, and argues that if trade unions give greater priority to cases of racial discrimination at industrial tribunals, then the success rate will improve.

Participation in unions
Although the density of union membership is higher among the black population than for white workers, the participation in union positions remains much lower, particularly at the senior level. (The most noticeable exception is the case of Bill Morris, the black General Secretary of the largest manual trade union in Britain, the Transport and General Workers Union, who was elected to that position in 1992, and re-elected in 1995.) The 1984 PSI study found that black members were much less likely to hold an elected post than white members even though they are more likely to join unions than white people, and attend meetings with about the same frequency (Brown 1984). In 1980 Phizacklea and Miles argued that an awareness of racial discrimination and racism at the place of work and within the union was a factor in explaining the lower level of black participation in workplace union activity. The reason there were so few black shop stewards was not because they were 'new' - they weren't - but rather because they weren't 'invited' through the usual informal processes. Furthermore, a black worker who felt that racism was a feature of the work environment would be less likely to take on a position which entailed making "personal sacrifices for the collective good" (Phizacklea and Miles, 1980).

White trade unionists have argued that the lack of participation by black workers is because of their inertia and lack of interest. Black /ethnic minority members themselves reply that after years of racism and neglect of their issues within unions, it is not surprising that they are reluctant to put themselves forward (Lee 1984). Black workers reported that at union meetings they felt that their issues were being excluded because of the apathy of the white majority. This was seen as the fundamental problem of being a minority in an organisation run by majority interest, and leads to the debate on whether there should be separate black structures of organisation within trade unions.

Many black/ethnic minority workers feel that the way to get their voices heard is by self-organisation *within* unions, in their own separate structures. Many white British trade unionists argue against separate organisation for black workers on the grounds that class-based interests as employees and workers take precedence over any other sectional interest such as race or ethnicity. The 'colour-blind' trade union approach argues that whatever problems minorities suffer from can best be resolved through a strategy that asserts from the beginning that all are equal. Autonomous organisations within the body politic, therefore, are considered as divisive and counter-productive (Virdee and Grint 1994). In reply to this position, the supporters of self-organisation deny that such structures detract from the mission of the union, and argue that, on the contrary, it provides an extra means of achieving the main goals of the organisation whilst ensuring that black/ethnic minority issues and rights are addressed by the trade union in a way acceptable to black members (Virdee and Grint, 1994). This debate is still proceeding within the British trade union movement.

In the mid-1950s in **Germany** an initial reservation displayed by trade unionists towards migrants gave way to a readiness to become concerned with their interests (Kuhne, forthcoming). Since that time, trade unionists have worked to ensure equal rights for foreign workers. The national trade union organisation, the DGB, was emphatic that workers recruited from abroad should receive equal wages and equal labour and social security rights, thus protecting the conditions of German trade unionists. When, in the early 1980s, the German government began to actively encourage migrant workers to return to their country of origin, trade unions reacted by demanding a secure right of residence and equal rights. Both the DGB and IG Metall (the union which organises more than half of all migrant members of trade unions) opposed the government's rule that drawing social security by foreigners rendered them liable for deportation. Unlike the government, the unions have no problem in seeing Germany as a "country of immigration".

Peter Kühne (1994) describes how the general policy of the trade unions towards the population of migrant origin is in advance of the government. They are in favour of voting rights at a local level, a demand that was rejected by the Constitutional Court in 1990. The Court argued that only the 'Volk' was sovereign, and those without German nationality did not belong to the 'Volk'. The trade unions are now pressing for dual citizenship. They argue that migrants living longer than eight years in Germany should have the right to obtain German citizenship without giving up their own.

The metal-workers' union IG Metall has proposed far-reaching legislation on migration and migrant workers' rights. The union is in favour of an immigration law allowing for regulated immigration according to a yearly quota defined by a group made up of representatives of parliament and social groups. Asylum-seekers, and those coming into Germany for family unification, should not be subject to the quota system. Within trade unions, and for shop stewards, and works councils for civil servants in companies, migrant workers have the right to vote and to be voted for.

These are the only German institutions within which the migrant population has equal rights. The trade union for chemicals, paper and ceramics has also made some suggestions for the improvement of the social and political situation of migrant workers: it asks for the right to residency after three years, dual citizenship, and the abolition of paragraph 19 of the 'Law concerning the promotion of labour' ('Arbeitsförderungsgesetz') which in theory prioritises indigenous and EU-workers for jobs. It is also in favour of deleting large sections of the 'aliens law'.

More recently trade unions have made strong stands on human rights issues with regard to the position of refugees and asylum seekers in Germany (Kühne, forthcoming).

In Germany, as in many other European countries, an awareness of the need for anti-discrimination measures has come more slowly in comparison with action of measures for integration and equal treatment. In November 1993, the DGB published for the first time its ideas for legislation protecting workers from 'ethnic discrimination'. This is a new action that has to be widely discussed within the union's own membership. Such a law should contain the following elements:

- Recognition of international legislation preventing any form of racism. The Federal Republic signed this legislation, but it remains largely unknown and unused.
- The paragraph in the Constitution outlawing any discrimination on the grounds of 'race, language, homeland, origin, faith or religion has to be made firmer in order to include the real disadvantages concerning the areas of work, housing, schooling and public services.
- Central documentation of cases of discrimination. The ombudspersons must be obliged to substantiate cases of ethnic discrimination to the relevant parliamentary agencies.
- Institutionalisation of a centre for those subjected to racism to report on their cases, and initiatives which mediate in cases of conflict.
- Checking and, if necessary, amendment of existing legislation prohibiting discrimination (e.g. in the media and restaurants).
(DGB-Informationsdienst, Nr. 15, November 10, 1993).

A survey has revealed that at the moment the main strategies in unions to prevent racism are seminars on the subject. Some concentrate on 'getting to know different cultures', helping workers to 'to get to know each other'. Although many trade union members and representatives talk about discrimination and racism at the workplace, this subject is rarely dealt with in official union publications on 'hostility toward foreigners'. The emphasis remains on the need for migrants themselves to become integrated, improve their qualifications, and have their culture explained to the majority population.

In trade union declarations in the early 1990s on the protection of refugees and asylum seekers, trade union members are reminded that they should make any manifestations of racism at the workplace the subject of company and staff meetings (Kühne, forthcoming). However, there is still resistance to special policies within unions themselves. In a study on 'Ausländerarbeit' (work with foreigners), Treichler (1994) asked eleven trade unions about their policy concerning migrant workers. Although the study was financed by the trade unions' research foundation (Hans Böckler Stiftung) only five of the trade unions answered. Some did not reply at all, others were annoyed that they had been asked, amongst them the union for construction workers, where a large number of migrant workers are found. The results show that the degree of organisation is high among migrant workers. However, in all unions except for the mining and energy union, the per centage of migrant *representatives* in companies was below that within the union. Although exact figures were not given, it was said that the per centage of migrants among people employed by the unions was even lower. In spite of this, no special measures were being implemented or thought of to increase their number, except for 'encouragement'.

Kühne concludes that although in the DGB and its member unions there are still many people who prefer not to talk about the specific interests of foreign workers, there are signs which point to a more open attitude of the trade union movement in general regarding both equal treatment measurers, and special policies for migrant workers. Foreign trade unionists have the opportunity to establish themselves as groups and make their voice heard within the organisation, but there is still a tendency to see their issues as the concern only of specialist bodies for foreigners, and for foreign members of works councils to be encouraged to deal with the problems of their compatriots (Kühne, forthcoming).

Generally speaking it is the metal-workers' union (IG Metall), which done most for migrant workers. They were the first (and, until 1994 the only union) to grant migrant workers the right to organise autonomously within the trade union. In 1983 the union general assembly decided to recognise migrant workers as a special group and to enable the setting up of migrant-specific committees. Migrant workers are allowed to hold their own conferences and to suggest measures for future union policy. Up to the present time, the directorate of this trade union is the only one with a member of migrant origin. Their leading position is no doubt due to the fact that they organise more than half of the migrant workforce, which in itself reflects the fact that they organise those sectors where migrants were, and are, traditionally over-represented. Nevertheless, even in this trade union, migrants are under-represented within the decision-making structures. Neither the metal-workers' union, nor any other union, has thought about any policies to increase the number of migrant workers within the union decision-making structures.

By international standards the trade unions in **Sweden** are very well organised and represent between 80 and 90 per cent of employees. The Swedish Trade Union Confederation (LO) is the umbrella organisation for national unions for blue-collar workers. The LO is therefore in a strong position to influence public opinion through its members, and played an active role in the regulation of immigration to Sweden. Over half of immigrants born abroad and in employment are members of blue collar unions and therefore affiliated to the LO.

Since 1979, the LO has had an immigrant policy programme which affirms the principle of equal treatment for all irrespective of nationality, race and religion. Various recommendations have been made and measures have been taken to improve the working lives of immigrants and their position within the trade union movement. These include:

- An immigrant committee or contact person in the LO section
- Weekly courses to shape opinion in immigrant and refugee questions
- The training of immigrants to be union representatives.
- Publication of the membership newspaper and information news sheet in five languages
- Conferences held together with the larger immigrant organisations.
- Activities for immigrant women who are not active in the unions.
- Provision of information to union representatives about immigrant questions.

The LO's 1991 Immigrant Political Programme stresses that trade union activities must be fair and equal for all members. The main principle guiding the LO's relations with immigrants is 'equal membership, and in order to achieve this, certain special measures for immigrants, especially during the earliest period of employment may be needed.

> It is LO's opinion that every union workplace organisation and employer in co-operation with one another ought to ensure, within, for example, the framework for work environment issues, that the necessary measures be taken to prevent and stop xenophobic expressions (e.g. graffiti) and harassment which can occur in the workplace. Information and shaping opinions are necessary measures in such preventative work. (LO 1991)

The 1991 Immigrant Political Programme also asked for a law against ethnic discrimination in working life, because of the growing body of evidence to suggest that ethnic discrimination occurs in different areas of working life and perhaps most frequently at the recruitment stage where the qualifications 'threshold' is raised unfairly so as to exclude immigrants (LO 1991). Although the law against ethnic discrimination does now exist, according to an LO representative it does not seem to have been particularly effective in practice so far.

Despite the LO's official policy against discrimination, there has been little in the way of any follow up in practice. There is a continuing need to get shop stewards and others to recognise discrimination when it happens, and greater efforts are being made on this on the information front. The Swedish report notes that although the LO stresses the need to prevent ethnic discrimination at local level through the efforts of local union representatives, this is not reflected in the motions presented at the LO's annual conferences which deal with immigrant questions. These have focused upon the language needs of immigrants and the importance of improving the language skills of members, the need to create a tolerant climate of opinion in society as a whole, and the need to strengthen the rules covering work permits for labour immigrants (Yalcin 1995). The Swedish reporters conclude that thus far the question of ethnic discrimination does not seem to have made much of an impression.

Collective agreements are an important part of the rule system governing the labour market in Sweden. As far as ethnic discrimination is concerned there is virtually no explicit regulation of agreements. An exception is the collective agreement of 1990 between the Swedish Metal Trades Employers' Association (SV) and the Swedish Metal Workers Union (Metall) on the introduction of immigrants into the workplace. The agreement states that local sections are to ensure that the parties will co-operate to prevent discrimination whenever necessary. The SV also recommends that its members encourage immigrants to join the union. As a consequence of the agreement, SV and Metall have together issued literature, intended for employers and union representatives. in which they express their determination to combat ethnic discrimination, The booklet informs new employees that it is illegal to discriminate in industry, and of the existence and role of the Ombudsman for Ethnic Discrimination. However, the booklet contains no concrete information on what an employee is to do if he/she considers themselves to have been discriminated against on the basis of ethnic background.

The Swedish report concludes that much of the information produced by trade unions is of a very general character. It does not come to grips with the practical realities of ethnic discrimination and the many different forms it can take in specific workplaces. When ethnic discrimination is examined it is often in the form of a general social problem, rather than something specific to the trade union itself. Indeed, there is relatively little awareness of the issue of participation of immigrants within union structures. For example, although many refugees have trade union experience in their countries of origin, there seems to be little recognition within unions of the valuable role they might play if they were able to participate more in union decision making structures.

In the **Netherlands** trade unions are not particularly influential in the political decision making process, representing roughly one quarter of the working population. There are no reliable figures on the degree of organisation of migrant workers. Trade unions agreed in principle to the post-war immigration of foreign workers as long as the influx was balanced and organised properly. The unions advocated in theory equal treatment, and formally were open to foreign workers joining. However, it seems that foreign workers were not particularly eager to join, and unions were not seen to be responding to their needs. Broader integration for migrants instead took place through religious and welfare organisations. In the 1970s pressure was put on unions to respond more to migrant workers. Documents were produced in different languages, and advisory committees were created. However, a study of a national strike in 1977 showed that unions made little attempt to inform foreign workers and involve them in their actions. In the 1980s the government and unions finally accepted that the Netherlands was a country of immigration with settled ethnic minorities, and trade union federations became more aware of the necessity of policies promoting their interests. In the 1980s they made more of a public stance against racism and extremism, and the Federation of Dutch Trade Unions (Federatie Nederlandse Vakbeweging, FNV) produced a manual on how to fight racism within the union movement, and decided that people who openly sympathised with racist organisations should be deprived of their union membership. After first strongly opposing any self-organisation of foreign workers, the FNV softened its line and conceded that a degree of self-organisation could play a role in the process of integration (Roosblad, forthcoming).

In 1990 unions came together with employers in the STAR agreement, which aimed to reduce the level of unemployment among ethnic minorities. However the agreement was not considered binding, and soon it became clear that it was not producing real change. One problem was found to be the indifferent attitude of many local union officials involved in the collective bargaining agreements, who were not sympathetic to the principles of the initiative decided at national level. In 1994 the law promoting the proportionate employment of 'allochtones' was passed, (Wet Bevordering Evenredige Arbeidsdeelname Allochtonen, WBEAA), and it is thought that this will have a greater effect - although it was noted that the trade unions did not lobby in favour of this bill (Roosblad, forthcoming).

In 1993, a non-discrimination code was formulated for the largest trade union organisation in the Netherlands, the Federation of Dutch Trade Unions (FNV). The code's objective is to achieve equal treatment for people from minority groups, on an individual level, as well as on an institutional level, and to attain the goal of proportional participation of minorities in the union and in the administrative body of the FNV and unions. The guidelines include non-discrimination stipulations, as well as positive action measures, aimed at the proportional entry and retention of people from minority groups. In the code, the establishment of a complaints and disputes procedure is also set out.

In March 1994, the FNV evaluated its non-discrimination code for the first time (FNV, 1994). However, the evaluation was made more difficult by the unions' lukewarm response. The Contact Committee Ethnic Minorities - the advice and consultation board of the FNV and unions for minorities policy - is reasonably positive about the outcomes, especially with regard to the increased amount of activities concerning the improved participation of members of ethnic minorities in the association's organisation. However, the labour market policy is still not yielding sufficiently concrete results, in spite of the increase in the number of Collective Wage Agreements (Collectieve Arbeidsovereenkomst, CAO) negotiations. This may be ascribed to the poor economic climate, which allows little new recruitment, and results in a great many job losses. Also, in practice, there is a lot of resistance against any sort of 'preference' policy, or positive action for minorities. The Contact Committee Ethnic Minorities feels that the recently established act for promoting the proportional labour participation of non-natives (Wet Bevordering Evenredige Arbeidsdeelname Allochtonen, WBEAA) is essential, in order to support the policy.

In **Belgium** the unions have had some influence in migration policies. Since the beginning of immigration by foreign workers - i.e. since the 1930s - the trade unions have always taken an interest in this section of the labour force: firstly, to limit abuses by employers by demanding regulations on the recruitment and employment of foreign workers so that they did not pose a threat to workers already in employment; and then, to ensure that these newly recruited members of the labour force were working under equal conditions, or conditions that were as near equal as possible. However, even though, as part of trade union strategy, the principle of equal treatment is indispensable in the fight for a general improvement in working conditions, it is a principle that is often contested by workers who are already in employment.

Although the principle of equal opportunities is accepted and propounded by trade union organisations, including both the Fédération Générale du Travail de Belgique (FGTB) [Belgian General Federation of Labour] and the Confédération des Syndicats Chrétiens (CSC) [Confederation of Christian Trade Unions], little progress has so far been made in its application. Only women can claim any real progress, though immigrants have some grounds for hope that the rights acquired by women may be accorded to them by extension.

Collective labour agreements No 38 of 6 December 1983 and No 38a of 29 October 1991 cover the selection and recruitment of workers and, in their Article 10, state that "employers who are recruiting workers may not treat applicants in a discriminatory manner. This means that employers may not, in principle, make any distinction on the basis of age, gender, civil status, medical history, race, colour, descent or national or ethnic origin, political or philosophical beliefs, or affiliation to a trade union organisation or any other organisation". However, the provisions of Article 10 are not binding and their violation is not subject to any penal sanction.

Both the CSC, which has 1.3 million members, and the FGTB, with 1.1 million members, have issued numerous statements and documents in which they explicitly state their wish to combat discrimination and promote equal treatment and opportunities for all workers: young people, women, immigrants or foreigners, the unemployed, etc.

With regard to the prevention of discrimination in the workplace, although the principle is established, the trade unions are certainly not putting it forward as a priority demand. Rather, the unions are looking to the courts and external bodies to do this. The law whose purpose is to repress certain acts inspired by racism or xenophobia (the Law of 30 July 1981) has recently been amended. It now includes discrimination in the recruitment and dismissal of workers. It is, however, too soon to assess its impact. A systematic assessment will, however, have to be carried out in the future to see whether immigrant workers, on the one hand, and trade unions and organisations whose object is to protect immigrants, on the other, are making use of the law and with what outcome.

There is also a new initiative: following research conducted in Antwerp and Ghent with some member organisations of the FGTB, and with the collaboration of trade union activists, a check-list has been drawn up (Rosvelds and Martens, 1993). This check-list should enable activists and members of works councils to measure and identify the "presence" or "absence" of foreign workers within their enterprise, to establish whether they are equally or unequally distributed and to assess the reasons and causes underlying any such (in)equalities: procedures of recruitment, selection, promotion, dismissal, etc. This check-list has been taken up and adapted by both the FGTB and the CSC.

In **Denmark** in the late 1960s and early 1970s some trade unions were very active in measures to prevent racism at the workplace. In recent years some trade unions have again become active, especially the Restaurant and Brewery Workers Union, which has a relatively high proportion of members of foreign origin. A couple of years ago this union persuaded the Danish Federation of Labour to set up a special committee to analyse the situation of foreign labourers on the Danish labour market. The committee published a discussion paper in 1991, which showed that foreign nationals were marginalised and subject to racial discrimination. To solve the problems, the paper agitated for more education in Danish, better guidance, and so on. It also proposed information and awareness activities to create better understanding among Danish workers of the situation of the immigrants and refugees. Shortly after publishing the paper the committee was dissolved.

The Restaurant and Brewery Workers Union remains the only trade union with immigrants on its board, and it is also the only one having an action programme for improving the situation of immigrants and refugees. In general there are few immigrant or refugee representatives in the Danish trade unions. The international Forum of the Danish Labour Movement, in cooperation with a number of trade unions and the Danish Federation of Labour, launched a big campaign against racism in the 1990s, and also put forward a proposal for an Act on ethnic equality at the workplace similar to one put forward by the Socialist Peoples Party (Socialistisk Folkeparti).

In **Ireland** the Irish Congress of Trade Unions is the umbrella organisation for most of the Trade Unions. While they have no policies dealing with the specific issue of race discrimination in the workplace they do have an equal opportunity clause contained in their constitution which commits them to ensuring equal employment opportunities and to oppose discrimination on any grounds including colour, ethnic or national origin, politics, race, religion and sex. SIPTU, the largest trade union in Ireland, has no specific policy relating to racial discrimination but does have a general equal opportunities policy in operation which would include this form of discrimination.

In **Luxembourg** interviews with senior officials of the Christian union, the LCGB [Lëtzebuerger Chröschtleche Gewerkschaftsbond] showed that discrimination is not seen to be a workplace issue. It is true that most of those workers in Luxembourg who receive the lowest pay are foreigners. However, all are seen to be treated according to employment legislation which draws no distinctions as far as race and nationality are concerned except, of course, in the case of provisions which relate to EU workers and those coming from third countries. The LCGB does not believe that a rule which requires the deposit of a bank guarantee for the employment of non-EU workers should be seen as discrimination. The union argues that this measure was designed to combat illegal employment, and it benefits any worker who is dismissed because his/her repatriation expenses are thereby covered.

There are no restrictions on joining a union, becoming an activist or seeking office. The union endeavours to arrange for the translation of documents and interpreting at meetings; there is also a special measure for immigrants in the form of their own structure which has direct links with the union's leadership and does not have to pass through the structures of the different branches.

In **France,** while the class struggle (CGT) and social catholicism (CFDT) traditions are more favourable to solidarity with immigrant workers than the corporatist closed-shop tradition, the weakness of French trade unionism is none the less evident, in a country where workers are free not to join unions, where the rate of unionisation is low, where the movement is split between rival organisation and where, overall, the unions achieve greater effect through their power to influence than through any legal or financial strength.

French unions do not follow the tradition common in countries such as the UK of putting centre stage problems of racism in relation to skin colour. The unions show a preference for the term "immigrant workers", usually synonymous with "foreigners", but indicative of the main premises on which they argue: it is because of their vulnerability as foreigners that these "new arrivals" suffer discrimination, and it is in their capacity as employees that they should benefit from the rights won by workers through their contribution to production. It is in this respect that the fundamentals of labour rights differ from those on which political rights are predicated. In France most social entitlements have been won by citizens in their capacity as workers (family allowances, pensions, unemployment benefits etc.). Nationality thus hardly has any bearing on the matter. Having said this, the trade unions, particularly manual workers' unions, have for a long time shown a keen awareness of the problems of racism, xenophobia and discrimination. They have produced a very large number of publications on the subject, and initiated many campaigns on the theme of equal social and trade union rights for migrants.

Trade union demands for immigration controls were voiced in terms of a rejection of discrimination: "legal" discrimination which deprived immigrants, at the time predominantly foreigners in the eyes of the law, of a number of social and organisational rights; and de facto discrimination by the non-application of rights common to all workers, made possible by their vulnerability. The main points of reference in this argument were the rejection of unfair competition, the dignity of labour and workers' solidarity. The unions maintained that their campaigning in this area represented a contribution to the fight against racism and xenophobia precisely because they opposed the working conditions imposed on relatively unskilled and exploited migrant workers.

Despite their commitment to equality for foreign workers, questions can be raised about the trade union position on the nationality clause governing employment in the public service. While they do not oppose the relaxations of the rule introduced in higher education and research, they also have not visibly contested the principle itself. Some lawyers (Lochak, 1990 and 1991) see this to be de facto union support for a protectionist policy, in view of the large number of public sector jobs having only a tenuous link with the exercise of powers of state. Others, on the other hand, accept the prevailing definition of public service as necessarily entailing, at all levels, the exercise of public authority.

In the private sector, it can be said that the unions generally combine pressure on parliamentarians to extend migrant workers' rights with the use of their muscle at local level to ensure that existing legislation is applied to all workers. Thus the 1960s and the beginning of the 1970s saw the parallel development of action at enterprise level and of representations to parliament for the recognition of foreign workers' eligibility to serve on bodies elected by the workforce (union-sponsored staff representatives on the comité d'entreprise) and for an end to abuses (for example, unpaid overtime forced on workers without residence permits).

For many years, the unions were the only legal and legitimate channel for the demands of immigrants, since it was not until 1981 that non-nationals obtained the right to form associations. These battles were part of the unions' fight for recognition of their right of action within the firm and of their status as lawful actors in the social arena. It is for this reason that the strike campaign of 1968 was so significant in the context of the fight against discrimination. Not only did it lead to the immediate abolition of certain practices (three-month contracts): it also heralded the extension to foreigners, until the 1980s, of many rights both within and outside the place of work. In allowing the unions to become active in the workplace, it brought about a major change in social relations within the enterprise, which also led indirectly to many immigrant workers taking on responsibilities at their places of work. This approach continues to be the one favoured by the unions.

Although France has over the years built up a body of legal provisions to combat discrimination, this has not in fact resulted in an increase in court cases involving discrimination against groups or individuals, singled out because of their national or cultural background or "race", in regard to their employment, pay or career prospects. Some interpret this as the unions being slow to take action. However, it should be noted that cases brought by trade unions are only legally admissible if the alleged discrimination can be classed as an act falling within the boundaries of an industrial dispute. In fact, trade unions are not legally recognised as anti-racist organisations and may not act directly as such within the context of criminal justice. They thus tend to refer such cases to the anti-racist organisations, the latter then serving as intermediaries between the victims and the law.

Now, the fight against racism is more likely to be carried out by trade unionists *outside* the workplace, particularly by those whose jobs put them in regular contact with deprived groups, such as those who work in local authorities. National trade union centres continue to make statements on immigration policy, on problems arising in relation to the immigrants' home countries, and on the Schengen Agreement, for example. They regularly join with the anti-racist movements and political parties in organising anti-racist demonstrations at national or local level.

Participation within trade unions
The unions have made efforts to integrate immigrants within their activities and structures. This has been particularly true of the CGT and CFDT. However, it is difficult to judge the extent of this as no trade union organisation lists its members according to their legal status, ethnic origins or racial characteristics. This they categorically reject, which is understandable in view of the illegality of keeping records in terms of ethnic or "racial" criteria.

During the 1960s all the trade unions set up committees to deal with the demands and special interests of various groups. The CGT has gone furthest down this road and has been most consistent in its practice (particularly in setting up a specialised press in different languages). These committees never had more than a consultative role and were meant to provide a point of contact between the union and the workers. Unions wished to avoid the segregation of workers into different groups, thus compromising unity. Certain unions reject any structure geared to special groups, arguing either that the special-interest needs of the groups in question have diminished, or that those needs are addressed more effectively by the union as a whole. In general, French unions have opposed the establishment of other associations serving particular groups or interests, especially those seeking to represent a given "nationality" or "ethnic group": attempts to set up an Arab workers' movement in 1973 were vigorously discouraged, as were moves to establish Comisiones obreras for Spanish workers in France during the Franco regime.

In **Spain** there has been no hesitation on the part of unions to organise and protect the conditions of migrant workers. The Trade Unions "Union General de Trabajadores" (UGT) and "Comisiones Obreras" (CCOO) expressed their concern about the problems involved in the emigration process and about the integration of immigrants. Thus, they have taken up the defence of the foreign residents who work in Spain as a basic union activity. This has been shown in various decisions taken in their congresses, and in the creation of specific union structures to deal with immigrants' problems, both within the union and through specific centres for immigrants. There have also been courses of professional training and union campaigns addressed to immigrants. The action endorsed by UGT and CCOO in terms of immigration policy moves along similar lines: support for policies of equal treatment for foreign and national workers, motivated by principles of solidarity and fighting inequality, discrimination, racism and social dumping.

The two Unions have created special centres of assistance for immigrants: the CCOO's "Centros de información para trabajadores extranjeros" (CITEs) [Centres of information for foreign workers] and the UGT's "Centros-guía de inmigrantes y Refugiados" [Centre-guides for immigrants and refugees]. They also organise other activities, such as training programmes and campaigns to facilitate the immigrants' integration into Spanish society. Often the working conditions of these immigrants are unacceptable: they have no contract or social security benefits, their wages are below the legal minimum, and some of them are even "dismissed" without receiving their wages at all. Sometimes they live in huts erected at the workplace and their "rent" is deducted from their wages (the Union CCOO found in 1990 100 immigrants working in these conditions in the north of Madrid). They have no union protection, and sometimes they run away as soon as they see a Union representative. However, the presence of unions is slowly improving among Moroccans: around 500 are members of CCOO and many of them recruit their fellow countrymen to the union.

Union measures include the provision of vocational training courses for immigrants, with leaflets in four languages, one of which is Arabic. There are awareness campaigns on immigration within the Union, through the training of union officials in these issues, and the organisation of conferences on union policy on immigrants, as well as on work with refugees. The CCOO and UGT Unions are currently carrying out numerous campaigns of support with regard to the immigrants' needs and rights, and have also promoted campaigns to increase the immigrants' membership in unions. In 1993, CCOO had 9,000 North African members.

The UGT has campaigned for a proper integration policy and has approved a plan of action in order to develop a union policy for immigrants. A press release of the UGT's Executive Commission of August 1992 stressed the urgency of carrying out an integration policy without further delay, covering all aspects of the immigration phenomenon including housing and health. It should be distinct from, but integrated with, other social policies. In the CCOO's last Congress a specific proposal on migration policy was approved, stating that the fight to regularise the immigrants' situation at all levels is an important element of union objectives. "The distribution of wealth in this country should benefit all those who have contributed to its production in an equal and non-discriminatory proportion". The CCOO also aims at creating more CITEs and a political platform where the following rights will be proclaimed:

- the immigrants' right to participate and receive advice at the Councils of Immigrants;
- the right to family reunion;
- the right to have residence and citizenship and access to nationality within 5 years;
- equal rights in access to employment, working conditions, promotion and vocational training;
- the right of adults and youngsters to education;
- a respect for the immigrants' cultural and ethnic difference, and for their national and cultural identity;
- the right to vote at regional and municipal elections;
- a respect for their right to housing;
- the opening of public centres of information and orientation;
- the right to return voluntarily with the transfer of acquired rights and social benefits.

The above issues are those of 'integration'; however, Spanish unions are also concerned with the issue of discrimination. The Spanish unions' actions show how the issue of discrimination is seen differently in many countries of Southern Europe in contrast to those of the north. Discrimination in northern countries of Europe tends to be seen as a problem of the exclusion of ethnic minorities from the best jobs, and the resulting higher unemployment for such groups, particularly of young people. In Spain and Italy, for example, there is more concern about the deliberate inclusion of migrants in highly exploitative or illegal work. The unions see their actions to pursue the equal treatment of foreign and national workers as alleviating discrimination and the social dumping which results from this. Similarly they see their campaigns for the regularisation of illegal workers as a step to end the institutional discrimination suffered by these workers: as long as their situation is irregular, they will be discriminated against in the labour market.

The unions plan to integrate more immigrants into the union structures. However, even though the immigrants' membership and participation in unions has improved in recent years, short term progress is not likely to take place. However, there has been some progress, in particular among North African immigrants. The presence of immigrants is particularly high in the union bodies specifically concerned with immigration issues, such as the CCOO's CITEs and UGT's "Orientation Centres".

Another important indicator of immigrants' participation in unions is the number of immigrants elected as union representatives. This should give an idea of the integration of immigrants in the union activities concerned with the general defence of workers' rights, rather than simply the issues specific to immigrants. However, data are not available on this, and it is assumed that the number of immigrants engaged in these activities is rather low. The large flow of immigration entered Spain after the union elections of 1990, and at that moment it was more difficult for immigrants to participate in elections. In late 1994 another period of union elections started, and it will be interesting to watch the progress of immigrants in the unions' structure.

Spanish Unions have a clear and well defined policy towards immigrants. However, the national union positions are not always accepted by all members at a local level, which sometimes results in a lack of correspondence between local actions and the principles of national policy. The Spanish report concludes that this shows the need for more training to promote discussion and awareness on the issue within the unions.

The **Italian** trade unions' attitude to immigration issues has been characterised by a willingness, from the outset, to act on behalf of the new migrants and to be relatively attentive to the issues and problems connected with immigration. This may be partly due to the tradition of universal solidarity, among both the Socialist and Catholic trade unions, whereby trade union action has never been limited to employees and has never given priority, in organisational terms, to "vertical" models (industry-based) over "horizontal" models (based on geographical distribution).

Until 1986, trade union initiatives were focused on solidarity with and assistance to migrant workers who were suffering material difficulties. During this period, the trade unions, often in close collaboration with voluntary groups of various kinds, took on functions ignored by the central State, which, over the years, had seemed incapable of perceiving immigration as anything other than a public order issue. Over the years, the focus of action has shifted from the voluntary activities of trade union officials in areas with a high concentration of immigrants to a more broad-ranging effort.

Initiatives from the unions cover both public campaigns and special measures within unions. Public initiatives covered the issues of solidarity, multi-culturalism and the fight against the threat of racism in society. Many activities have been developed, particularly since the latter half of the 1980s, and are intertwined with initiatives whose purpose is to solicit Government engagement in the legal domain and, thereafter, the implementation of regulations passed by Parliament. Particular importance is attached to countering the information provided by the media. Information and guidance activities have been provided for workers, especially in the industrialised regions (though sometimes also in mining centres and less urbanised areas). Major demonstrations have also been organised, such as the one against racism held in Rome in October 1989, during which, for the first time, the trade unions clearly stated their belief that the traditional sphere and mode of intervention adopted by organisations within enterprises, which concerned labour relations alone, are no longer an adequate framework for tackling some of the urgent problems relating to the circumstances of immigrants.

Other union actions have included the production of bilingual leaflets, the first, in Italian and Arabic, being distributed in the late 1970s in Sicily by the agricultural workers' union which is part of the CGIL. Since then, others have been produced across Italy. At the organisational level, the unions are beginning to make a more systematic effort to recruit members among foreign workers and the unemployed. Foreigners are now found among the ranks of trade union officials and activists, a considerable number of whom will later be elected or co-opted onto regional and provincial executive bodies, as well as local and sectoral executives. Also, all the confederations are encouraging the establishment of national planning and co-ordination bodies to take responsibility for organising consultations and exchanges of experiences on immigration issues between officers in the various Italian regions.

The period since the 1980s has seen the emergence not only of information and anti-discrimination campaigns and protection and assistance schemes, but also of mainstream examples of specific consultations and activities at regional, sectoral and even enterprise level. This has happened first and foremost in the provinces of Northern Italy, where employment in industry, and especially in small and medium-sized enterprises in the iron and steel industry, ceramics and foodstuffs sector, as well as the building trade, now involves large numbers of immigrants in secure jobs

Two main questions are seen to be important: how to enrol the unemployed and illegal immigrants, and how to form relations with immigrants' associations. All confederations took a similar approach by refusing to draw a distinction between "regular" and "irregular" immigrants and saw the latter's condition as a consequence of legislation that needed to be improved and as one of the issues that needed to be tackled with regard to rights. They established special membership conditions, issuing union cards at a reduced price, or free.

Even when workers are not "irregular" there are issues for the unions to be concerned about. The document on "Immigrants and collective bargaining" drafted by the CGIL's national co-ordination body in Emilia Romagna, looks at the presence of immigrant workers in industrial enterprises and the service sector: although irregular, insecure employment relationships do exist, most immigrants are working under proper contracts and are in employment relationships that are secure over time. However, occupational integration is concentrated in the lower strata of the labour market; usually, immigrant workers' occupational skills are not recognised, and this implies a longer term threat to career prospects to which the trade unions must respond. The report concludes "It is essential, then, at all levels of confrontation and bargaining and, in particular, in the next round of bargaining at enterprise level, to include specific issues concerning these workers, whose presence is structural and bound to increase." The problem is "to take cognisance of their working conditions, on the basis of a cultural diversity that exists and is to be respected".

Foreign workers who are heavily involved in the trade unions, despite their positive opinion of the role the unions play, sometimes speak of a sort of "paternalistic welfare-ism" by some union officers, particularly with regard to the first years of intervention. The shock of the murder of a South African immigrant in Villa Literno (Naples) in 1989 and the national demonstration against racism in October 1989, marked a decisive turning-point in trade union engagement in immigration issues. However, even after this dramatic change, many trade union officials continued to exhibit a sort of "polite racism", according to one immigrants' national coordinator. It was felt that some people are sympathetic towards social policies to promote racial equality, and consider themselves to be free of prejudice, but in fact hold negative beliefs and feelings towards the groups that are discriminated against. Some trade union officials are in favour of a commitment to immigrants, provided it does not compromise the achievements of the trade union movement or reduce employment opportunities for Italians.

The **Portuguese** report contains interviews with union officers. One is from the CGTP, the General Portuguese Workers' Confederation, which has a specific department on issues of migration (both emigration and immigration). The unions have immigrant union members and officials, and maintain that the unionisation of immigrants is relatively easy. They support a policy of integration (not assimilation), recognising the cultural identity of immigrants and also their entitlement to the rights and duties of the host country's citizens. They also support the right of immigrants to vote in local authority elections. They support the legalisation of irregular immigrants and they fight against all forms of discrimination in the area of pay or working conditions. They condemn discrimination attributable to racism and they fight against all manifestations of racism and xenophobia. At the same time they are against positive discrimination of a 'paternalistic' nature.

Also interviewed for the Portuguese report was the president of the Construction and Public Works Union, which has many immigrant members and some union officials from third countries. They largely agree with the sort of policies suggested by the CGTP, with a desire for better integration and living conditions for immigrants and their families to prevent their marginalisation, and an improvement in the bureaucratic procedures for legalisation of work and residence in Portugal. The construction sector involves poorly paid work under poor conditions, and the union is very concerned over the lack of safety at work, attributable to the low level of technology among employers, the very widespread use of the subcontracting system and the pressure for greater profit. The union is therefore beginning some initiatives to tackle this issue. They state that they also fight against racism and xenophobia, although they do not regard this as a major problem in Portugal, with no major problems of racism among workers

The **Greek** report could find little to say about trade union policies on minority or migrant issues, because the trade unions had taken very little interest in either of them. Work permits for legal migrants have been kept very low; illegal migrants take the jobs which locals avoid, and unions do not seem to have any interest in calling for their legalisation, or in calling for equal pay for equal work. Some of the unions belonging to the GCGL - the main union confederation - accept foreign workers as members, but hardly any foreigners actually join. Other unions refuse to accept foreigners as members, such as the PSF (Panhellenic Seamen's Federation) which voted not to accept foreigners in any of its 14 craft unions.

In **Norway**, immigration policy was not a central issue for the labour unions until the late 1960s. In 1968 there was an initiative from the hotels and restaurants industry, which comes under the umbrella of the Norwegian Confederation of Trade Unions (LO). According to Thorud (1985), it was no surprise that the initiative came from the hotel and restaurants union, as many of the immigrants living in Norway at that time were employed in this industry. The union made several suggestions:

- Trade Unions should have control in the recruitment of foreign workers.
- Immigrants seeking work should need to be members of a Trade Union.
- Training should be given in the Norwegian language, free of charge.
- Trade Unions should take responsibility for finding a place to live for Union members of foreign origin.

These suggestions were central to the immigration policy of the Confederation of Trade Unions. However, despite the official policy of the Trade Union, members were in practice both passive and restrictive, because they were afraid that the immigrants would take scarce jobs (Thorud, 1985). After the political election in 1995, issues relating to immigrants in Norway became important, with the Norwegian Confederation of Trade Unions establishing a permanent working group on immigration. The major aims of the working group are first, to concern themselves with the current labour market situation, particularly ways of reducing the number of unemployed, and second, to work to change people's attitudes. There is little specific concern with issues relating to discrimination.

In **Finland** the proportion of employees in unions is among the highest in the world - around 80 per cent of employees are union members. Immigrant members are found in all of the three main unions. However, they are not active as trade union members, due to their small numbers, and the Finnish report could find no example of an immigrant shop steward. The unions have produced information literature in different languages, and have participated in anti-racist campaigns, but discrimination at work has not become an issue.

In **Austria** the highly centralised and well-financed structure of the labour organisations enabled them to become central to the political process. Officials of the Austrian Trade Union Federation (ÖGB) regard the Federation's permanent entry into national policy making in 1961 as its greatest political achievement. For over three decades there has been no economic or social policy-making without their consent. This centralisation led to a trade union focus on national level collective bargaining and to the inclusion in it of a great many issues other than pay, ranging from working conditions to workers' rights. The central role in the state of the labour movement means that it is not at the company level, therefore, at which the labour movement develops its main thrust, but the national level, far removed from the actual workplace.

The trade unions in Austria have tended towards highly nationalist or protectionist labour market policies. The primary objective of trade union policies was always was to keep the current number of immigrant labour market participants as low as possible. It should be noted that this goes far beyond keeping new immigration low, for it also entails actively reducing the number of foreign nationals participating in the labour market and living in the country (Gächter 1995, 1996).

The legal environment of immigrant employment was shaped by the trade unions. Immigrant workers were meant to be employed mostly for part of the year, and the policy of employing immigrants at all was meant to be provisional, and to lapse as soon as productivity gains would make it possible to do without immigrants. In 1975, with the promulgation of the Foreigners Employment Law, the general policy of employing immigrants became accepted by the trade unions. The trade union and national policy since then could be described as accepting immigrant employment as permanent but keeping each individual immigrant's employment and residence provisional. Thus the relative powerlessness of foreign workers in Austria and the ease of their exploitation by employers (as described in Section 2.2.1) is a direct consequence of the policies of the Trade Union Federation.

The other area of concern in Austria is the relationship of foreign workers to works councils. In a 1986 survey only one quarter of foreign workers thought the works councils in their enterprises took care of their interests. Of Turkish workers surveyed only 14 per cent felt represented by their plant's works council (Wimmer 1986). The situation improved with the size of the plant but decreased with the share of foreign nationals in the workforce. Subsequent research confirmed that works councils themselves do at times perceive immigrant workers as a marginal part of the workforce, irrelevant to the works council's concerns (Meggeneder et al, 1992).

The union movement itself does not seem to be putting great effort into moves to remove the legal barriers which prevent foreign workers from being elected to works councils. In October 1991, the Federation, endorsed the right of foreign nationals to be elected to works councils, but no action followed. One of the trade unions most affected by the ban on foreign works council members, the Hotel, Restaurant, Personal Services Union of Wage-earners (HGPD) endorsed works council membership, but this trade union is small and has little weight within the Federation. Since then a number of provincial trade union executives have voted in favour of the right to works council membership. However, two powerful trade unions, the Metalworkers Union and the Union of Construction and Timber Wage-earners, are known to oppose membership, as do the Textile Workers. At the 13th Congress, in October 1995, a resolution to endorse the right of foreign nationals to join works councils was passed once more. In quick sequence thereafter, resolutions of the same basic content were passed by the council of the Vienna Chamber of Labour, by the ÖGB's women's organisation, and by others. The chairman of the Salaried Employees Union at an organising rally held shortly before the 13th Congress declared that his union - the largest - would come out publicly in favour in Spring 1996.

Because works council membership is the stepping stone into advancement within the trade unions there are virtually no foreign nationals among trade union officials. Nor, it is reported, do the majority of officials support the view that foreign nationals should be represented at all levels of the Federation. In the early 1990s the Federation changed its statute to allow the employment of foreign nationals by the trade unions but there are only very few foreign employees so far.

The nationality of trade union members is not known. At the end of 1983 a survey found 55.7 per cent of the foreign workforce to be union members, which roughly coincided with the national average at the time. The sole trade union activity in combatting racism has been by means of educational efforts. In 1990-91 courses for works council members were started, educating them on fascism and right-wing extremism and on how to hold speeches on the topic. The subjects are now included in the three-year trade union school's syllabus as well as in week-long and weekend courses on trade union matters. It was estimated that roughly 200 people may so far have received this kind of education.

At the beginning of this chapter the point was made that the practical significance of trade union policies in this field depends on the power of the trade union movement in a particular member state, and its influence in the political system. The unstated assumption here might be thought to have been that trade union influence would be a force for more positive policies towards migrant workers. The final example of Austria shows that, to the contrary, the consequence of the formal incorporation of a powerful trade union federation into the political process can be the bolstering of exclusionary policies which directly contribute to the exploitation of and discrimination against foreign workers.

6. OBSTACLES TO PROGRESS

The national reports have pointed to the existence of a number of problem areas. The first are as follows:

1. The occurrence of overt racism towards migrants/ethnic minorities, and direct racist exclusion from employment opportunities

2. Practices at work of indirect discrimination. These include the use of family connections and informal 'acceptability' criteria in recruitment.

3. The lack of social, economic and political rights of 'denizens' and the related effects of 'discrimination in law' which excludes non-nationals from certain jobs.

Illustrations of, and implications of, these problem areas have already been set out and discussed in earlier chapters of this report. However, other problem areas need further explanation. The rest of this chapter discusses in more detail further obstacles to progress, grouped under four headings:

1. A lack of specific information and research on the employment circumstances of migrants and on the occurrence of discrimination in many European countries.

2. Problems of attitudes and knowledge of key actors. This could include ignorance and a lack of awareness of the problems of racism and discrimination in employment, misconceptions about the concepts of racism and discrimination, or outright hostility to anti-discrimination measures.

3. Weaknesses in national legislation against discrimination in employment or in the implementation of legal measures .

4. Broader developments in the economy and labour market which undermine progress towards anti-discrimination protection.

These four problem areas will be considered in turn in this chapter. A fifth problem - the absence of anti-discrimination measures at European Union level - will be discussed in the final chapter.

6.1 A LACK OF INFORMATION AND RESEARCH

The detail provided in many of the national reports is limited because of an absence of statistical information which might otherwise point to the existence of a problem, and a lack of research evidence on this issue. The omissions fall into three main groups:

- an absence of national statistics on ethnic background
- a lack of information on migrants in the labour market and their working conditions
- a lack of information on discrimination in employment

6.1.1 An absence of national statistics on ethnic background

In countries where migrants tend to remain as foreigners, and where citizenship is relatively difficult to acquire, then migrants only slowly become 'ethnic minorities', and official statistics cover a large proportion of the migrant population and descendants. In such countries the extent of unemployment amongst foreign nationals would be known, but not amongst ethnic minorities. In countries where migrants acquire citizenship more easily, through colonial ties perhaps, or where citizenship is granted by reason of being born on the soil, then statistics on 'foreigners' alone become less useful. (The UK is one of the exceptions in noting the ethnic background of its citizens.) Where ethnic background is not recorded it is possible to gain a more accurate impression of migrants who have become naturalised by noting their country of birth and that of their parents. Sometimes academic research can produce more accurate statistics, but in some countries such research is also rare.

The lack of statistical evidence on ethnic background in a country could be a function of two factors: there may be laws or regulations forbidding the collection of statistics which enable the identification of ethnic background, or there might be an assumption that such statistics are not important. Sometimes the two factors go together.

For example, in **Denmark** the Register Acts prohibit any official or private registration of people according to race, culture, religion or ethnic background Residents are registered by nationality. Thus no exact figures on ethnic minorities exist in Denmark. The statistics on nationality do not reveal ethnic identity. It is only by examining information on those immigrants who have kept their original nationality, and assuming that the situation of the others is comparable, that it is possible to get a rough idea of the situation of the new ethnic minorities on the Danish labour market as a whole.

For many years Danish politicians and government officials believed that the immigration of foreign labour was a temporary phenomenon. It was assumed that immigrant workers would return to their countries of origin as soon as there was no longer any need for them. The problems of adapting to Danish society would disappear when the migrants went home, so no systematic research was initiated which might have indicated how the problems of integration could be solved. When it became clear that many migrants were settled in Denmark the Danish Social Science Research Council initially granted funds for a number of projects, but it remains a fact that Denmark has very few experienced social researchers examining issues in the field of migration.

In **France** the terminology employed in official circles is almost completely absent of any "ethnic" or "racial" categorisation. Collection of data on this basis is forbidden by law. For example a 1987 French act specifies that data on racial origins may not be stored electronically without the express agreement of the person concerned, with penalties of up to five years in prison for breach of this law.

There are no longitudinal statistics on "immigrants". Thus French researchers have found it impossible to keep track of what happens to population groups of foreign origin in different social areas (employment, housing, social and political involvement etc.), because of their "disappearance" from the statistics once they assume French nationality and, in particular, when the children of foreigners become French by birth. Because of the lack of reliable data on those of foreign origin and their descendants after they arrive in France, researchers do not have a reliable overall picture of the social circumstances of these groups, and in particular of the sorts of patterns of inequality which might suggest the operation of discrimination.

However, the French report points out the contradiction that this lack of official categorisation contrasts strongly with unofficial processes of categorisation. Firstly, there is the increasing readiness of the press and the 'man in the street' to classify immigrant or minority groups and generalise accordingly. More worryingly, there are the secret, sometimes illegal, classification methods employed by the public authorities: police, and officials responsible for welfare, social security and education. In fact, many French public authorities are far from being as "colour-blind" as the Republican principles would have them be. There is a discrepancy between what the law says and what the authorities do: the police have their own criteria for locating people; agencies responsible for allocating subsidised housing openly apply quotas in the name of "population mix" or "social balancing"; some temporary employment agencies resort to coding the job offers submitted by prospective employers who will only take on "persons of French stock", and so forth.

Things are perhaps beginning to change with regard to official and academic research. Recently a demographic definition of immigrants, suitable for use in statistics, was provided (Tribalat, 1989). and has been used in recent official enquiries. Certain official statistics make a distinction between "immigrants from the European Community" and "immigrants from outside the EC". There are some officially authorised exceptions to the 1987 act on computer information, allowing some social research projects to use data on ethnic origins, and French social scientists are beginning new research involving identification of the population of migrant origin.

In most countries information on non-indigenous ethnic or racial groups is limited. For example, the **Irish** census of population does not include questions on racial or ethnic background. The only information available from census statistics is a profile of the population by place of birth. This profile, while useful for illustrative purposes, is not a reliable guide to national or ethnic background of people living in the Republic of Ireland. There are other limitations with statistical information available. The figures are not broken down into those employed/unemployed or those available for work and those unavailable for work, for reasons of age, retirement etc. These factors are important as Ireland is a popular holiday and retirement location for people from the US, Britain and other parts of Europe, who are unlikely to have any links with the labour market at all. In **Portugal** a community of many thousand Cape Verdeans, the largest visible minority, who live near Lisbon, is relatively invisible in any statistical indicators as they hold Portuguese citizenship. In **Germany** 'ausländers' such as Turks show up in the census unless naturalised, and the fact that the degree of naturalisation of migrants in Germany is one of the lowest in Europe means that most will be covered. Those who do take German citizenship will not show as 'ethnic minorities' as only German nationals such as gypsies, Sorb and Danish minorities are officially classified as ethnic minorities, but these groups will not appear in the statistics of companies and trade unions.

Even when the simple category "foreigners" is used in a census, this may still severely underestimate the numbers of foreign workers in cases when part of the workforce lives in the border zones of a neighbouring country. For example, in **Luxembourg** one quarter of the workforce live outside the country in such border zones and so go unrecorded in the national census.

In **Greece**, only rough estimates can be made about the size of the foreign population in the country. Estimates are based on the 1991 census figures, the data of registered foreigners of the Ministry of Public Order and the number of deportations and expulsions. However, evidence shows clearly that many foreigners did not register at the 1991 General Population Census. They also show that although the data on the registered foreigners given by the Ministry of Public Order on a year to year basis are more realistic, they cover, at least in recent years, just over half of the actual foreign population in the country. Similarly, due to the lack of statistical information, the numbers of ethnic, religious, cultural, linguistic and other minorities in Greece are rough approximations based on estimates.

6.1.2 A lack of information on migrants in the labour market and their working conditions

In many countries statistics are able to show that migrant workers are concentrated in the worst areas of work, in jobs which, for example, expose them to greater possibilities of industrial injury. Such patterns can be identified more accurately in countries where a relatively recent migrant population remains 'foreign' and therefore has not started to become invisible in national statistics. Some labour market statistics are available from data on work permits. For example, the information available on immigrants in the **Spanish** labour market is found mainly in the statistical data on work permits provided by the Ministry of Labour and Social Security. The "Encuesta sobre poblacion activa", EPA, [Active Population Survey] submitted by the "Instituto Nacional de Estadistica" [National Institute of Statistics] collects data obtained through sampling every three months on foreign residents who live in family housing, but does not include those who have found accommodation in hotels, hostels or other arrangements. Thus the EPA underestimates the total number of foreign workers (Alvarez, 1992). In **Italy** most foreigners who are resident will show in the statistics on work permits or family residence permits, but these give a poor indication of employment status as sometimes the type of permit does not correspond with occupational status in reality. In **Greece** only rough estimates can be made about the participation of the foreign population in the labour force, and as for ethnic minorities, the assumption is simply made that the economically active who belong to those minorities have about the same participation rate in the labour force as that of the total population in the area they live in.

The most obvious omission from statistics in all countries is the level of participation in the illegal labour market. Information on migrant and ethnic minority participation in this sector is only likely to be provided by specific pieces of research.

In most countries there remains very little information about what happens to migrant workers *at enterprise level*. There is relatively little information on working conditions which would show to what extent immigrants, ethnic minorities and refugees have to perform heavy lifting, work under noisy conditions, do monotonous work, are involved in accidents, work anti-social hours, or are absent from work. There is little exploration of the extent to which young people of migrant origin have difficulty in finding vocational training. There has been little research into the reasons for the higher unemployment rate of migrants and ethnic minorities; for example, the extent to which the language ability of immigrants and refugees prevents them from getting jobs, or to what extent under-valuing of the education and experience of immigrants and refugees is responsible for a higher rate of unemployment.

6.1.3 A lack of information on discrimination in employment

Even less common than information on the working conditions of migrants and ethnic minorities is research into processes and experiences of discrimination. Even in countries where there is an established tradition of researching the experiences of migrants, this research is nevertheless is more likely cover the migrant communities themselves and their potential for integration, rather than experiences of discrimination. The **German** experience is typical of many others. Research carried out in the 1970s (Esser 1980; Kremer and Spangenberg 1980) concentrated mainly on migrants themselves: on their cultural characteristics, their willingness to integrate, and their qualifications. Researchers concluded that the problem of integrating the migrant population was mainly a problem of socially-disadvantaged groups, reinforced by language and culture barriers on the part of the migrant population. The researchers proposed a broad integration policy, covering housing conditions, work conditions, schooling and training. Following this study, the main body of research into migration has been on the migrant population and their 'willingness' or ability to integrate or to assimilate. Far less attention has been paid to structural and subjective factors (discrimination and racism) as a hindrance to integration and equal access to social resources. This is especially true for research into the employment situation of migrants workers. As far as racism and discrimination are concerned, publications focus on right extremist politics, and since 1990, mainly on young right extremists (Stöss, 1989; Farin & Seidel-Pielen, 1992; Benz, 1989; Heitmeyer, 1989).

There are some exceptions. Seifert (1994) has shown that within companies migrant workers are much less likely to get promoted than are indigenous workers, and this was also demonstrated in Biller's study (1989), focusing on a large car production company. It was assumed that discrimination might play a part, as difference in qualifications was not a significant factor, yet neither of these studies was able to demonstrate this. Clearly, more detailed research is necessary on what goes on within companies. For example, migrant workers are under-represented in training and qualification programmes, mainly in those offered during working-hours. There is some indication that this may partly be due to discrimination, including on the part of shop stewards who participate in the decision-making process of selecting workers for further training. Research is necessary to shed some light on the reasons for the under-representation of migrant workers on training courses and its possible connection with discriminatory practices within companies and trade unions.

In general, with the exception of the UK and the Netherlands, the national reports could find relatively little research into discrimination itself. Most significant of all is the absence of 'discrimination testing' in recruitment in most member states, which is one of the most effective ways of determining whether or not there really is 'no problem here'. The International Labour Office plans to expand its programme, but at the moment only a minority of countries have applied this method.

In general, the lack or research and statistical evidence in a country exacerbates the next obstacle: that of problematic attitudes.

6. 2 Problems of attitudes and knowledge

Some reports found that employers could be quite hostile to any thought of introducing equal opportunities and anti-discrimination measures. For example, a 1992 study of 70 companies in the Brussels region revealed that employers were hostile to any intervention by the public authorities that may restrict their freedom in the selection process, and even rejected the suggestion that certain sentences should be added to job advertisements to encourage immigrants to apply (Van Roost and Buyse, 1992). Even without open hostility there can exist a sort of passivity, as described in the Belgian report, whereby neither employers nor the trade unions have any sense of haste or urgency in conducting awareness campaigns or actions to prevent racism in the workplace. Those who want to approach the problem will be tolerated, maybe with a degree of goodwill but certainly not with any overwhelming enthusiasm. Whether it is hostility or simple passivity which is encountered, the reasons behind them can often be the same: a general lack of understanding of the main points of the issues. It is possible to categorise many of the misunderstandings and misconceptions commonly expressed. The reports revealed seven different types:

- A lack of recognition of the problem of racism and discrimination in employment - the syndrome of "no problem here"
- A 'colour blind' attitude of 'equal treatment' which cannot countenance any special measures for migrants
- A tendency to 'blame the victim'
- Misconceptions about the concepts of racism and discrimination
- A confusion over anti-discrimination concepts
- A confusion of 'multi-cultural' or 'integration' policies with anti-discrimination or anti-racist policies
- A confusion of protest policies with anti-discrimination policies

6.2.1 A lack of recognition of the problem of racism and discrimination in employment - the syndrome of "no problem here".

"No problem here" is one of the most commonly expressed views. In general, in societies with egalitarian ideologies and where racism and discrimination are viewed as objectionable, there is a tendency to deny that a problem exists. The 'denial of racism' is found at many levels, from whole nations to individuals. National politicians often emphasise how in their respective countries the word "racism" cannot be applied in the context of their laws, their traditions and their populations (van Dijk, 1993). It is noticeable that in different countries there are often different arguments as to why racism is not part of their society. For example, where a country has no history of major colonial oppression of non-white people, this is seen to be the reason for an 'absence of racism' in society. In traditional countries of emigration it is often stated that people are sympathetic to the experiences of migrants. These and others reasons are used as explanations as to why there is 'no racism here'. In fact, whether the issue is recognised as a problem or not bears little relationship as to whether in reality there is a problem.

A national lack of awareness on the issue can be reflected lower down in the institutional culture of organisations. In **France** the Central Services of the Paris Labour Inspectorate, told the report authors that they had never undertaken any research on racial discrimination and, accordingly, were unable to provide any information whatsoever on the subject. The French authors could see that this might be seen to be surprising, coming from institutions which specialise in labour law and in litigation between workers and employers. The reason is quite simply that racism and discrimination have never been central to their concerns. Cases are based instead on more traditional and 'safer' arguments. One labour inspector pointed out that racism and racial discrimination at places of recruitment and employment are "not part of our working culture. Discrimination on grounds of trade union activity and sex, yes, but racism and racial discrimination, no."

Employers readily subscribe to this view. One French employer stated: "In the 25 years I have worked (in this department), I have never heard anybody say 'I don't want anybody from another race'. I have my doubts as to what happens in reality. It is the foreign workers themselves who are most worried about it ...They are afraid of being rejected. If they are turned down for a job, they reassure themselves by putting it down to the colour of their skin, though in fact, if they are not taken on, it is because they are not profitable".

The author of the **German** report sees that both at national and company level, one of the main obstacles to preventing racism and discrimination is the lack of awareness about the existence of everyday racism and discrimination at the workplace. Conflicts are either not seen, or are suppressed. In the research done for the German report, management representatives all claimed there were no conflicts between migrant and indigenous workers. This is also the official opinion of the employers' federation (Arbeitgeberverband). In an issue of their journal they assured the public: 'In companies, integration of migrant fellow-citizens is a reality and social equality is realised. The pragmatic relationship between colleagues who work together towards a common goal and depend on each other does not know of any resentments against aliens.' ('Der Arbeitgeber', Nr. 20/45, 1993, p.721) The same thing is said by works council representatives and indigenous shop stewards. Correspondingly, German companies were found to have very few measures for preventing racism, reflecting the general view in Germany that anti-discrimination policy is unnecessary, because there is no general discrimination against the migrant population.

In **Luxembourg** there was found to be a certain amount of sensitivity about discrimination problems among both employers and trade-unionists, but this goes no further than declarations of principle. Foreigners are thought to be well integrated, and this has always helped to make an explicit integration policy superfluous. There is an almost complete absence of publications and papers on discrimination produced in Luxembourg itself. There is no problem of unemployment to highlight the issue as Luxembourg continues to enjoy a boom in employment, with workers are still being hired from outside to fill the new jobs being created there. Although there is unemployment in **Ireland**, the Irish researchers described the common perception that racial or ethnic discrimination is not an issue in Ireland, with a very low level of public awareness on the issue.

Of course, this is not to say that a "no problem here" attitude is automatically to be seen to be problematic. It is in theory quite possible that a "no problem here" opinion could indeed largely reflect reality. The problem arises when such opinions are expressed in a context where there is at least tentative or prima facie evidence from other sources that racial or ethnic discrimination exists, and where there is an absence of research or other investigation into the circumstances and experiences of migrants, using the sorts of methods and sources of evidence illustrated in Section 2.3.

6.2.2 A 'colour blind' attitude of 'equal treatment' which cannot countenance any special measures for migrants.

Individual employers will emphasise their own colour-blindness, with statements such as "I don't care what colour they are - white, black or blue - we treat them all the same" (see: Lee and Wrench, 1983; Jenkins, 1986; van Dijk, 1993). This (often mistaken) view that minorities are always treated the same as everyone else leads to a refusal to concede that there could be any special policy needs. The problem is that as problems of racism and discrimination only affect the visible minority part of a workforce, then certain measures to address the resulting inequality will often only apply to those groups. However, many employers and trade unionists were strongly opposed to any measures which did not apply to all workers. For example, the policy of the **Danish** Employers' Association (Dansk Arbejdsgiverforening) is that refugees and immigrants should not be regarded as a special group. The rights and obligations of foreign nationals are regulated by the same laws and regulations as apply to Danish citizens. Thus foreign nationals are guaranteed equal conditions of employment, pay, vacation and unemployment insurance as Danes, and there is no need for any special measures. The **Belgian** report describes how in the early 1980s the reason for not including protection against discrimination in employment in Belgian law was that such protection would be seen by other workers as a privilege "and might therefore reinforce rather than combat xenophobia".

Similar hostility to special measures was expressed by **German** employers in response to the questionnaire administered as part of the German report. However, the German report observes that when migrants are not 'ethnic minority citizens' they automatically start from a position of difference in relation to the national population. In this sense, 'equal treatment' might be quite inappropriate. A study of employers in Hamburg (Haugg, 1994) found an under-representation of migrant apprentices, but also that interviewing panels rejected the idea of encouraging migrants to apply. They even felt that the sentence "We welcome applications by young people of migrant origin" would contravene the principle of equal treatment. 'Equal treatment' is seen solely as migrant workers getting the same pay for the same work. The fact that there are hardly any other German workers doing the same work is not seen to be a problem, and the factors which have led to this segregation or work are not critically examined.

With trade unions the emphasis on equal treatment and the opposition to 'special measures' for migrants and ethnic minorities is usually voiced in the view that class-based interests as workers should take precedence over sectional interests such as 'race' or ethnicity, and that any special policies for one group would therefore undermine membership and class unity. In **France** the unions subscribe to the rational vision of the enterprise as a world governed by rules and abstract principles - responsibilities, specialisation, seniority - which should be applied impartially to all workers. These impersonal rules, replacing the old system of paternalism and management prerogative, have facilitated an abstraction of industrial relations with points of reference in universal categories - the workforce, the mass of persons employed by a particular firm, the working class etc. - rather than in specific groups. Thus measures relating to ethnic minority or migrant groups are alien to this view.

6.2.3 A tendency to 'blame the victim'.

'Blaming the victim' is very common in public discourse and in the literature on the origins of racism. Discriminatory practices are often rationalised or legitimated by the perpetrators, and a common device is to explain it away in terms of the character of those who are discriminated against. There are different versions of the 'blaming the victim' syndrome. One is to see the major problem to lie within a lack of education, qualifications, language or experience on the part of the migrant workers. The other is to emphasise the factor of 'cultural difference' to explain patterns of inequality.

In the **UK**, a noticeably higher rate of industrial injuries for ethnic minority workers was assumed to be the result of factors to do with the "newness" of a migrant population: for example, rural migrant workers might be unfamiliar with industrial work; language difficulties might lead to problems in understanding safety instructions; or injuries may reflect a syndrome of maladjustment and stress from the social disruption of the migration process. There was even the idea that a "cultural proneness" might exist for those ethnic minority groups which exhibited a cultural "fatalism" towards the occurrence of injuries. In fact, a study of 4,000 accidents in the Midlands demonstrated that the apparent predisposition to suffer injuries was entirely attributable to the fact that migrant and ethnic minority workers were over-represented in the more dangerous jobs. The common sense "blaming the victim" explanations had been entirely inappropriate (Lee and Wrench, 1980).

The **French** report encountered the view that if discrimination occurs, it is exclusively due either to legal criteria or to objective conditions governing the recruitment and employment of persons, i.e. differences in levels of qualification, language comprehension, or physical aptitude. Thus interviewees for the French report would dismiss complaints of racism as advanced by people who do not have the cultural and behavioural attributes that fit naturally into the openings provided by the labour market. In France the reasons for the "handicap" experienced by foreign population groups in the labour market are sought in the first instance in the particular characteristics of the groups in question, such as poor levels of skill, difficulties in adapting, a poor command of French, and so on. Differences between individual foreign population groups are also seen as deriving from their respective "cultural characteristics": some are seen as experiencing more difficulty in "integrating within the firm", whilst others show more "dynamism".

In **Germany** migrant workers were seen as a problem because of their assumed lack of qualifications or poor command of the German language. The unequal distribution of migrant workers within a company's hierarchy is not seen to be an effect of direct or indirect discrimination (if unequal distribution is acknowledged at all) but rather as a consequence of migrants' lack of skills and qualifications. Either they do not speak German well enough, or do not have the skills necessary for a better position. In spite of this opinion, though, there are no specific programmes to improve the qualifications of the migrant workforce. This again is often explained away by an assumption that migrants are not interested in gaining qualifications, but are motivated primarily by a desire for 'quick money' instead. Although the German report noted that this was a widespread opinion heard often from staff in employment bureaux, there is no research or evidence to substantiate this view. The 'cultural' argument is also current in Germany, with the idea that migrants have an 'alien culture' and do not fit well into German society. The assumption was reported in the German report that the 'more distant' the culture of the migrant is from the culture of the host country, the more problems there will be.

In **Denmark** a 'blaming the victim' discourse has evolved in which the alleged lack of knowledge of the refugees and immigrants of the language and culture of the majority and their insistence on maintaining their own cultural and religious traditions are seen as the cause of all their problems. The Danish report concludes that this ideology enables people to ignore the fact that the absence of ethnic equality in society is mainly caused by social, economic and political factors In the **Netherlands** there was reported a shift in some official thinking towards more of a 'blaming the victim' emphasis. Lutz (1993) describes the developing official view that ethnic minorities exhibit high rates of unemployment because they were previously treated by the government as a 'care' category and have therefore become dependent on public money. In a 1986 report by the Minorities Research and Advisory Commission, (Adviescommissie Onderzoek Minderheden, ACOM) had argued in favour of positive action measures in order to ameliorate the position of ethnic minorities in the labour market, and to reduce discrimination. However, the Social Economic Council (Sociaal Economische Raad, SER) which advised the Government emphasised instead the low qualification level of minorities, stressing the need for more training and education for them.

A key emphasis of anti-discrimination measures is that they are directed at the practices of the majority population, not at the characteristics or practices of the minorities. Thus although educational programmes for migrants can be very important, if they are not accompanied by anti-discrimination policies in recruitment and promotion, their effects will be limited.

6.2.4 Misconceptions about the concepts of racism and discrimination

It is often the case that politicians and policy makers are willing to condemn racism if it is seen as the activity of unrepresentative right-wing extremists. They are less willing to undertake action which would imply that racism in both its ideological and practical manifestations forms part of the structure of their society, operating routinely in the allocation of services, housing and jobs. A number of reports identified the view that racism could be defined only as the sort of untypical behaviour exhibited by extremists. It was therefore seen as a marginal problem originating from deprived youth or right-wing fringe groups. Sometimes only direct, overt violence is regarded as racism. It is true that, in **Germany** for example, racism or 'hostility towards foreigners' has only become a serious object of concern for companies and trade unions since violent racist attacks against people of migrant origin have substantially increased. But precisely because of this, the problem has mostly been located outside the factories (Neo-Nazis, right extremists) or within individuals (prejudices). Structural and individual discrimination inside their own organisations is not yet a main focus of concern for companies or trade unions.

Reports revealed an unwillingness to define some activities as 'racist', or a lack of awareness of the nature of racism itself. The **French** report describes how a workplace sub-culture of the use of jokes and stereotypes is not seem to be problematic, with a wide toleration of a sort of "bar-room racism", which is not in itself felt to pose any real risk of discrimination or exclusion. Another conclusion of the French report was that there existed a blindness to *patterns* of racist behaviour. Even those respondents who were clearly not indifferent or complacent with regard to racism or racists, had not integrated this dimension into their analysis of the workings of the labour market. It is as though everything could be put down to isolated cases, with acts of racism or discrimination resulting from individual behaviour described as "foolish" or "clumsy" and relegated to the level of anecdotes.

The French report also encountered the view that the existence of racism and racial discrimination cannot be widespread because it would amount to an economic aberration. The argument runs as follows: "Why should employers introduce into the enterprise elements which are alien to its function as a producer, i.e. elements unrelated to economic or financial profitability? The enterprise is a place of rational decisions, and racism is irrational; the two are therefore incompatible".

Another misconception revealed by interviewees in reports was that racism was due to an "information deficit". Because racism is mainly seen as an individual problem of prejudice due to false information, a logical emphasis of anti-racist activities should therefore consist in providing correct information. The **Danish** report encountered the belief that although it is acknowledged that racism plays a part in marginalising immigrants and refugees, more information on the situation of migrants and refugees will do away with this discrimination. Consistent with this view is the response of several companies surveyed in the **German** report, who argued that because of the international character of their company and the fact that many of their German employees also worked in other countries for some time, they had no problems with discrimination. This argument presumes that discrimination and racism are due to a lack of knowledge of 'another culture'. In some European countries there are training initiatives in employment which work from this assumption: programmes to encourage 'inter-cultural awareness' and promote better communication and understanding, which provide demographic facts and figures on migrants, their countries of origin, their current employment patterns, and cultural information on migrant and ethnic minority communities. Implicit in this approach is the idea that the provision of correct information and raising trainees' cultural awareness is enough to reduce discriminatory behaviour (see Wrench and Taylor, 1993).

6.2.5 A confusion over anti-discrimination concepts.

A 1989 survey of employers in the **UK** revealed ignorance and misconceptions on the part of many employers on some of the basic concepts of the Race Relations Act. For example, when asked to state what they understood by indirect discrimination, about half of respondents gave incorrect answers. Some respondents appeared to believe that intention to discriminate was necessary for there to be indirect discrimination. Others thought that it referred to a willingness to recruit but not to promote; or to unconscious prejudice or reverse discrimination. Just fifteen per cent of employers gave correct replies (CRE, 1989). A 1991 project revealed that major UK employers still confuse equal opportunities - and more specifically, positive action - with positive discrimination and giving an unfair advantage to ethnic minorities. Some employers argued that there was no need for an equal opportunities policy in their organisation because they didn't want to "give preference to anybody or any group" (Wrench et al, 1993). This confusion of equal opportunities initiatives with positive discrimination or quotas was found in other countries. For example, the **Danish** Employers Association was against equal opportunities measures because it did not believe the that problems of the high rate of unemployment among immigrants and refugees could be solved by introducing "positive discrimination" or "quotas". They argued that there would be many other marginalised groups which should also have such arrangements. In **Luxembourg** a trade union official wrongly considered some special arrangements for migrants within the union to be positive discrimination; and in some countries people believed that any extra provision for migrants was 'positive discrimination'.

6.2.6 A confusion of 'multi-cultural' or 'integration' policies with anti-discrimination or anti-racist policies.

Related to the above misconceptions and confusions is a lack of understanding of what anti-discrimination measures entail. For example, in the **German** report many of the companies who were asked about their measures against discrimination replied in terms of their 'social' or 'education' policy. One company financially supported projects which worked for integration. Other strategies included organising the seminars on 'knowledge of different cultures', and 'encouraging people to get to know each other'. In **France** a number of educational programmes have been devised for policemen, magistrates, teachers, social workers with the general aim of instilling a professional awareness of the diversity of population groups and cultural origins represented among those they have to deal with. With the same aim in mind, specialised agencies have been set up, such as the Agence pour le Développement des Relations Interculturelles (Agency for the Promotion of Inter-cultural Relations). However, the above mentioned occupations are all concerned with making service delivery more culturally sensitive, rather than combating discrimination.

Anti-discrimination measures are less concerned with changing attitudes than with changing practices. It is seen to be more important to produce changes in behaviour on the grounds that even if racist attitudes remain unchanged, at least the actual practice of discrimination may be effectively reduced. "Research on the relationship between attitudes and behaviour has created substantial evidence that changes in behaviour may have more potent and lasting effects than changes in attitudes, *per se*" (Bovenkerk 1992). Minorities are hurt more by racist practices than racist attitudes, it is argued. Moreover, the added attraction of this argument is that in the long term, changing behaviour may even produce a corresponding change in attitudes. Over time the climate and operations of the workplace may be changed by the new behaviours, and ideological change is likely to follow this (Chesler and Delgado, 1987).

6.2.7 A confusion of protest policies with anti-discrimination policies

This seventh 'misconception' is more likely to be found amongst trade unions than employers. Some trade union respondents say that the unions' commitment to the fight against racism and discrimination is demonstrated by their public stands against racism. Although these activities are welcome, the problem is that these are relatively uncontroversial among the membership and are often easier for unions to carry out than those anti-discrimination measures which imply changes in the behaviour of members within the union itself. For example, the UK unions for a time seemed far more ready to support the activities of the Anti-Nazi League and the boycott of South Africa during apartheid than they were to introduce measures against racists within the union. The German and French unions make a public stand for the rights of migrants or asylum seekers; Italian, Spanish and Portuguese unions actively support major demonstrations against racists and racist violence - but all have been less ready to reflect critically on the position of migrants within the union itself. In Germany, some companies have paid for major advertisements in national newspapers denouncing 'hostility to foreigners'. All these activities have an important educational and political value, but they are complementary to, and not an alternative to, anti-discrimination measures.

Although all the above 'misunderstandings' have been separated out for the sake of analysis, in practice they often merge together. For example, in the German report three respondents (airline, insurance, and telephone companies) reported that there were no conflicts between migrant workers and indigenous workers, and that there was no need for any special measures in their workplace as the migrants they employed had been born in Germany and spoke German perfectly; they therefore posed no problem. This simple response contains elements of many of the misunderstandings listed above. There is the possibly complacent 'no problem here' assumption; an implicit 'blaming the victim' (it is a migrant's inability to speak perfect German which causes problems); misconceptions about the nature of racism, (a failure to realise that racism can be easily experienced by someone speaking German as a first language if the colour of their skin is not white), and an implicit view that racism is due to false information or cultural misunderstanding, in that someone "born in Germany" will therefore escape it. There is also an apparent ignorance about the nature of anti-discrimination measures.

6. 3 WEAKNESSES IN LEGISLATION AND ITS IMPLEMENTATION

Chapter 3 set out legal approaches against discrimination at a national level. For some countries there was very little to be described; for others, even when policies existed in theory, there were problems in practice. The **French** report typifies a number of problems experienced with the use of legal measures against racism and discrimination. In general it is difficult to secure information on racism and discrimination in the workplace and to ensure that it is recorded and defined as such with a view to taking legal proceedings. The fight against racism runs up against a number of obstacles: the victims do not speak out; unions or anti-racist associations are not always in a position to defend them; there are difficult choices to be made as to the best way of proceeding; legal proceedings are often inconclusive and may even be risky for the victims.

Although cases of discrimination in the rejection of job applicants are cited as an everyday occurrence by the victims themselves and by French trade unions and anti-racist organisations, such cases are seldom brought to court for lack of concrete evidence, and in practice the employer is free to take on whoever he likes, provided he does not openly show that his decision was based on criteria prohibited by law. Since he has no obligation to justify his choice, it is easy for him to dismiss any accusation of discrimination. Thus, the employers' organisations and officials of the Agences Nationales pour l'Emploi (public employment offices) are able to argue that such refusals are extremely rare.

Furthermore, the legal framework does not offer adequate safeguards for a case to be properly defended. Infringements of the law are hardly ever punished when committed by a public service. Directors of Agences Nationales pour l'Emploi who allow the publication or posting up on their premises of discriminatory advertisements have seldom been found guilty of an infringement, despite a Ministry Circular of 1972 drawing their attention to the unlawful nature of such advertisements and requiring them not to accept them.

The decisions of tribunals do not always help. In cases where a job applicant is rejected by an employer on the grounds that "the company already employs enough foreign workers", the findings of the tribunals tend to contradict one another. One employer was judged to be in breach of the law in claiming to limit his foreign workforce to 25%, and arguing that "beyond that level there would be a deterioration in the working environment". The tribunal found that it was incumbent on the head of the enterprise "to organise the work in such a way as to avoid antagonism between French and foreign workers". By contrast, another was exonerated by the judges who considered this excuse a valid one since, "despite the appearances" it was not "inspired by racist or xenophobic motives" (see GISTI, 1994).

Here too, when a public authority is involved, any reference to racial or ethnic criteria in recruitment generally goes unpunished. Persons charged have in effect been exonerated from all responsibility by the tribunals on the pretext that they have no personal authority to hire people for work. As has been pointed out by the Mouvement contre le Racisme et pour l'Amitié entre les Peuples (MRAP), "it seems that charges brought against holders of public office often founder on 'buck-passing' within the authority concerned".

In France, the "natural" vehicle for the defence of victims of racism and discrimination at work are the trade unions, the only organisations having a legal right to be present on the shop floor. However, French unions seem poorly equipped for dealing with discrimination against French nationals on grounds of their ethnic origin, or for the defence of the victims of racist acts. There are a number of reasons for this state of affairs. It has to be recognised that the rate of unionisation is very low (10%) and that many small and medium-sized firms do not have union representation. The potential power to act against discrimination will vary greatly according to workplace circumstances. In some cases the victims of racism are isolated, in others they form more or less established groups, and in others they constitute the majority of the workforce. The militancy and strength of the unions will determine how well victims can be defended. The most virulently racist and discriminatory climates are more likely to develop where the climate of the workplace is harshest and most hostile to individual and collective rights; in other words, those most difficult for a union to defend. This factor is important since French unions, anarcho-syndicalist by tradition, more naturally resort to a show of strength in defence of the victims of racism and discrimination in order to force the perpetrators to back down, rather than automatically resorting to law.

Furthermore, proceeding against an employer or his representatives for discrimination is not a matter to be taken lightly. Success may sometimes result in a reversal of the discriminatory act (a dismissed person would then have to be reinstated), and, in most cases, the employer is ordered to pay damages with interest; failure, however, could mean the employer suing the victim for defamation.

In order to prove that somebody has been excluded from the normal line of promotion on grounds of ethnic origins, it is necessary to draw up a report (only a labour inspector may do this) demonstrating that other persons, comparable in every respect save this one, have fared better during their service with the firm. This is a daunting task for a labour inspector to embark on. Because of all the difficulties, informants to the French report stated that remedies are usually sought on more traditional, safer and, in practice, more effective grounds. For example, a labour inspector reported a case in which a group of shop stewards had been dismissed, all of them "Africans"; he based his opposition on the articles of the Labour Code covering the protection of shop stewards, without mentioning the element of racial discrimination, even though this was blatant in this case.

As effective defence of workers tends not to make use of legislation outlawing discrimination, this in itself contributes to its non-recognition and reinforces the general tendency to disregard it in future cases. The Office of the Chairman of the Paris Industrial Tribunal told the French researchers that never once, in all the 17 000 cases dealt with each year by the Paris conciliation system, has there been a plea of racist conduct.

In **Ireland** it is reported that people fail to report incidents of racial discrimination in the workplace. One important reason is that the only legislative protection for workers who may have experienced racial discrimination in Ireland is the Unfair Dismissals Act (1977), and there are serious limitations to the protection this legislation actually provides. To date, only two cases of racial discrimination have been taken under the terms of this Act. Furthermore, the latest research available from the Task Force on the Travelling Community shows very low aspirations on the part of Travellers with regard to entering the formal labour market because of discrimination (Nexus Research, 1994).

In **Belgium** racial discrimination is seen to be difficult to identify and even more difficult to prove before the courts. During 1991 and 1992, 440 cases were brought before the courts, of which 334, or 75%, were not pursued. With respect to the cases that were pursued, there were only five "guilty" rulings, one acquittal and six out-of-court settlements. The results are somewhat disappointing and several factors can explain the lack of effectiveness of the law. These are the unwillingness of public prosecutors to apply the law, the unwillingness of judges to adopt a clear and consistent stance *vis-à-vis* this law, and major gaps within the law itself.

To encourage public prosecutors to pursue more cases, legislators have made provision for some more severe penalties in their 1994 amendment to the law, and some of the gaps in the law have been eradicated. The new provisions of Article 2a on discrimination in matters of employment provide an opportunity for combating discrimination with regard to work. However, as with other countries, the problem is to prove that there has been discrimination. A victim may not be sure of the reason for dismissal or disciplinary action or may have difficulty in proving that discrimination is the reason.

The Belgian report concludes that courts need to be more open to the use of proofs such as the use of statistical data or surveys that seem to indicate *prima facie* discrimination. Use of statistics of this kind could have the effect of creating a refutable presumption of discrimination, as already exists in the case of the dismissal of a pregnant woman. The Centre pour l'Egalité des Chances et la Lutte contre le Racisme has suggested that this presumption be inserted in Article 2a, but the proposal was rejected by the Senate Commission in Belgium.

The Belgian report summaries the weaknesses in the current state of things:

- There is still only a very slim chance of seeing acts of racism in connection with employment and work being punished by the courts;
- There is a latent, or even manifest, reticence of workers' representatives to raise this issue publicly within enterprises, or launch actions to counter these practices;
- The local social institutions that support actions to raise awareness and prevent discrimination are both precarious and vulnerable.
- There is public-sector resistance - a resistance that is often shared by unions - to employing and promoting workers of immigrant origin. This situation offers the private sector an easy alibi for not having to take responsibility on this issue.

Even in countries where stronger legislation exists with a greater tradition of thinking in terms of racism, there are problems. In the **Netherlands** legislation is not applied frequently as a means to combat discrimination. People do not go to court as easily as they do in, for example, the United States or Great Britain. Victims of discrimination are often insufficiently acquainted with the legal machinery. Furthermore, a policy of active prosecution is lacking, and in only a small amount of cases will notification of a complaint lead to actual criminal prosecution. In principle, the onus of proof is with the plaintiff, and demonstrating the occurrence of discrimination is very difficult. Litigation is often a lengthy and costly matter, and sanctions are often too light. Complaints are often not dealt with seriously enough by the Police or the Public Prosecutor, and furthermore, most cases do not lead to conviction of the perpetrators. Even when they do, the penalties imposed are insignificant. All these factors contribute to the fact that few victims report discrimination. There is also the fear of being viewed as over-sensitive, or a fear of retaliation at work (for example, that a promotion might be withheld) that deters victims from going to court.

In some cases, pressure groups will avoid resorting to the law, but will try to bring about social policy changes by means of negotiations with government. Although in 1985 the National Bureau for Combating Discrimination (Landelijk Bureau Racismebestrijding, LBR) was established in Utrecht with the aim of preventing and fighting racial discrimination in the Netherlands, the bureau does not have any legal power, and accordingly, it does not have a legal enforcement function.

In **Sweden** there are already seen to be problems with the new 1994 law against discrimination in employment. While preparing the law the government was keen to stress the law's effect on public attitudes. It was thought that a number of successful cases would also help to establish legal praxis (Reg. Prop. 193/94:101). Seen in this perspective, the current law is not without problems. According to the Ombudsman the desired 'signal effect' for the public is unclear. For example, part of the law can be interpreted as saying that negative special treatment is allowed, and is even acceptable according to the law, as long as the discrimination does not become too 'obvious'.

Another difficulty associated with the law's 'signal effect' is the problem of finding cases that can be taken up at a work tribunal so that legal praxis can be developed. Given the way the law is formulated today, this is extremely difficult. To begin with the law requires that negative special treatment is only based on the factor of ethnicity. In reality, this is seldom the case, as usually several factors are involved. The law can therefore only be applied in an extremely small number of cases. The situation is excacerbated by the fact that ethnic discrimination cannot be said to have occurred until an employer has completed the process of employing an applicant and has rejected other applicants on the basis of ethnicity.

The law states that the Ombudsman's primary goal is to reach a settlement between the partners in a dispute. It is only after such an attempt has failed and the conflict remains that the Ombudsman can move on to other measures. However, it is more logical for an employer to agree to a settlement, even if this entails certain costs, than to risk losing in court. Thus, if cases do not come to tribunal, it becomes impossible to develop an effective legal praxis, and thereby to "shape public opinion".

The Ombudsman is of the opinion that the law is unnecessarily restricted in its application to be able to be effective. Instead, the law ought to be formulated so that it can be used in every case where an employer is seen to discriminate on the basis of the factor of ethnicity. The Swedish report finds it strange that not a single case has been brought to a work tribunal with the help of the law. If the perceptions and experiences of discrimination in working life mentioned earlier in this report are true, then the Swedish law does not yet seem to be able to deal with the problem.

The **UK** has the strongest and most extensive legislation against discrimination in the European Union, covering both direct and indirect discrimination in employment; allowing victims of unlawful discrimination to receive compensation from employers; and allowing employers and training organisations to undertake certain types of positive action. There is a growing awareness of equal opportunity and anti-racist measures in Britain. Some private sector employers and a larger proportion of local authorities have made efforts to advance equal opportunities practice. A significant minority of employers have adopted equal opportunity measures in line with the CRE's Code of Practice, and a smaller amount of these have instituted some form of positive action.

However, by other indicators, the success of the Race Relations Act has been limited. Complainants who bring legal cases of discrimination have a relatively low success rate, with many factors acting to discourage them from resort to legal remedies. In 1986 a survey into the experiences of 377 complainants was carried out on behalf of the CRE. This found that the majority of the complainants withdrew their cases before a tribunal hearing was reached, most of them without having obtained a settlement. Of the cases which went to a hearing only 20 per cent resulted in the complaint being upheld by the tribunal. When related to the original number of applicants this proportion is even smaller: only 9 per cent were able to conclude their cases successfully (Zegers de Beijl, 1991). The findings demonstrate the importance of professional assistance for the applicant. Applicants who were represented by the CRE had a far better chance of bringing their case to a successful end. The survey also found that trade unions had been slow to accord due importance to cases of racial discrimination, in that only 8 per cent of complainants received any assistance from their union in proceedings (Kumar, 1986).

Most of the complainants who withdraw their applications do so as a result of pressure exerted on them by their employers or in stages of negotiation and conciliation. A recent overview concludes:

> Given the vulnerability of the individual employee and the employer's monopoly over information which may be vital for presenting a complaint, it is very difficult for a complainant to prove to tribunal members that the treatment he or she has received was in fact discriminatory .... The few complainants who win their cases receive little by way of award or compensation. Probably they will have to face relationships with their employers that are seriously disturbed ... up to the point where their prospects for finding other employment might be severely hampered. The individual road to equality obviously is a very difficult one (Zegers de Beijl, 1991)

There remain weaknesses in British legal provision against discrimination, and arguments for strengthening the Race Relations Act. Nevertheless, most commentators agree that the relatively limited progress in this area is not due so much to failings of the Act and its provisions, but rather a lack of effort in applying them.

Slow progress in facilitative measures
One consequence of having anti-discrimination legislation that is weak, or weakly applied, is that there remains little pressure on employers to adopt more 'voluntary' measures such as the use of codes of practice, or positive action, in those countries where such measures are officially allowed or encouraged. Positive action is one tool in the drive to correct for past discrimination and disadvantage. It is argued that if equal opportunity policies are not merely intended to eliminate discrimination but are also seen as programmes aimed at producing 'equality of results', then elements of positive action must be involved. For example, where an organisation has gained an image as one unsympathetic to ethnic minority employees, and where previous discrimination has left an all-white workforce, then simply removing previously discriminatory practices within an organisation will not be enough. Positive action policies are needed to provide the extra encouragement and/or training which may be necessary.

In the **Netherlands** the evidence is that codes of practice are not observed meticulously, and their effects are relatively insignificant. Although positive action has been discussed for a considerable amount of time now in the Netherlands, it appears that companies are still reluctant voluntarily to make an effort to employ more persons from ethnic minorities. The new Act for the Promotion of Proportional Labour Participation of Non-Natives aims to alter this situation.

In the **UK**, research in 1994 concluded that employers had made patchy use of the various types of positive action available under the Race Relations Act and that its overall impact is probably limited. The most common activity was measures to encourage more ethnic minority applications, such as messages included in advertisements and advertising in the ethnic minority press. Far less common was positive action training. Only a third of employers felt that 'encouragement' measures led to a significant increase in applications, whereas there was evidence that positive action training often led to 90% or more of trainees subsequently gaining employment. The implication of this is that the most widespread forms of positive action have been least effective, whilst those which appear more effective have been less widely undertaken, and conducted on a relatively small scale. It is therefore likely that the positive action measures taken to date have had a relatively limited impact in terms of the overall numbers of ethnic minority individuals entering employment. The conclusion is that positive action measures can be effective, but at the moment there is not enough incentive for employers to adopt them.

It remains the case that there is relatively little incentive to encourage employers to adopt good practice in this area, over and above the avoidance of unlawful discrimination. There is therefore an argument for strengthening the powers of the CRE and imposing greater requirements on employers to introduce equal opportunity measures.

6.4 BROADER DEVELOPMENTS IN THE ECONOMY AND THE LABOUR MARKET

There are a number of broader developments in work, the labour market and the economy which provide a somewhat unsympathetic context for the adoption, or effective implementation, of new anti-discrimination measures. These include the growth of unemployment, the trend to work 'flexibility' and job insecurity, the expansion of the illegal labour market, and new developments in the organisation of work.

6.4.1 Unemployment

Unemployment in the Union now stands at 11% and has averaged close to 10% for a decade. It is seen as the gravest social problem throughout the Union. Special concern focuses on the lack of prospects for new entrants to the labour market - young people and women especially - and on those who have become excluded from regular work particularly when they are long-term unemployed. (EC, 1994).

The unemployment situation in the EU is worse than that of the USA and Japan - for example, the share of long-term unemployment stands at more than 40% of the total in the EU, but 11% in the USA. The burden of unemployment remains very unequally distributed. "Disparities of unemployment rates persist between men and women, young and adult, particularly in countries such as Italy, Belgium and Portugal. Here the well-organised 'core' workforce has been able to ensure its security and social protection, whilst more vulnerable groups are left in a seriously exposed position (Room, 1995). As Rhodes and Braham (1987) argue in the British context, "effective action to overcome the problems of black workers proved difficult enough when there was excess demand for labour; in conditions of deepening recession and rising unemployment, effective action will be still more difficult, though by no means impossible". There are several reasons why the context of structural unemployment makes anti-discrimination initiatives harder. When companies are shedding workers rather than recruiting, polices to remove racist barriers to recruitment will not produce much overall change. Furthermore, indigenous workers may well be more resistant to the introduction of such measures. If there is no general expansion in employment, all other things remaining equal, then an improvement in the position of ethnic minority workers would require a deterioration in the position of other groups (Rhodes and Braham, 1987). Although the operation of the labour market is more complex than this, the problem is that many white workers will believe this to be the case.

More broadly, unemployment provides an unsympathetic climate for foreigners and migrants in general, as they are more likely to be seen as competitors for work, or as a potential drain on the welfare state. Unemployment amongst immigrants reduces the opportunities for work contact, thus reducing the general social contact between nationals and migrants. Differences within this can be seen in **Italy**. In Northern Italy, the fact that immigrants are in more structured, permanent employment and work side-by-side with Italian workers means they have contact with each other in broader social and institutional networks. The entire local population experiences daily contact with immigrant families in school, leisure and neighbourhood. This helps to reduce any alarmist images which can be fostered by a lack of direct contact. In Southern Italy - and in urban areas in particular - where work is less structured and not readily available, the only social identity that immigrants have is that of immigrants. Their identity is not mediated by any broader social relations. This situation encourages social marginalisation, where public and private welfare structures become the sole point of reference. This state of dependence feeds negative images in the public imagination, thus producing a vicious circle of marginalisation and hostility.

In response to unemployment, there have developed across Europe active labour market programmes to promote the employment of the young or the long-term unemployed. However, "much of the employment that is found is 'precarious' and is marked by the absence of rights in relation to collective bargaining, social security, dismissal and redundancy" (Room, 1995). It is also the kind of work not easily protected by equal opportunity policies and anti-discrimination measures.

6.4.2 Work 'flexibility' and insecurity

The trend towards flexibility in work makes more insecure the working population, and makes the adoption of anti-discrimination policies more difficult. The trend towards deregulation and job insecurity is developing in many economies, with an increase in part-time work, sub-contracting and short-term contracts. Pressures in highly competitive sectors encourage larger firms to use sub-contractors (which may or may not use 'irregular' labour). Similarly, firms across the EU increasingly draw on temporary and part-time workers, often recruited through agencies. All these factors taken together make it harder for equal opportunities policies to take hold. The conclusion of the Portuguese report holds true more broadly: integration policies and anti-discrimination measures are inhibited by the significance of the illegal economy, insecure, unskilled and poorly paid employment, and the dominating corporate culture of short-term management of manpower. In these circumstances anti-discrimination law has severe limitations, and this is particularly so when such workers are undocumented migrants themselves, engaged in 'illegal' work.

6.4.3 Illegal work

In southern European countries many migrants are found in 'precarious' work, with low wages and bad working conditions, employed without a contract or social security benefits, where employers pay lower wages than those stipulated or agreed with unions, and where working conditions are worse than those of the corresponding nationals. Illegal employment is thought to be getting more common. For example, in France recent laws against migrants and asylum seekers have forced workers into the clandestine labour market, especially construction, textiles, and catering, and particularly with sub-contraction. Similarly the processes of tightening the EU borders has helped to increase people with insecure employment status, including undocumented workers and asylum seekers.

Descriptions of the illegal labour market in Greece, Italy, Spain and Portugal have been presented in earlier sections of this report. However, the issue of the illegal labour market is not one restricted to the countries of southern Europe. Unregulated labour is expanding in countries of Northern Europe, often fed by workers from the former Eastern European bloc. The process of transformation to market economies in countries of the former Warsaw Pact area means that more people there are becoming unemployed. Often workers move to countries where they have geographical or cultural proximity. Agreement has been reached between countries of the EU and four Eastern European neighbours that their nationals no longer need visas to enter relevant member states. Now, in Germany and Belgium, for example, there is currently a question of Poles who enter as tourists for short periods and work illegally, and who have the freedom to move (and continue working illegally) in other European countries (Rea, 1995).

The issue of the illegal labour market is related to the issue of anti-discrimination measures for migrants and ethnic minorities in employment. Firstly, illegal work undermines the effects of fair employment practice and anti-discrimination measures in the regular labour market. The deregulation of the labour market and expansion of insecure and 'illegal' work means that people are often not in a position to claim the protection of anti-discrimination legislation. Secondly, discrimination in the regular labour market is one factor which is likely to contribute to the entry of ethnic minorities and migrants into the unregulated and illegal labour market.

6.4.4 Work organisation

Finally, there may be new developments in the organisation of work which potentially undermine anti-discrimination policies even when they have been long established. In the UK, where there has been some move towards the adoption of centralised equal opportunity initiatives in companies, there have been other developments which could counter their effects. A trend has been noticed towards devolution and decentralisation of managerial power and responsibilities, often to a 'cost centre', making 'cost-consciousness' the responsibility of members of staff lower in the hierarchy. The locus of decision making in recruitment shifts down towards lower-level line managers/supervisors, weakening the control of professional personnel specialists. This has implications for equal opportunity and anti-discrimination measures - the professional guidance of equal opportunities specialist personnel staff is weakened, and financial considerations become paramount for line managers. "In the absence of a clear appraisal sanction or budgetary implication for non-compliance, equal opportunities is likely to have a low priority" (Jewson and Mason, 1991).

This chapter has set out the main obstacles to progress in the prevention of racism and discrimination at work. The next chapter suggests the various strategies which may be adopted in order to overcome, or at least reduce the effect of, these obstacles.

7. CONCLUSIONS AND STRATEGIC OPTIONS

Exclusion and the labour market

It has been said that the most important social integration occurs via the labour market. Now this particular means of integration has been severely undermined for many people of migrant descent. Through processes of economic change, the decline in old industries which first employed migrants, and the re-location of production out of geographical areas inhabited by migrants, they are faced by persistent and structural unemployment. This is made worse by the discrimination they experience in the labour market. Discrimination can lead to the alienation of those discriminated against from civil society. As Castles and Miller (1993) put it: "Discrimination endures despite the integration policies of many Western European governments. Disadvantage, therefore, is often intergenerational and this poses a grave challenge to Western European social democratic traditions."

We can see that exclusion from and disadvantage in the labour market has its roots in a number of different factors. The first one considered in this report is legal exclusion at EU or national level. These include exclusion from mobility rights of legally-resident third-country nationals, the restrictive access to formal citizenship rights of such migrants and their descendants, and the restrictions denying access of non-nationals to some jobs. These legal and formal exclusions are considered to be a form of discrimination, even though they may not fit the conventional view of individual discriminatory actions which are the focus of standard anti-discrimination legislation and actions.

Many of those who agitate for the abolition of these legal restrictions and the greater extension of citizenship rights assume that fairness in the labour market will thereby follow. In fact, the experience of member states where most post-war migrants have citizenship and civil rights and face no legal barriers to employment opportunity shows that there are still major problems of discrimination and exclusion. It is true that the exclusion and inequality experienced by such ethnic minority citizens are not simply a product of racial discrimination (See Chapter 2). However, discrimination is one factor in social exclusion whose importance is often underestimated, and an understanding of it has direct implications for important areas of social policy, both at member state and EU level.

Migrants, the second generation and exclusion

It is particularly important to be concerned about the circumstances of young people of migrant origin. The problems facing the first generation were of a different order. Often they held inferior employment conditions precisely because they migrated to fill these jobs. In some countries, access to jobs may have been legally restricted. This is less likely - and less defensible - for second and third generations, who have similar rights to indigenous white workers but are excluded by forces of direct and indirect racism. Sometimes language barriers provided a genuine barrier to better jobs; again, this is much less likely to apply to the "second generation", and there can be no justification for discrimination against a population raised and educated in the receiving country.

The racism experienced by young ethnic minorities reflects a 'paradox of integration'. Whereas their parents often remained relatively 'invisible', separated out in sectors of work where few indigenous people worked, these young people put themselves forward to a much broader range of occupations, thereby putting themselves in positions where they are more likely to encounter racism and discrimination.

More than educational disadvantage
Evidence has emerged from a number of member state reports that young ethnic minorities and second generation migrants are disproportionately concentrated amongst the unemployed and those with only a tenuous hold on regular employment. The national reports have shown that there are many people who subscribe to over-simple explanations as to the reasons why this is so, usually restricted to the 'blaming the victim' kind. It is true that many within migrant communities are disadvantaged by education, and for many, their inferior labour market status is a reflection of their lower qualification level. However, there has been research in some members states - the UK, Germany and the Netherlands, for example - to show that higher qualification of migrant workers does not lead to their employment in qualified jobs. As described in Section 2.3.1 above, a major UK study of 28,000 school leavers found that even after taking account of factors such as educational attainment, young people from an ethnic minority background were far more likely to experience both higher rates and longer spells of unemployment. In a German case study of a car manufacturer (Biller 1989) there was no correlation between qualification and upward mobility. Migrant workers, especially Turkish and Greek workers, did not get better jobs even if they were better qualified than their German counterparts. On the other hand, after some time in the company, German workers quickly moved further upwards from low-paid, low-qualified jobs even if they had no formal qualifications. A pilot study carried out for the German report (Räthzel and Sarica) found a number of cases where migrant workers were not employed according to the level of their qualifications, even if they had been trained in Germany, and made applications for job vacancies as they occurred

In the Netherlands several pieces of research have demonstrated that the level of education or poor command of language are only of marginal significance in explaining the high per centage of unemployment among ethnic minorities (Kloek, 1992; Veenman, 1990; Van Praag, 1989; Roelandt and Veenman 1992). The fact that command of the language is not a decisive factor in finding a job is also demonstrated by the high per centage of unemployment among Surinamese and Antilleans, who speak Dutch fluently. Therefore, researchers have concluded that there have to be other factors which account for the high level of unemployment among ethnic minorities, such as discrimination. Evidence for this was strengthened in the discrimination testing carried out by Bovenkerk et al. (1995), as this demonstrated that ethnic minorities with a high educational level were still discriminated against in one out of every five applications.

It is clear from previous research that a conventional "human capital" approach is inadequate in itself in explaining the labour market exclusion of young migrants. Instead the processes of labour market integration and exclusion are multiple, diverse and highly complex. For example, it is not necessarily the case that the greater level of unemployment found in one social group reflects simply and directly the lack of human capital skills achieved through education. It can also work the other way round - a perception of poor opportunities and a lack of fairness in the labour market for ethnic minorities reduces educational motivation and performance and the desire for vocational training after school. Young people from these groups lose faith in the advantages of further education for themselves and simply opt out.

Unemployment and the 'underclass'

An important question to ask in this context is: what might be the long term social implications of persistent unemployment over two or perhaps three generations of migrant-descended populations in Europe? Are we witnessing the early stages of an "underclass" formation, with the increasing isolation and alienation of second and third generation descendants of migrants in Europe? The concept of underclass has come to signify a segment of people at the bottom of or beneath the class structure, permanently removed from the labour market, with no power or stake in the economic system. More specifically, in the USA the term has come to represent the black urban poor. The underclass debate has been increasingly discussed in the European context.

It has been argued that so far the concept of underclass is not yet transferable to immigrants in advanced industrial European countries, even though they do occupy low socio-economic positions. For one thing, European immigrants come from a tradition of above average participation in the labour market, albeit in inferior employment, and they are not completely disconnected from mainstream social institutions, often creating their own social and political organisations. 'Whether the emergence of an underclass is a strictly American phenomenon or an emergent characteristic shared by all advanced industrial societies is an empirical question that can only be fully addressed by systematic comparative research' (Heisler, 1991).

After studying the Dutch empirical evidence, Roelandt and Veenman (1992) conclude that at present there is no ethnic underclass in the Netherlands. However, they conclude that some groups of migrants who are concentrated in the inner-city neighbourhoods of the country's largest cities are at risk of becoming an underclass, in the sense of their marginalisation from the labour market and their bleak prospects for any sort of social mobility. They also conclude that their poor prospects are caused less by the characteristics of the minority labour force than by the nature of the labour market's selection processes, including the discriminatory practices of employers.

7.1 Problem Areas Revealed by the National Reports

It now is possible to bring together and group into a number of categories the problem areas and obstacles to the prevention of racism and discrimination at work as discussed in Chapter 6 and the preceding chapters. (Not all of these apply equally to all the European countries studied.) They are categorised and summarised as follows:

   1. Inadequate specific information and research on the employment circumstances of migrants/ethnic minorities, and on the occurrence of discrimination.

2. The occurrence of overt racism towards migrants/ethnic minorities, and direct racist exclusion from employment opportunities

3. Practices at work of indirect discrimination. These include the use of family connections and informal 'acceptability' criteria in recruitment.

4. A general ignorance and lack of awareness of the problems of racism and discrimination in employment on the part of many employers and trade unionists.

5. Hostility and misunderstandings on the part of employers and unions about equal opportunity and equal treatment policies, and anti-discrimination practices, as well as misconceptions about the nature of racism and discrimination.

6. Broad ideologies of resistance to anti-discrimination measures. These might be rooted in economic or market theories; alternatively they could be related to philosophies about the principle of racially or ethnically specific policies as opposed to universalistic measures.

7. Weaknesses in existing legislation against discrimination in employment in many countries, and problems with the implementation of legal and administrative measures against discrimination. Sometimes there is the absence of political will at a national level to implement the legislation which exists.

8. The lack of social, economic and political rights of 'denizens' and the related effects of 'discrimination in law' which excludes non-nationals from certain jobs.

9. The absence of anti-discrimination measures at European Union level.

10. Broader developments which undermine progress towards anti-discrimination protection, such as the spread of illegal/undocumented work, structural unemployment, etc.

These problem areas and obstacles are:

- factors which lead to discrimination against migrants/ethnic minorities
- barriers to the adoption of anti-discrimination measures
- obstacles to the effective implementation of anti-discrimination measures once they have been adopted

Some of these problems can be effectively addressed by improved social policies. Others, realistically, can only be partially addressed, perhaps only the final one is beyond the remit of policies discussed in this report.

7.2 Areas for Action

The national reports have shown that discrimination operates in different ways and at different levels. Some of the action which needs to be taken is that at the EU level; others are at member state level. This report concludes that there are eight main areas for action:

1. Improvement of the rights of third-country nationals
2. EU directive on racial discrimination
3. EU initiation of a code of practice
4. Member state action on citizenship rights
5. Anti-discrimination legislation at member state level.
6. Voluntary measures against discrimination by employers and trade unions
7. More information and research
8. General employment protection

7.2.1. Improvement of the Rights of Third-Country Nationals

The first issue is that of the anomalous status of third country nationals in the EU, and the discrimination and disadvantage related to this. "It is difficult ... to justify a two-tier workforce - one with the right to work anywhere in the EC, and the other restricted to a single EC country" (Dummett, 1994). The Commission issued a communication on immigration in 1994 which recognised that "integration policies must be directed in a meaningful way towards improving the situation of third-country nationals legally resident within the Union by taking steps which will go further towards strengthening their rights relative to those of citizens of the Member States." This has been backed up by a number of recent reports, such as the De Piccoli report to the European Parliament in 1993 on racism and xenophobia, which have stressed the importance of equal rights for all EU residents, regardless of nationality, so that people who live and work in an EU country should have the normal rights and duties of a citizen of that country.

The Commission's view is that an internal market without frontiers, in which the free movement of persons is ensured, logically implies the free movement of all legally resident third-country nationals for the purpose of engaging in economic activities, and that this objective should be realised progressively. Although there was a commitment to provide for the free movement of all EU residents at the Edinburgh summit in December 1992, there has been little movement to implement this (Mirza, 1995). As a CRE report puts it:

> The distinction between EC nationals and legally resident third-country nationals carries real dangers. As the single market develops there will be more opportunities for jobs, business and cultural activity, but third-country

nationals will not be able to move in order to take advantage of them. In fact, the more the Community offers, the greater their disadvantage. The gap between them and their EC national neighbours can only widen unless their legal rights are improved throughout the EC (Dummett 1994).

The national reports have given examples of the ways in which this disadvantage is experienced. This is a particular problem at a time when sectors and enterprises are undergoing restructuring, and in the case of enterprise closure and mass redundancies The clearest example quoted in the report is when the Limbourg coal mines in Campine [Kempense Steenkoolmijnen (KS) - Charbonnages de Campine] in Belgium were closed down in 1987/88. This closure affected some 5800 workers, a significant proportion of whom were Italian (13%) and Turkish (10%). The latter had permanent jobs and average pay that was higher than that of Belgian workers. A survey of a representative sample of former miners two years after the closure of the mines revealed some manifest differences between Belgian, Italian and Turkish workers' chances of occupational reintegration (Denolf and Martens, 1991). Two years after the closure, 82% of Belgian miners had found another job. By contrast, 30% of Italian miners and 83% of Turkish miners were still unemployed. Some 78% of Turkish miners had not worked at all since the closure of the coal mines. One of the extra disadvantages faced by the Turkish miners in comparison with the other two groups was that they were not free to find work over the borders in neighbouring countries.

7.2.2. EU Directive on Racial Discrimination

This report has shown the problems stemming from the wide variation in anti-discrimination legislation between member states. Across EC countries, measures to combat discrimination are variable in their scope and effectiveness, and in some cases hardly exist. Many member states are at quite different stages of developing law and practice to deal with racial discrimination in employment.

> It is clear that protection within individual states against racial discrimination is wholly inadequate and that it will take many years for states to summon the requisite will to introduce measures which are truly effective. In order to realise fully the aim of the Single Market and in order to allow for the free movement of workers .... in pursuit of that aim, legislation at the European level is both desirable and necessary (Mirza, 1995).

The argument has been advanced that the Treaty of Rome and the Single European Act do not confer any competence on the Union in the field of racial or ethnic discrimination. There are therefore pressures for the amendment of the Maastricht Treaty to provide explicitly for Community competence on discrimination against migrants and ethnic minorities, in the same way that it covers sex discrimination. Some people argue that measures against racial discrimination should remain the concern only of individual member states. Others argue that there are good reasons why action at EU level is important. Mirza (1995) concludes:

> It may be argued that legislation at Community level is justified because race discrimination is an issue of a transnational nature and will not be adequately

tackled at state level; the lack of Community action combined with the erratic nature of protection against racial discrimination at state level conflicts with the requirements of the Treaty to correct distortions of competition and to strengthen social cohesion; and action at Community level, because of its standardising effect, would prove beneficial to an extent that is not possible if action were taken at member state level.

A committee of experts appointed after the EU Corfu summit in June 1994 produced a report in 1995 recommending the amendment of the Maastricht Treaty to provide explicitly for Community competence on discrimination against migrants and ethnic minorities, in the same way that it covers sex discrimination. It recommends directives and regulations at Community level to cover issues which include discrimination in employment. An EU directive sets out certain goals which have to be met by a given deadline. Each member state must then pass the necessary laws.

> Protection against discrimination in the member states needs to include elements that are common to the whole Community - so that there is some uniform protection throughout the EC. But complete uniformity would be impossible, given the different legal systems and conditions in the 12 countries. A directive is therefore the ideal instrument laying down a common basis in firm goals to be achieved through legislation but allowing each national government the flexibility to deal with its own particular problems (Dummett, 1994).

The obligations of the Equal Treatment Directive led to every EU country introducing legislation to guarantee equal treatment between men and women in the labour market (Forbes and Mead, 1992). The same should now be done for racial discrimination.

> By its very existence, European sex equality law recognises the need to interfere with the operation of 'free' market forces. It is a major inconsistency in European policy that legal protection is available to address the unequal treatment of women workers, but that parallel provisions are not available for racial and minority ethnic groups. There is no evidence to suggest that the cost advantages to employers from discriminating on grounds of race are any less than for sex discrimination (Sales and Gregory, 1995).

A proposal for amending the European Community Treaty in 1996 has been set out by the 'Starting Line Group', a group of independent experts. They argue that in principle there appears to be no obstacle in amending the Treaty; already all member states of the European Union have ratified the UN Convention on the Elimination of all forms of Racial Discrimination (except Ireland, which is committed to doing so). They have also ratified the European Convention on Human Rights and Fundamental Freedoms, and include in their laws or constitutions some form of condemnation of racism. There are already EU restrictions on the broadcasting of racist material.

The suggested amendment to the Treaty would place the elimination of discrimination among the guiding aims and principles of the European Union. The experts feel that the present situation in Europe urgently requires that the Union should make this unequivocal statement of principle, and make its rejection of racism explicit in 1996.

This is not only because of the widely publicised manifestations of racial hatred and violence but also because of the "everyday unjust discrimination which large numbers of people living in Europe suffer when they are denied access to employment, decent housing, and other social goods and needs because of their race, colour, religion, or national, social or ethnic origin". As the current report shows, this 'everyday discrimination' operates across member states in employment, yet it is often not publicly recognised.

7.2.3 EU Initiation of a Code Of Practice

As this report describes, codes of good practice against discrimination in employment are currently in use in the UK and the Netherlands. A code gives guidance to help employers and others to understand the law, and sets out policies which can be implemented to help to eliminate racial discrimination and enhance equality of opportunity in the workplace. A code can give practical guidance to explain the implications of a country's anti-discrimination legislation, and can recommend measures to reduce the possibility of unlawful behaviour occurring. Although a code itself does not impose legal obligations and only has advisory status it is possible that failure to observe its recommendations could result in breaches of the law. In the UK, evidence about the performance of the code's recommendations can be taken into account by industrial tribunals in deciding whether an act of unlawful discrimination has occurred and assessing the degree of liability by employers for any such acts.

In order to encourage the adoption of such a code at member state level it would be possible for the EU to initiate a code of practice to combat racial discrimination in employment, similar to the code it initiated on sexual harassment. Such a code could cover the full range of employment issues, such as recruitment and selection procedures, opportunities for training and promotion, disciplinary procedures for racist harassment, dismissal and redundancy procedures, and taking account of particular cultural or religious needs. A code could encourage organisations to adopt an equal opportunity policy, and anti-discrimination training for staff. There might be variation in codes so that different codes could be drawn up to relate specifically to trade unions and employment agencies, as in the Netherlands.

The July 1994 White Paper (European Social Policy: A Way Forward for the Union) stated the Commission's intention to consult the social partners at European level on the possible adoption of a code of good employment practice against racial discrimination. The Commission asked the European Human Rights Foundation to put together a draft of such a document to serve as a basis for discussions between the social partners. This draft, entitled "A Code of Practice to Combat Racial Discrimination and to promote Equal Opportunities at Work" was produced in 1994 (Coussey and Hammelburg, 1994).

So far the EU social partners have failed to agree on a common code of practice. As a first stage, at the Social Dialogue Summit in Florence in October 1995, they agreed on a "Joint declaration on the prevention of racial discrimination and xenophobia and promotion of equal treatment at the workplace". This sets out a range of means that have made a positive contribution towards preventing racial discrimination at the workplace, and also sets out various possible approaches for evaluating the progress made by such measures. The social partners will seek to use this declaration to raise their members' awareness on these issues.

7.2.4 Member State Action on Citizenship Rights

In those countries where it is not easy to achieve citizenship, there are employment disadvantages which are unacceptable, particularly when this applies to legally-resident people born in the country of migrant parents. It is difficult to talk about measures against racism and discrimination when a barrier to improving this situation is the legal status of the population of migrant origin. Easy access to citizenship for permanently settled migrants can be regarded as an effective means to help remove disadvantages in employment which are based on legal restrictions linked to the non-citizen status. Moreover, an 'open' citizenship policy can also be seen as an important symbolic step, because it recognises the increasing heterogeneity in the country's population and incorporates migrants politically and legally on an equal basis.

There are a number of European states where naturalisation is not easy, and this could, and should, be rectified. Nevertheless, it must be realised that, even when naturalisation is made easier, the inclination of migrants to apply for naturalisation remains relatively low, primarily because of the necessity of giving up their citizenship of origin. This is the case, for example, in Germany, where migrants argue for the right to *dual* citizenship. Scholars suggest that after decades in which migrants have been "differentially incorporated" into a nation state they tend to develop strong ethnic structures and an ethnic identity. Therefore, the giving up of the original citizenship might be regarded within ethnic communities as 'an abandonment of national identities' (Bauböck, 1992). In addition, it appears that many migrants reject the idea of being exclusively German and thus a member of a community which they feel rejects and discriminates against them (Brandt, 1996).

The situation with regard to dual citizenship in Germany is in fact more complicated in reality than it initially seems in theory. The German governments' line is that dual or multiple citizenship is something to be avoided and officially discouraged. However, in practice, dual citizenship is tolerated on a large scale. For one thing, dual citizenship emerges "naturally". It has been estimated that the marriages of Germans to "foreigners" between 1950-1990 could produce between one and two million children with potential dual citizenship. In addition to this, the Aussiedler, or ethnic Germans, are allowed to keep their original citizenship when naturalised. Therefore, scholars have argued that the official government opposition to dual citizenship begins to look somewhat selective, not so much based on an issue of principle and international law, but rather reflecting a resistance to the naturalisation of permanently settled migrants (Brandt, 1996).

In Germany, proposals for the formal acceptance of dual citizenship were put forward in the early 1990s by the Bundesrat, the Beauftragte der Bundesregierung für die Belange der Ausländer, and various political parties (Bündnis90/Grüne, Social Democrats), supported by immigrant associations, trade unions, ombudspersons and even parts of the Liberal Party, and Christian Democratic Party. An initiative launched in the early 1990s was able to collect one million signatures in favour of dual citizenship within eight months. As long as dual citizenship is formally discouraged the per centage of naturalisation of migrant workers will remain low. This means that the migrant population is not only discriminated against in everyday life, but initially by legislation, which prohibits employers from employing migrants without an EU-nationality, so long as EU-nationals can be found.

The examples quoted in this report of German and Austrian legal and administrative barriers to the equal treatment of migrant workers are perhaps the most visible and extreme examples of a more general point which is applicable to many other countries. Where rules exist which make it difficult for migrants - including 'second generation' migrants - to be regarded as equal in the labour market, then these legal discriminations would need to be removed before other anti-discrimination measures could become fully effective.

Some scholars argue that we may not necessarily have to think in terms of citizenship as such, in the removal of such legal barriers. Layton-Henry (1990) writes:

> foreign residents who live in a country for longer than a temporary stay gradually become members of their country of residence, and this fact should be recognised, even if most may not want to become naturalised citizens of their new society. We suggest that a new status of denizenship should be granted to them, entitling them to all the rights of citizenship within their country of residence, including the right to participate in national elections. This would give them rights similar to those of dual nationals, who have rights in more than one country.

Forbes and Mead, in their 1992 review of measures to combat discrimination in EU member states, argue that voting rights transform an outsider pressure group into a significant bloc of potential voters, given the way that visible minority groups tend to be concentrated in urban areas, and ensure increased access to the political process. This has the long term effect of altering the agenda of political parties. Thus "the lack of voting and full citizenship rights is a very good indicator of the absence of adequate legislation dealing with racial discrimination".

7.2.5 Anti-Discrimination Legislation at Member State Level.

In 1991 a comparative analysis of measures to combat racial discrimination covering the then 12 member countries of the European Union (Forbes and Mead 1992) came down heavily in favour of specific legal measures to combat discrimination. The authors conclude that existing international *conventions* on racial discrimination, such as the ILO Convention 111 on Discrimination in Employment and Occupation, only have substantive effects when they lead to and inform domestic *legislation* on discrimination. International provisions on racial discrimination in employment are not in themselves enough - there must also be domestic legislation. A starting principle of domestic legislation is to make racial discrimination a criminal and /or a civil offence. Although in some countries racial discrimination in employment is covered by criminal law, many commentators are not convinced that this is the best way of countering it. Whereas racist attacks, harassment and propaganda are threats to public order and these can be dealt with by criminal law, civil proceedings may be more effective for racial discrimination. This is for a number of reasons, including the fact that the standard of proof is less rigorous, and that in civil law the applicant can initiate proceedings, whereas usually only the police initiate criminal proceedings (Banton, 1994).

Banton points to France, where the primary remedy for all kinds of discrimination lies in criminal law. Statistics show that by 1991 the annual number of convictions had risen to 101, almost entirely for offences against public order, namely for incitement to racial hatred, insult, and so on. There were just four convictions for racial discrimination in employment. This "scarcely suggests that criminal remedies are effective in this field." For Banton, the French experience shows that while criminal law can be effective in dealing with racial defamation by the published word, as in the press, it is ineffective in dealing with discrimination in the workplace. (Some other countries rely on *labour* law to combat workplace discrimination; however, this leaves the victim dependent upon support from a trade union.) British experience suggests that remedies in civil law are more effective Forbes and Mead (1992) argue that "Racial discrimination can be a criminal *and* civil offence, thereby opening up two quite different avenues for the aggrieved individual, with important implications for the educative effect of convictions".

Legislation must include both a strong prohibition of racial discrimination in all its forms, together with a committed prosecution policy (Forbes and Mead 1992). The following are likely to be components of legislative action against discrimination in employment. Legislation could:

- make it unlawful to discriminate at any stages of recruitment on the grounds of colour, 'race', nationality, ethnic or national origins, or religion.

- forbid an advertisement which indicates that an employer is intending to discriminate on the above grounds.

- make it unlawful to discriminate against employees, once recruited, in regard to their terms of employment or opportunities for training or promotion.

- render unlawful "pressure to discriminate", i.e. inducing another person to perform an act of unlawful discrimination,

- make unlawful racist insults, harassing, threatening and bullying by other employees.

- protect against victimisation individuals who bringing a complaint of discrimination or give information in proceedings brought by another person.

- give individual victims a right of direct access to the courts and tribunals for legal remedies against unlawful discrimination.

- make racist attacks, harassment, propaganda and general incitement to racial hatred a criminal offence.

It is also important for legislation to recognise the distinction between direct and indirect discrimination, and outlaw both. Indirect discrimination occurs in employment with any job requirement or condition which, although applied equally to all, in practice affects members of one 'racial' or ethnic group less favourably than another, and has the effect of excluding a higher proportion of members of certain groups than members of others.

It is quite acceptable for legislation to contain provision for exceptions. These might include work in a private household, or jobs where 'race' or ethnic background is allowed to be a 'genuine occupational qualification', such as for artistic performances, or in ethnic restaurants for reasons of authenticity. In certain circumstances exceptions might apply for jobs which entail providing people of a particular 'racial' or ethnic group with personal welfare services. These provisions for exceptions would equally allow the recruitment of ethnic minority or white applicants.

Some countries have industrial tribunals to deal with employment discrimination cases. Forbes and Mead (1992) suggest that separate tribunals should be set up to handle all discrimination cases, or that only specialist personnel should deal with such cases within the established tribunal framework, so as to allow a body of specialist expertise to develop.

Enforcement agencies
Some people argue that the fact that few racial discrimination cases appear before the courts means that discrimination is rare. However, the real reason is that there is either a lack of legal mechanisms for bringing a case, or the mechanisms for doing this are inadequate. "The fact that individuals do not have access to the courts and tribunals constitutes a fundamental criticism of the limited measures that have been introduced by individual states" (Mirza, 1995). Forbes and Mead (1992) argue that anti-discrimination measures cannot be effective without a range of measures of implementation. These include the creation of an agency backed by law and central government to undertake advisory and litigatory functions. They see the existence of an agency as a key indicator of a country's commitment and progress in dealing with discrimination. Governments in several countries have established special enforcement agencies to initiate legal action and help individual litigants. This is particularly important when individuals are without the resources or skills to pursue their cases to tribunals. An agency could have both an educational role and formal investigative powers, with the ability to take cases to court. An enforcement agency may also (as in Britain and the Netherlands) be authorised to prepare codes of good practice, advising employers what they should do to avoid discrimination. (Banton, 1994). Forbes and Mead (1992) conclude:

> Government-funded and semi-autonomous commissions and bureaux are needed to specialise in anti-discrimination measures, and a range of tribunals to deal with complaints is required. The appointment of an ombudsman with an operating policy of voluntarism and co-operation, but backed up by an enforcement authority, is another possibility. There is also a place for non-

government organisations to provide assistance, take cases to court and champion the cause of ethnic minorities, if necessary by acting as a spur to government bodies.

Contract Compliance

It is possible for national legislation to enable anti-discrimination to be pursued by administrative action, such as contract compliance. This is when the government or local authorities encourage companies and agencies supplying goods or services to comply with minimum requirements on employment practices, including on equal opportunities. The main impetus for equal opportunities contract compliance came from the United States. During the Kennedy administration contractors were required to file compliance reports to contract compliance offices in government departments, and non-compliance on issues of racial equality led to termination of contract. Experience in the USA and the UK has shown that contract compliance can lead to greatly improved equal opportunities practices in the companies involved. Forbes and Mead (1992) conclude:

> This practice does result in a faster spread of good practice throughout the economy, since it concentrates minds and changes practices more quickly than would otherwise be the case. Should they choose to use this approach, central and local governments find themselves in a very strong position, given their vast and often concentrated purchasing power, to establish a vigorous timetable for implementation and assertive evaluation techniques.

The conclusion of a recent international overview of legislative measures to combat discrimination can be repeated here: "In short, a comprehensive anti-discrimination statute in civil law, backed up with measures to promote equal opportunity and a specialised redress mechanism, appears to be the most effective way to tackle discrimination by legal means" (Zegers de Beijl 1995).

7.2.6 Voluntary measures against discrimination by employers and trade unions

Experience in the United States shows that anti-discrimination legislation is a necessary but not sufficient means of reducing racial discrimination in employment. The effect of such legislation is often that racism becomes more subtle, and that indirect, institutional or unintentional discrimination becomes more important. As two American researchers put it:

> The effects of legal and intentionally discriminatory practices remain long after court decisions and social customs signal the reduction of overt discrimination. Racial oppression and privilege have become institutionalised, embedded in the norms ... and roles ... in a variety of social, economic and political organisations (Chesler and Delgado, 1987).

Therefore, as well as laws against discrimination, there is a need for the stimulation of a range of social policy initiatives against racism and discrimination, including equal opportunities programmes, codes of practice, positive action, education and information provision, and training. The law can be used not just to prohibit, but to allow, to encourage and to facilitate. It can provide a stimulus for organisations to undertake 'voluntary' action, such as adopting equal opportunity policies.

Equal Opportunity Policies
Laws against discrimination need the support of equal opportunity policies implemented at the workplace. An equal opportunity policy consists of a set of aims and procedures adopted by an organisation which should be summarised in a public statement and made known to all employees. An equal opportunity policy could include the following:

- an audit of ethnic minority employees;
- ethnic monitoring of job applicants;
- equality targets for recruitment;
- equality targets for entry to management posts;
- recruitment initiatives to encourage ethnic minority applicants;
- training for recruiters and selectors on avoiding racial discrimination;
- positive action measures to stimulate ethnic minority applications
- positive action training for ethnic minority employees
- procedures against racial harassment

Ethnic Monitoring
Ethnic monitoring entails the collection of statistics on the ethnic origin of all employees and trainees in order to identify where ethnic minority staff are employed in the organisation and to compare their progress with that of white staff. Monitoring of the workforce and of decisions made at recruitment, selection, promotion and redundancy stages has an important contribution to make in cases of both direct and indirect discrimination. Such statistics can reveal unintentional discriminatory outcomes and allow employers to deal with problem areas by reviewing standard practice and providing specific training to increase awareness and introduce new techniques to ensure fairer outcomes (Forbes and Mead, 1992). The ethnic profile of the workforce provides a baseline against which progress can be measured. Experience in the USA has shown that firms usually discover advantages in the practice of monitoring, not least the fact that the very process of recording and returning data gives a degree of systematisation of recruitment and selection procedures and criteria which might previously have been absent.

Codes of Practice
One of the roles of the enforcement agency may be to prepare codes of good practice in conjunction with employers and trade union representatives. A code of practice gives practical guidance to employers on policies which avoid discrimination (see above, Section 7.2.3). It would cover the full range of employment issues, such as recruitment and selection procedures, opportunities for training and promotion, disciplinary procedures for racist harassment, dismissal and redundancy procedures, and taking account of particular cultural or religious needs. A code would encourage organisations to adopt an equal opportunity policy, and anti-discrimination training

for staff. There might be separate codes for trade unions and for employment agencies.

Positive Action
Positive action seeks to do more than simply attack discrimination; it also includes measures to tackle the causes of under-representation by devoting extra resources to encourage and assist members of under-represented groups to compete for employment. Examples of the sorts of positive action measures which could be adopted are in existence in some members states. These include organising special recruitment campaigns targeted at in ethnic minority areas, or advertising in ethnic minority publications. The national reports show that some people still confuse 'positive action' with 'positive discrimination'. Employers can encourage the interest of those they are trying to attract, and take other positive steps, but should then select candidates solely on the basis of their suitability for that job. This is different from the use of quotas, which would constitute positive discrimination. Setting a quota for people from ethnic minorities would almost certainly involve selection on the basis of 'race' rather than on merit alone, which would be undesirable.

In the UK the law allows for positive action training for groups before they enter the labour market, or for groups of employees who are under-represented in particular work within companies. However, in the UK this does not allow for 'reverse' or 'positive' discrimination or 'quotas'. Unlike positive discrimination, positive action stops at giving ethnic minorities more favourable treatment in competition for jobs. Positive action in employment is the promotion of ethnic minority interests and chances *within existing procedures* for distributing and allocating jobs and training. Positive discrimination on the other hand involves *overriding* existing allocation practices by allowing a degree of preference for minority group members.

Another sort of positive action measure is that found in the Netherlands, where the law allows positive action elements stronger than those allowed in the UK, namely the preferential treatment of minority applicants in the case of sufficient or equal qualification for a post. This does not, however, mean lowering the qualification requirement for the vacancy in order to recruit the minority applicant - this would be seen as unacceptable 'positive discrimination'.

Equality Targets
Equality targets consist of a figure of ethnic minority employees which employers would aim to reach by a specific date, through both positive action and through measures to eliminate direct and indirect discrimination (see Chapter 4). They may relate to numbers or proportions of under represented groups in particular jobs or grades, and be defined in relation to the per centage of ethnic minority population in the relevant area or local labour market. Where an organisation is recruiting, for example, graduates for professional jobs, the basis for setting targets might be the national labour market. Targets are not quotas and must not be reached by discriminatory selection decisions.

Anti-Discrimination Training
The national reports show that a great deal of ignorance exists about the employment circumstances of migrants and ethnic minorities, and the discrimination they suffer.

Anti-discrimination training can form part of consciousness-raising activities on this issue, and is recognised as an important tool within the range of techniques for combating discrimination against migrants and ethnic minorities. Anti-discrimination training is to be differentiated from positive action training. Positive action training can be important as a means of compensating for years of discrimination and increasing the recruitment of minorities to employing organisations. However there is a danger that such training carries with it the assumption that there is a general deficiency within the minority group which needs to be addressed by training. In reality, one of the main factors which remains to blight the opportunities of such minorities is discrimination on the grounds of race, colour or ethnicity. A strategy for tackling this is anti-discrimination training. Whereas positive action training provides skills and knowledge to individuals to improve their own opportunities, anti-discrimination training is aimed at people who can affect the opportunities of others, and seeks to reduce discrimination by giving skills and knowledge or by changing attitudes or practices (Brown and Lawton, 1991).

There are many different types of anti-discrimination training. Some of the different areas covered in the training content are as follows:

- imparting cultural information to prevent misunderstandings at work;
- making people aware of the racism underlying their own attitudes and behaviour, and helping them to develop strategies to deal with it;
- making people aware of the history and mechanisms of racism and discrimination, and helping people to develop strategies to oppose racial injustice;
- developing skills and work practices to stop discrimination in personnel management;
- explaining the meaning of an organisation's equal opportunities programme and the duties that it puts on individuals;
- explaining anti-discrimination legislation and its implications for the organisation and for the individual. (Brown and Lawton 1991).

Throughout the training literature runs a debate as to whether it is better to attempt changes in attitudes or in behaviour. Initially the predominant training goal was seen to be the promotion of awareness and sensitivity amongst whites, focusing mainly on changes in attitudes and feelings (Luthra and Oakley, 1991). The assumption of this approach was that attitude change would lead automatically to changes in practices, an assumption which later came to be questioned. For one thing, research has shown that there is no simple and direct relationship between attitudes and behaviour - in some instances employers have been shown to discriminate although they were not prejudiced; in others, racist employers have been shown not to discriminate in practice (Bovenkerk, 1992).

It became recognised that this initial over-emphasis on training to produce attitude change was flawed. The pendulum of consensus swung more the other way - it was seen to be more important to produce changes in behaviour on the grounds that even if racist attitudes remain unchanged, at least the actual practice of discrimination may be effectively reduced. "Research on the relationship between attitudes and behaviour has created substantial evidence that changes in behaviour may have more potent and lasting effects than changes in attitudes, *per se*" (Bovenkerk, 1992). Minorities are hurt more by racist practices than racist attitudes, it is argued. Moreover, the added attraction of this argument is that in the long term, changing behaviour may even produce a corresponding change in attitudes.

In reality, this simple attitude/behaviour dichotomy is flawed. Attitudes and behaviour are tied in a way that makes their logical separation difficult to sustain. Most jobs allow people a degree of discretion, and therefore "even when people stick to the letter of their formal duties there is plenty of scope for prejudiced attitudes to find an outlet in discrimination" (Peppard, 1983). Nevertheless, much training, implicitly at least, still subscribes to one or other emphasis. It is possible to recognise a rough typology of different anti-discrimination training approaches according to differences in strategy and content (Wrench and Taylor, 1993). These are categorised as follows:

1. Information Training
2. Cultural Awareness Training
3. Racism Awareness Training
4. Equalities Training
5. Anti-Racism Training
6. Diversity Training

(1) Information Training

In many European countries there would appear to be much training effort which could fall into this category: programmes to encourage inter-cultural awareness and promote better communication and understanding, training directed at those dealing with the integration of migrants which provides demographic facts and figures on migrants, their countries of origin, their current employment patterns, etc. A broader type provides cultural information but also includes factual information on prejudice and racism, the evidence and processes of discrimination, etc. The assumption behind this approach is that most people are fair, but are often unaware of the extent and effect of racial discrimination. Training is required to inform them about discrimination and disadvantage in society, so that they will be disposed to implement measures to tackle it. The underlying assumption is that the provision of correct information is enough to lead to behavioural change.

(2) Cultural Awareness Training

This not only provides cultural information, but actively engages trainees in exercises to change their attitudes; for example, role play exercises, or intensive group discussions. Sometimes these involve invited representatives of migrant/ethnic minority communities. Courses of cultural awareness might include material on the majority culture of the trainees on the grounds that thinking critically about their own culture will help in understanding others better. Courses on the theme of "living/working together with foreigners/migrants" will often fall under this heading. Although Cultural Awareness Training, unlike simple Information Training, is more active in trying to produce attitude change in the trainees, it still remains similar to

Information Training in seeing behavioural change as relatively unproblematic. Implicit in this approach is the idea that raising trainees' awareness and changing prejudiced attitudes will thereby automatically reduce discriminatory behaviour.

(3) Racism Awareness Training
This approach is typified by the "Human Awareness" or "White Awareness" programme of Katz (1978) in the USA and those who follow her model. The premise of Racism Awareness Training is that racism is located in white people and operates to their interests; it is therefore their responsibility to tackle it. White people need to be made aware of their own racism as a precondition of being able to tackle the problem in their own lives. (Luthra and Oakley, 1991: 24). The methods are generally techniques to induce self-awareness in a group setting, with trainers sometimes using confrontational techniques, along with role-play and other self-awareness exercises. "The training thus aims to create a heightened awareness of racism within each participant, and largely presumes this will give rise to motivation at the behavioural level.

(4) Equalities Training
In complete contrast to Racism Awareness Training which seeks to change attitudes, Equalities Training refers to training which is designed primarily to affect behaviour. The training seeks to side-step attitudes by seeing them as private and irrelevant to the job, and simply aims to instruct the trainees in legally or professionally appropriate behaviour. This is defined as precisely as possible in terms of the appropriate norms and behaviour, and the required skills (Luthra and Oakley, 1991:27). In many countries the starting point of Equalities Training will be that the law proscribes racial discrimination and that agencies and professionals must therefore make sure that discrimination, whether deliberate or unintentional, does not occur. This type might also be known as "Equal Opportunities Training".

(5) Anti-Racism Training
Anti-Racism Training was developed after disillusion with Racism Awareness Training, retaining a strong commitment to combating racism directly, whilst seeking to change organisational practice rather than individual self-awareness. The premise of this approach is that racism cannot be simply reduced to a problem of (white) individuals, and yet neither can it be tackled purely in terms of discriminatory behaviour without addressing the level of personal attitudes and awareness. The goal is to secure the support of individuals in challenging the racism which is endemic in the culture and institutions of the society, and so training exercises are geared to developing both self-awareness and job performance. Although producing change at the behavioural level is the target, the tackling of attitudes is seen as a necessary condition of effective behaviour change. An important characteristic of this training approach is that racism and discrimination are still seen to constitute the main problem within the organisation, and the main reason for the training programme.

(6) Diversity Training
This is the most recent development, perhaps best typified by "Managing Diversity" programmes in the United States (Thomas, 1990; MacDonald, 1993). It has been argued that Diversity Management is the logical next step after measures such as equal opportunities initiatives and affirmative action programmes have broken down

barriers to the employment of minorities, producing a more diverse workforce. Diversity management is seen as a strategy of fully tapping the resources within an organisation, getting people to perform to their potential. The training, which is mainly directed at managers, emphasises the importance of valuing difference. It argues that ethnic, racial and sexual groups have different cultural styles of working which should not be negatively labelled by white managers. Fairness is not seen as treating people equally but treating people appropriately. Managers should carry out a "cultural audit" to discover what it is that is blocking the progress of "non-traditional" employees; this may uncover the organisation's "institutional racism". The objective is not to assimilate minorities (and women) into the dominant white (and male) organisational culture but to create a dominant *heterogeneous* culture. It is different to the previous training approaches in that it is broader in emphasis, more ambitious, and long-term in perspective.

The International Labour Office has recently commissioned a survey on the extent and character of anti-discrimination training in several European countries, as part of its broader programme of work on "Combating discrimination against (im)migrant workers and ethnic minorities in the world of work" (see Wrench and Taylor, 1993). One aim of this programme is to come to some conclusions about which type of training is most useful for combating discrimination, and in which circumstances. At the time of writing this report, the results of this survey are not available. However, it already seems clear that training which simply concentrates on information provision on aspects of 'culture', or which restricts its focus to attitudes, will be inadequate, and that training must cover behaviour modification and tangible anti-discrimination practices.

Recommendations for trade unions
Although many of the above 'voluntary' measures are relevant to trade unions as well as employers, there are some specific issues of particular relevance to unions. For one thing, there is a need for more accurate data on membership levels of migrants in unions. The availability of data, and the density of union membership amongst migrants, seem to vary a great deal between different member states. Some trade unionists have assumed that the right to join a trade union should be limited to those who are nationals of a country. In many member states migrant workers are under-represented in unions, reflecting the fact that unions have not been seen to be sympathetic or relevant to their issues. They have therefore turned to other organisations to protect their interests. In other countries, unions have positively welcomed migrants, appeared to be sensitive to their issues, and have even set up specialised departments within the unions to deal with them

Unions have an important and special role to play in the integration of migrant workers both in the workplace, and in broader society. Special measures are needed for unions to adopt in countering racism and discrimination. These might include:

- union educational programmes which tackle racism and discrimination. These should not simply cover, for example, issues of right extremism - they should also attempt to develop awareness on discrimination in the workplace and the union, and measures to tackle it.

- the adoption of an equal opportunities policy and code of good practice with regard to the union's role as an employer itself, as well as in looking after the interests of its members.

- a readiness to take vigorous action on employment grievances concerning racial discrimination, including a willingness to support victims as far as industrial tribunals.

- procedures for dealing with racial harassment at the workplace, with a readiness to take disciplinary action against union members guilty of racist action.

- a commitment to countering racist propaganda, including involvement in national demonstrations and campaigns to raise public awareness on these issues.

- the production of union material in relevant ethnic minority languages when necessary. This could include recruitment material and broader information such as health and safety regulations.

- encouraging employers to take on board anti-discrimination measures by, for example, the inclusion of equal opportunity clauses in collective agreements, and encouraging employers to use voluntary measures such as codes of practice, fair personnel procedures for recruitment and promotion, etc.

- encouraging migrants not only to join unions, but also to share union responsibilities, working to remove barriers which prevent migrant and ethnic minority workers from reaching union office.

In general, unions should not simply restrict their activities to the workplace, but should also concern themselves with the broader position of migrant workers in society.

Some trade unionists feel that the right to join a trade union should be limited to those who are legally resident in a country. However, increasingly, European unions are seeing it as important to secure rights and protection for all workers, including undocumented migrants. This report has shown that formal measures against discrimination are undermined by the illegal labour market. Thus unions should make it a priority to extend protection to workers in the illegal labour market, including undocumented workers.

The business case for equal opportunities
The measures for employers described in Section 7.2.6 can be described as 'voluntary', in that although they would be allowed for in law, they would not be mandatory. Nevertheless, many employers do implement these measures. This might be for reasons of social justice, or a concern to avoid broader social problems. Their implementation does not, however, have to be simply altruistic. It is recognised that there can be a number of potential advantages stemming from equal opportunities practice. For example:

- if qualified people are locked into a secondary labour market of poor and unskilled work, this is an inefficient use of human resources and a waste of talent.

- if workers are employed below their capacity, this can lead to poor motivation and low productivity.

- migrants tend to be a young population, and in some local labour markets form an increasingly significant proportion of school leavers. Therefore, an employer who presents a negative image to ethnic minority young people may have difficulty recruiting appropriate trainees.

- the introduction of a well-managed equal opportunities programme which includes the accurate monitoring of both the existing workforce and new applicants can give new and helpful insights into aspects of the organisation's human resource management.

- if employers fail to recruit and use ethnic minorities in a culturally diverse region they will lose an opportunity to increase their attractiveness to potential customers.

- there is a danger of bad publicity if an organisation is suspected of operating racial discrimination. Whereas a high profile equal opportunities policy can be very good for the corporate image, a tribunal case for discrimination can severely undermine it.

The balance between voluntarism and compulsion
While it is true that there can be identifiable advantages for an employer in the introduction of equal opportunity measures, and that in some member states individual employers have embraced them willingly, it is also true that without further encouragement by legal measures their widespread adoption is unlikely. Even in countries such as the UK and the Netherlands it remains the case that there is relatively little incentive to encourage employers to adopt good practice in this area, over and above the avoidance of unlawful discrimination. There is therefore an argument for imposing greater requirements on employers to introduce equal opportunity measures.

A legal framework might be established to impose a duty on employers to work for equality in a number of ways. For example, employers might be under a duty to monitor the ethnic origins of their workforce, and make annual returns to the appropriate enforcement agency. Alternatively, the agency might simply be given the power to require them on demand. Employers might be given the duty to adopt goals to be achieved over a certain period of time - such as their workforce proportionately reflecting the ethnic breakdown of the local labour market. Contract compliance measures by local and national government might be used to encourage these activities. In other words, such measures would make some of the above-listed 'voluntary' measures less voluntary.

In the UK the CRE has asked, without success, for something similar to be introduced. It points out that the Race Relations Act relies entirely on voluntary action to achieve change, provided only that employers avoid actual racial discrimination.

Few in positions of power and authority have adopted, implemented and monitored the kind of comprehensive equal opportunities policies that would help end discrimination and enable all to realise their potential regardless of ethnic origins. Accordingly, the CRE is calling for a new legal framework for achieving equality which emphasises achieving equal opportunity beyond the basic elimination of unlawful racial discrimination.

One model which swings the pendulum a little more away from voluntarism towards compulsion is that recently considered by the Netherlands. A 1989 report to the Dutch government by the Scientific Council for Government Policy (WRR) recommended an Act for the Promotion of Labour Opportunities, based upon the Canadian 'Employment Equity Act'. This act, which had been in effect in Canada for two years, commits companies to employ minorities to bring about a proportional reflection of the country's population breakdown. In order to achieve proportional representation of minorities in the workforce, employers should, in consultation with employees' organisations, formulate a public plan with goals and timetables. Although no sanctions are imposed if a company does not reach its target, the act makes it a legal obligation for employers to release public reports annually, in which they have to set out the number and proportion of minorities in their workforce. The rationale behind this is that because of the figures are made public, social pressure will be exerted on the company to increase the representation of minorities in the workforce. This measure is sanctioned; when a company does not make its annual report, it will be fined. As an additional sanction, the government will be able to use contract compliance to encourage firms to perform well; it therefore has the ability to cancel a contract with a company that is not striving hard enough for a more proportional representation of minorities. (Kosten, 1994). The Canadian act was one of the influences of the Act for the Promotion of Proportional Labour Participation of Non-Natives (Wet Bevordering Evenredige Arbeidsdeelname Allochtonen) which was passed in the Netherlands in 1994 (see Chapter 3).

Although many of the equal opportunity measures implemented by employers in countries such as the UK and the Netherlands are 'voluntary', they may well be motivated by a desire to avoid falling foul of anti-discrimination legislation. A major study of employers' equal opportunities practice, financed by the UK Department of Employment, concluded that a successful policy needed to have the commitment of organisational power holders such as senior directors, but that this commitment was unlikely to be 'voluntarily' secured without some sort of pressure.

> "There are a number of ways in which their attention might be engaged, including: moral pressure and example from government; financial incentives, such as those entailed in contract compliance; legal sanctions and penalties; and the emergence of perceived business advantage. In our research almost all the initiatives we encountered had their origins in some sort of outside pressure (investigations, riots, accusations of malpractice, and so on.) A significant number of managers also made the point that equal opportunities were costly of time and resources. They often said they would be inclined to do more if there were an obvious business pay off, or, more frequently, a discernible price to be paid for inaction" (Mason and Jewson, 1992).

The conclusion has to be that where a 'business pay-off' is not immediately obvious, some extra pressure will need to be applied via the legal framework.

7.2.7 More Information and Research

Chapter 6 of this report described how national reports were hindered by incomplete national statistics, and more specifically by lack of research on the experiences of migrants in employment, and on discrimination. In many of the 12 member states there was relatively little or no such research to refer to, little public awareness of discriminatory practices, and therefore little debate as to their implications for social exclusion. The acceptance of a notion of 'no problem here' means there is little incentive for research, the absence of which then reinforces the idea that there is no problem. Some reports explicitly made the point that until broader awareness of the various processes of discrimination and exclusion is achieved through identification and discussion, there can be no progress in related social policy developments against exclusion.

It is important to raise public awareness through comprehensive studies on the experiences of non-nationals of different ethnic backgrounds, including those who may be working illegally. Better information on working conditions is needed, in order to show to what extent migrants have to perform heavy, unpleasant or monotonous work, suffer noisy or dangerous work conditions, work anti-social shifts, suffer higher accident or absenteeism levels, and so on. Research could focus on, for example, what is happening in traditional and declining sectors of industry where migrant workers are over-represented. Are they unfairly selected for redundancy, and do they subsequently have less chance of re-employment? What keeps them from being employed in newer industries: education, geography, or discrimination? Research should also focus on immigrants who have taken the nationality within a member state, and the circumstances in which this has a positive impact on employment It might show, for example, that the acquisition of nationality, although desirable, is still not sufficient in itself as a remedy for the problems faced by immigrants.

In many countries at present, official statistics provide information only on foreign nationals. As the Danish report puts it, when immigrants and refugees have become naturalised, this changes neither their colour nor their name, and they are just as much subject to racial discrimination as immigrants and refugees who still have foreign citizenship. When official statistics lack detail, researchers can therefore play an important role in filling in some of the gaps in knowledge by carrying out specific surveys. Surveys which produce evidence of inequality or disadvantage can, by 'controlling' for other possible causes, demonstrate that the residual disadvantage is likely to be a result of discrimination.

This report has recommended that equal opportunity and anti-discrimination initiatives should be implemented in companies and trade unions. However, it is clear that research will also need to be carried out on the circumstances of migrants in companies and trade unions before many key people in these organisations will be convinced of a need for such measures. When equal opportunities and anti-discrimination measures have eventually been adopted, there will need to be case studies of organisations which have operated them, in order to disseminate knowledge of good practice to others.

Discrimination testing
As argued elsewhere in this report, statistical indicators of inequality are not enough in themselves.

> Statistics of inequality are snapshots of complex and continuing processes. ... No one can ascertain the extent to which disadvantage is the result of discrimination without first understanding the process which has produced it ... It is essential to understand how the system works before looking to see if it is operated in a manner that gives some an advantage at the expense of others (Banton, 1994).

Therefore, further types of research are needed. Discrimination testing, where people of different ethnic origin but having the same qualifications apply for jobs, is an invaluable way of finding out the degree of discrimination. The International Labour Office (ILO) initiative "Combating discrimination against (im)migrant workers and ethnic minorities in the world of work" is extending its programme of discrimination testing (Bovenkerk 1992), and the Netherlands carried out the first national study of this programme in 1994 (Bovenkerk et al, 1995). In many countries, no such discrimination testing has ever been carried out, and it is important that such work is undertaken as one of the first stages in a programme of research.

Qualitative research
Discrimination testing such as carried out by the ILO is effective, and is an important first stage, but it has limitations in its explanatory value. It clearly demonstrates the existence of the problem, but gives little further insight into the processes behind it. Qualitative research can complement and add to the research already being done by exploring in detail the attitudes, motives and practices of key labour market players, including employers, trade unionists, and migrant workers themselves. It can bring to light practices in the labour market which contribute to the exclusion of migrants and ethnic minorities, even though they may not be motivated by racism or intentionally discriminatory.

In addition, research on discrimination that takes into account the opinions and experiences of migrant workers is badly needed. Most research done on the subject focuses on statistics or on interviews with managers. Fewer studies incorporate direct information from migrant workers themselves. Qualitative research on the experiences of migrants at the workplace can bring out their subjective experiences of inequality and discrimination, their perceptions of barriers to occupational mobility, and a whole range of first-hand experiences which are otherwise invisible to outsiders. Such material has the power to undermine the complacency of those who feel that there is no problem.

Research can usefully cast light on the relationship between educational performance and employment status. The extent to which language ability prevents migrants and refugees from getting jobs has not been subject to detailed research. It is not known to what extent under-valuing of the education and experience of immigrants and refugees is responsible for their higher rate of unemployment. Information on vocational training is often inadequate. It is known that young people of foreign origin often have great difficulty in finding places for practical training, but to what lies behind this is often not known. Within companies, migrant workers are under-represented in training and qualification programmes, mainly in those offered during working-hours. Some evidence from trade unionists indicate that this could be partly due to discrimination, even on the part of shop stewards who participate in selecting workers for further training. Research is therefore necessary to shed some light on the reasons for the under-qualification of migrant workers and its possible connection with discriminatory practices within companies and trade unions.

Little qualitative research has been carried out to explain the incidence of discrimination in terms of the various motivations and interests of the respective actors and gatekeepers in working life, and the degree to which it results from fear, prejudice and intolerance, taste or profit. Is it among employers, managers, workers or clients that the real opposition to employing immigrants and ethnic minorities is to be found? As long as the reasons why, and the ways in which, people discriminate are not clearly identified, it will prove to be difficult to design effective means to tackle this.

Research on the illegal labour market
The issue of discrimination and the illegal labour market is qualitatively different from the issues of employment discrimination and the 'second generation' being discussed in many EU countries. Nevertheless, the two issues are related. The existence of the informal labour market undermines anti-discrimination measures, and creates a class of workers who are unable to draw upon the protection of such measures. The national reports describe the difficulty in discovering the detail of the over-exploitation immigrant workers are subjected to. Immigrants rarely report such practices, often because they have no documents. This is one reason for the need for further research. There should be qualitative research to bring to light and expose these practices to public knowledge. There should also be sensitive, ethnographic work on workers in the illegal labour market to fill in the picture of how people enter such employment, the operation of informal networks, and the relationship of the informal with the formal labour market.

To conclude, it is clear that major issues relating to the employment exclusion of migrants and ethnic minorities in Europe are the discrimination which keeps them out of good jobs in the regular employment sector, and the discrimination which keeps them in the worst jobs and in the unregulated sector. Already there is some evidence at the statistical level which confirms this distribution. What is particularly lacking is detailed qualitative work which will allow more insight into the processes at work here. Such an insight will not only be of academic relevance in facilitating an understanding of forces at work in the European labour market, but will also have important implications for social policies aiming to protect vulnerable groups in the labour market. Furthermore, dissemination of the findings of this research, whether in the media, or by education or training programmes in employment, will help to overcome some of the problems of misunderstandings and lack of awareness described in Section 6.2.

International exchanges of information

There should be international exchanges of experiences on issues such as citizenship and anti-discrimination legislation, the experiences of equal opportunities policies, etc. This is best co-ordinated by international organisations. The ILO is carrying out such comparisons as part of its current programme: one is a comparative analysis of national measures against discrimination in employment in different countries (e.g. Zegers de Beijl 1991). A second part is its comparison and evaluation of anti-discrimination training measures in employment, currently under way in the UK and the Netherlands and planned for a number of other European countries.

There could be similar comparative research and international exchanges of information which could be of great value. The EU's ETUC and UNICE could arrange such exchanges of information on a European level. Managers and officials of companies and trade unions should meet with those from other countries to exchange both good and bad experiences in the field. For example, a meeting of personnel managers at a European level could be initiated, where managers from companies with an equal opportunity policy would inform their colleagues about the advantages of, and the problems concerning, such policies. The European Union and initiatives launched by the European Commission or other European institutions can be valuable facilitators of such activities. One of the national reporters discovered during the course of research for this project that often the mere mention of a European institution would open the door to many informants.

7.2.8 General Employment Protection

Even with the best measures, anti-discrimination law and practice will have a limited impact in the context of a general degradation of work. Anti-discrimination protection can only be effective in the context of reasonable minimum standards of employment protection. At an EU level this issue has been addressed through the Social Charter and the social chapter of the Maastricht Treaty. Included in the 1989 Community Charter of the Fundamental Social Rights of Workers - the Social Charter - are principles relating to the improvement of the well-being of EU workers, covering employment and remuneration, better working conditions, worker participation, health and safety at work, etc. Britain alone refused to adopt the Charter. The social chapter of the Maastricht treaty also deals with the social rights of workers in the EU, and, unlike the Social Charter, is legally binding. Again, Britain alone refused to sign this.

The dispute between member states on this issue symbolises the tension between economic strategies and social objectives of European policy (Sales and Gregory 1995). The European Union was always supposed to be more than economically driven. It was conceived from the start as having an important social dimension to ensure fair competition and free movement of labour, thus giving wider legitimacy to processes of economic integration. However, since the early 1980s, the UK has led an attack on harmonisation in this sphere, diluting and blocking social legislation, and perhaps setting a precedent for other new states opting out of unpalatable social provisions The UK government sees measures of employment protection such as those in the social chapter of the Maastricht Treaty as an unnatural interference with the free operation of the labour market. This philosophy is reflected in what is happening within the UK: for example, the government recently abolished wages councils which had set minimum hourly rates in sectors such as hotels and catering, retail, hairdressing and the rag trade, fast food outlets, hotels and department stores. A quarter of all ethnic minority employees work in such low paid, low status jobs (*Guardian* 10 February 1993). Dismantling wages councils leaves Britain as the only EU country without some form of legally enforceable minimum wage protection. Also relevant here is the UK government's undermining of trade union rights in a series of Employment Acts, so that union rights are inferior to those in many other member states. The recent failure of a year-long union campaign in the Midlands to improve the pay and conditions of a group of highly exploited ethnic minority sweat-shop workers was largely attributed to the reduction in union power brought about by the government's legislation (Wrench and Virdee, 1995).

This is the paradox: the UK maintains the strongest anti-discrimination legislation in Europe, with its measures in many ways providing a model for others to emulate. Yet its standards of general employment protection are among the weakest in the EU, which means that in practice the anti-discrimination measures are practically irrelevant to large sections of its ethnic minority workforce. In some other EU countries standards of general employment protection are higher and these often benefit migrant workers along with indigenous workers, but the lack of anti-discrimination measures means that its migrant and ethnic minority workforce are unable to seek protection those extra disadvantages suffered only by visible minorities. Clearly, what is needed are both elements: general employment protection measures, and more specific anti-discrimination measures in all EU member states.

> In the absence of a high general standard of employment protection, the existence of such (anti-discrimination) laws merely accentuates the hierarchy of employment. Only those people with secure, permanent jobs and the protection of a strong trade union may be in a position to insist on their rights. Those at the bottom of the hierarchy - who are most vulnerable and disadvantaged and so most in need of legal protection - are precisely the groups who have the least access to the law. This is leading to a greater polarisation, whereby an ever increasing proportion of people find themselves in a twilight zone of temporary, casualised, unregulated work (Sales and Gregory, 1995).

Furthermore, anti-discrimination law does not touch the large numbers of workers who are outside the formal labour market in highly exploitative illegal work. For people with insecure employment status, including undocumented workers and asylum seekers, anti-discrimination law is almost irrelevant. This partly explains the lack of concern with equal opportunities and anti-discrimination measures in countries of Southern Europe, whose national reports describe the super-exploitation of large numbers of migrants in poor or illegal work, suffering conditions which would not be tolerated by native workers, but which they are not in a position to reject.

The national reports have shown how in Greece the informal economy forms up to 30% of total economic activity, with migrants working illegally in jobs which locals avoid, in small firms which avoid labour inspection, in seasonal work, and in low status jobs in catering and tourism. It also noted that undocumented migrants are being increasingly employed in more 'regular' jobs. In Spain unregistered immigrants were estimated to represent 40 to 60% of all immigrant (non-EU) workers, working with no contract or social security benefits and often suffering exploitative working conditions in terms of wages, quality, intensity or duration of their work, and arbitrary dismissal, sometimes without wages. In certain sectors employers prefer to employ immigrants because of the low cost, pliability and vulnerability of this type of labour force. The Italian report showed how the current policy of restrictions with regard to immigrants who are already resident in Italy and the difficulties they have in securing the legalisation of their position are thus perpetuating and reinforcing conditions of marginalisation. In Portugal it was estimated that about 50% of ethnic minority workers have no employment contract, with no legal protection, welfare rights, or protection against abuses of safety or working hours.

In these countries, racism and discrimination are seen to operate in the sense of the concentration of ethnic minorities in poor working conditions, and sometimes in the ideologies of rationalisation which help to maintain their segregation in such work. Unlike countries of Northern Europe the issue is not expressed in terms of a concern is with the unjustified exclusion on 'racial' or ethnic grounds of migrants and ethnic minorities, particularly the 'second generation', from the employment opportunities they reasonably aspire to. In countries of Southern Europe immigrants are actively preferred and recruited because they are cheaper, more vulnerable, and more pliable - they are less able to resist over-exploitation in terms of work intensity or working hours. They experience a perverse kind of "positive discrimination" in the selection process and then, within work, suffer the "negative" discrimination of conditions which indigenous workers would not tolerate. Therefore, 'anti-discrimination' measures in this context are seen to include union campaigns for the regularisation of illegal workers as a step to end the discrimination suffered by these workers resulting from their irregular status.

It is possible to speculate that the different emphases of Northern and Southern Europe may converge in the long run. As well as struggling with the problem of the exploitation of migrants in irregular work, countries in the South will need to develop an awareness of equal opportunity and anti-discrimination measures which will become increasingly relevant for settled migrants in regular work, such as found in the industries of Northern Italy, for example. Meanwhile, the issue of the illegal labour market is not one restricted to the countries of southern Europe. The illegal labour market is said to be expanding in countries of the North, particularly from the EU's eastern borders. For example, agreement has been reached between countries of the EU and four Eastern European neighbours that their nationals no longer need visas to enter relevant member states. Now, in Germany and Belgium there is currently a question of Poles who enter as tourists for short periods and work illegally, and who have the freedom to move (and continue working illegally) in other European countries. (This gives them an advantage compared to migrant workers who are third-country nationals who do not have the freedom to move to other countries - Rea 1995). The issue of the illegal labour market is the 'other side' of the issue of anti-discrimination measures for migrants and ethnic minorities in employment. Firstly, illegal work undermines the effects of fair employment practice and anti-discrimination measures in the regular labour market. Secondly, discrimination in the regular labour market is one factor which contributes to the entry of ethnic minorities and migrants into the unregulated and illegal labour market.

It has been argued that there is a "fundamental contradiction" at the heart of European Union policy. Whilst on the one hand there are moves to develop more social and economic rights and raise the living and working conditions of citizens of member states, on the other hand, many of the most vulnerable groups are denied access to these rights, including some 15 million migrants from non-member states who are currently residing within the Union. "This is producing an ever widening gulf between formal and substantive equality, between theoretical and actual access to the labour market, between those with high status, well paid and relatively secure jobs and those who are excluded from the labour market altogether or exist at its margins in various forms of precarious employment" (Sales and Gregory, 1995). If this gulf is allowed to develop, it will lead to a "dual society". A report for the European Foundation for the Improvement of Living and Working Conditions (Ball, 1994) argues that in the 1990s, the choice facing Europeans lies between a dual society and an active society:

> A "*dual*" society in which wealth is created by a highly qualified labour force, using capital equipment based on advanced technology, and income is then transferred to the non-active, through social security payments, as the basis for some measure of social justice.
>
> An "*active*" society, in which there is a wider distribution of income, achieved by means other than social security transfers, and in which every person feels that she or he can contribute, not only to production, with all those who wish to work having a reasonable chance of access to employment, but also by participation in the life and development of society.

The report argues that a "*dual society*" is unlikely to be socially cohesive. It will mean that some citizens will be doomed to long periods, even lifetimes, of unfulfilled potential at best and poverty at worst. It will also mean the persistent undermining of the economic competitiveness of Europe, because where social cohesion is lacking there is a cost. Therefore, it is argued, the choice must be for the "active society". "It alone can be socially cohesive, and indeed allows meaning to be given to the term: a society which aims to reduce inequalities generated by social and economic imbalances, not just by social transfer payments, but by offering the opportunity for participation to all". When one marker of this dualism becomes ethnicity or colour, then the social implications of a "dual society" are even more severe. One way of assisting the access to employment and participation in the development of society of all groups is via both the legal and voluntary anti-discrimination measures discussed in this report.

8. REFERENCES

Abell, J.P., M.C. Groothoff en I.L.M. Houweling (1985) *Etnische minderheden bij de overheid.* ISBP, Amsterdam

Addal-Jeboah et al. (1991). *Tør vi satse på en innvandrer?* Prosjektforum for arbeidslivsstudier Oslo

Alvarez, F., (1992) "La inmigración americana en España", Ponencia presentada en la Conferencia de la Unión internacional para el estudio de la población sobre "El poblamiento de las Américas", Veracruz, mayo

Andersson, L. (1992) *Det tar tid att bli svensk. En enkät- och intervjuundersökning av flyktingars och företags beteende på den svenska arbetsmarknaden* CAFO Högskolan i Växjö

AMS. (1991) *Arbetsförmedling som informationskanal bland arbetsökande. Rapport från Utredningsenheten* AMS Stockholm

Ball, C. (1994) *Bridging the Gulf* European Foundation for the Improvement of Living and Working Conditions, Dublin

Banton, M. (1991) "The Effectiveness of Legal Remedies for Victims of Racial Discrimination in Europe" *New Community* Vol.18 No.1

Banton, M. (1994) *Discrimination* Open University Press, Buckingham

Bauböck, R. (1992) *Immigration and the Boundaries of Citizenship* Monographs in Ethnic Relations No.4, University of Warwick

Beauftragte der Bundesregieiung für die Belange der Ausländer (ed) (1994) *Bericht der Beauftragten der Bundesregieiung für die Belange der Ausländer über die Loge der Ausländer in der Bundersrepublik Deutschland,* Bonn

Becker, H.M. en G.J. Kempen (1982) *Vraag naar migranten op de arbeidsmarkt.* Erasmus Universiteit Rotterdam, Rotterdam

Beek, K.van (1993) *To be Hired or not to be Hired: The Employer Decides* University of Amsterdam, Amsterdam

Benz, W. (1989) *Rechtsextremismus in der Bundesrepublik.* Frankfurt am Main, Fischer.

Berg, B. and Vedi, C. (1995) *Fra holdning til handling* Rapport, SINTEF.

Biegel, C. en K. Tjoen-tak-sen (1986) *Klachten over rassendiscriminatie* VUGA, Den Haag

Biegel, C., A. Böcker en K. Tjoen-tak-sen (1987) *Rassendiscriminatie... Tenslotte is het verboden bij de wet* Tjeenk Willink, Zwolle

Biller, M. (1989) *Arbeitsmarktsegmentation und Ausländerbeschäftigung* Campus. Frankfurt/Main, New York

Biffl, G. (1995) *SOPEMI Report on Labour Migration: Austria 1994/95* WIFO, Vienna

Boos-Nünning, U., Jäger, A., Henscheid, R., Sieber, W., and Becker, H. (1990) *Berufswahlsituation und Berufswahlprozesse griechischer, italienischer und portugiesischer Jugendlicher. Beiträge zur Arbeitsmarkt- und Berufsforschung* Bundestalt für Arbeit, Nürnberg

Bouvier, P. (1989) *Le Travail au Quotidien* Presses Universitaires de France, Paris

Bouw, C. en C. Nelissen (1988) *Gevoelige kwesties. Ervaringen van migranten met discriminatie.* Centrum voor Onderzoek van Maatschappeliijke Tegenstelligen, Rijksuniversiteit Leiden, Leiden

Bovenkerk, F. en E. Breunig-van Leeuwen (1978) "Rasdiscriminatie en rasvooroordeel op de Amsterdamse arbeidsmarkt" in: F. Bovenkerk (red.) *Omdat zij anders zijn; patronen van rasdiscriminatie in Nederland.* Boom, Meppel

Bovenkerk, F. (1986) *Een eerlijke kans. Over de toepasbaarheid van buitenlandse ervaringen met positieve actie voor etnische minderheden op de arbeidsmarkt in Nederland.* Ministerie van Binnenlandse Zaken, Ministerie van Sociale Zaken en Werkgelegenheid, Den Haag

Bovenkerk, F. (1992) *Testing Discrimination in Natural Experiments: A Manual for International Comparative Research on Discrimination on the Grounds of 'Race' and Ethnic Origin* International Labour Office, Geneva

Bovenkerk, F., Gras, M.J.I. and Ramsoedh, D. (1995) *Discrimination against Migrant Workers and Ethnic Minorities in Access to Employment in the Netherlands* International Labour Office, Geneva

Brandt, B. (1996) "The Policy of Exclusion: The German Concept of Citizenship" *Migration* Sondernummer

Brassé, P. en E. Sikking (1988) *Discriminatie van migranten binnen arbeidsorganisaties.* In: Migrantenstudies, 2, pp.13-24

Brown, C. (1984) *Black and White Britain: The Third PSI Survey* Heinemann, London

Brown, C. and Lawton, J. (1991) *Training for Equality: A Study of Race Relations and Equal Opportunities Training* Policy Studies Institute, London

Brown, C. (1992) '"Same difference": the persistence of racial disadvantage in the British employment market' in P. Braham, A. Rattansi and R. Skellington (eds) *Racism and Antiracism: Inequalities, Opportunities and Policies* Sage, London

Brown, P. and Scase, R. (1994) *Higher Education and Corporate Realities: Class, Culture and the Decline of Graduate Careers* UCL Press, London

Cachón, L. (1994) "Inmigrantes en España: de la discriminación institucional a la segmentación del mercado de trabajo", *Revista Española de Investigaciones Sociológicas* (en prensa).

Calvo, T. (1990) *España racista? Voces payas sobre los gitanos*, Anthropos, Barcelona

Castles S. and Miller, M.J (1993) *The Age of Migration: International Population Movements in the Modern World* Macmillan, Basingstoke

Chesler, M, and Delgado, H. (1987) "Race Relations and Organisational Change" in J.W. Shaw, P.G. Nordlie and R.M. Shapiro (eds) *Strategies for Improving Race Relations: the Anglo-American Experience* Manchester University Press, Manchester

C.I.R.E.S. (1992) "Actitudes ante los inmigrantes" en *La realidad social de España (1990-1991)* Madrid

Colectivo IOE (1991) *Foreign women in domestic service in Madrid, Spain* O.I.T., Ginebra

Commission of the European Communities (1992) *Moyens Juridiques pour Combattre le Racisme et la Xénophobie* Commission of the European Communities, Office for Official Publications of the European Communities, Brussels

CRE (1989) *Are Employers Complying?* Commission for Racial Equality, London

Cross, M., Wrench, J., and Barnett, S. (1990) *Ethnic Minorities and the Careers Service: An Investigation into Processes of Assessment and Placement* Department of Employment Research Paper No.73, London

Coussey, M. and Hammelburg, H. (1994) *A Code of Practice to Combat Racial Discrimination and to Promote Equal Opportunities at Work* Volume 1, European Human Rights Foundation

Daniel, W.W. (1968) *Racial Discrimination in England* Penguin, Harmondsworth

Denolf, L. and Martens, A. (1991) *Van 'mijn'werk naar ander werk: Onderzoeksrapport over de arbeidsmarktpositie van ex-mijnwerkers* Permanente Werkgroep Limburg, Brussels

Dijk, van, T. (1993) "Denying Racism: Elite Discourse and Racism" in J. Wrench and J. Solomos (eds) *Racism and Migration in Western Europe* Berg, Oxford

Drew, D., Gray, J. and Sime, N. (1992) *Against the Odds: The Education and Labour market Experiences of Black Young People* Employment Department Research and Development Paper No.68, Sheffield

Dummett, A. (1994) *Citizens, Minorities and Foreigners: A guide to the EC* Commission for Racial Equality, London

EC (1994) *Growth, Competitiveness, Employment: The Challenges and Ways Forward into the 21st Century* White Paper, European Commission, Brussels

Echardour, A. and Maurin, E. (1993) *Données Sociales* INSEE

Edwards, J. (1988) "Facing up to Positive Discrimination" *New Community* Vol. 14 No.3

Esmail, A. and Everington, S. (1993) "Racial discrimination against doctors from ethnic minorities" *British Medical Journal* 306, March

Essed, Ph. (1984) *Alledaags racisme*. Feministische uitgeverij Sara, Amsterdam

Esser, H. (1980) *Aspekte der Wanderungssoziologie. Assimilation und Integration von Wanderern, ethnischen Gruppen und Minderheiten. Eine handlungstheoretische Analyse* Darmstadt/Neuwied, Luchterhand.

Farin, K. and E. Seidel-Pielen (1992) *Rechtsruck. Rassismus im neuen Deutschland*. Rotbuchverlag, Berlin

FNV-secretariaat etnische minderheden (1994) *Eerste evaluatie non-discriminatie code voor FNV en bonden*. FNV, Utrecht

Forbes, I. and Mead, G. (1992) *Measure for Measure* Employment Department Research Series No. 1, London

Gächter, A. (1995) "Forced Complementarity: The Attempt to Protect Native Austrian Workers from Immigrants" *New Community* Vol.21 No.3

Gächter, A. (1996) "Austria: Protecting Native Workers from Immigrants" in Penninx, R. and Roosblad, J. (eds) *Trade Unions, Immigration, and Immigrant Workers in Western Europe, 1960-1993* University of Amsterdam, Amsterdam

Giraud, M. et Marie, C.V. (1990) *Les stratégies socio-politiques de la communauté antillaise dans son processus d'insertion en France méropolitaine* Rapport de recherche, Ministère de la Recherche, Paris

G.I.S.T.I. (1994) *Les discriminations dans l'emploi.* Contribution à l'"European Guidelines to good employment practice to combat discrimination" (à paraître). Paris, G.I.S.T.I. (multigr.).

Gribbin, J. (1994 "The British code of practice against racism at the workplace" *Proceedings of the European Conference on Migration and the Social Partners - Dublin 1993* European Foundation for the Improvement of Living and Working Conditions, Dublin

Haagensen, E. et al. (1990) *Innvandrere - gjester eller bofaste?* Gyldendal Oslo

Haugg, S. (1994) 'Wir vertreten die, die hier im Hause sind' Landeszentrale für politische Bildung, Hamburg

Heisler, B. S. (1991) "A Comparative Perspective on the Underclass: Questions of Urban Poverty, Race and Citizenship" *Theory and Society*, Vol.20 No.4

Heitmeyer, W. (1989) *Rechtsextreme Orientierungen bei Jugendlichen.* München, Juventa

Hooghiemstra, E. (1991) *Gelijke kansen voor allochtonen op een baan? Wervings- en selectieprocessen op de arbeidsmarkt voor on- en laaggeschoolden.* In: Migrantenstudies, 1

Hubbuck, J. and Carter, S. (1980) *Half a Chance? A Report on Job Discrimination against Young Blacks in Nottingham* Commission for Racial Equality, London

Izquierdo, I. (1994): "Las encuestas contra la inmigración", in Martín, L., Gómez, C., Arranz, F. y Gabilondo, A., (1994): *Hablar y dejar hablar (Sobre racismo y xenofobia)*, Universidad Autónoma de Madrid, Madrid

Jenkins, R. (1986) *Racism and Recruitment* Cambridge University Press, Cambridge

Jewson, N. and Mason, D. (1991) "Economic Change and Employment Practice: Consequences for Ethnic Minorities" in M. Cross and G. Payne (eds) *Work and the Enterprise Culture* Falmer, London

Jones, T. (1993) *Britain's Ethnic Minorities* Policy Studies Institute, London

Kalpaka, A,, W. Kopp and D. Leskien (1992) *National Study for the Federal Republic of Germany on Legal Instrments to Combat all Forms of Discrimination, Racism and Xenophobia and Incitement and Hatred and Racial Violence.* Institut für Migrations- und Rassismusforschung, Hamburg.

Kalpaka, A, and Räthzel, N. (1994) *Die Schwierigkeit, nicht rassistisch zu sein* Mundo-Verlag, Köln

Kartaram, S (1992) *Final report on legislation against racism and xenophobia in the Netherlands.* Landelijk Bureau Racismebestrijding, Utrecht

Katz, J. (1978) *White Awareness: Handbook for anti-racism training* University of Oklahoma Press

Kloek, W. (1992) *De positie van allochtonen op de arbeidsmarkt* Centraal bureau voor de statistiek, Heerlen

Kosten, A. (1994) *Kleurenblind in gekleurd Amerika; een literatuurstudie naar het beleid van positieve actie in de Verenigde Staten* Sociaal en Cultureel Planbureau, Rijswijk

Kremer, M. und Spangenberg, H. unter Mitarbeit von L. Jäger und S. Schitzler (1980) *Assimilation ausländischer Arbeitnehmer in der Bundesrepublik Deutschland.* Forschungsbericht. Königstein/Ts., Peter Hanstein Verlag.

Kühne, P. (1991) "Interessenvertretung von ausländischen Arbeitnehmerinnen und Arbeitnehmern: Eine bleibende Herausforderung an die deutschen Gewerkschaften" in *WSI-Mitteilungen* 1991,1

Kühne, P. (1994) Arbeitsmigration in die Bundesrepublik und nach Westeuropa. Gewerkschaftliche Gestaltungsvorschläge in Kühne, P and N. Öztürk, K-W. West (eds.) (1994) *Gewerkschaften und Einwanderung,* Bund-Verlag, Köln

Kühne, P. (forthcoming) "Immigration: support or resistance?" in Penninx, R. and Roosblad, J. (eds) *Trade Unions, Immigration and Immigrant Workers in Western Europe 1960 - 1993,* University of Amsterdam, Amsterdam

Kumar, V. (1986) *Industrial Tribunal Applicants under the Race Relations Act 1976* Commision for Racial Equality, London

Layton-Henry, Z. (1990) (ed) *The Political Rights of Migrant Workers in Western Europe* Sage, London

Lee, G. and Wrench, J. (1980) "Accident-Prone Immigrants: An Assumption Challenged" *Sociology* Vol.14 No 4

Lee, G. and Wrench. J. (1983) *Skill Seekers - Black Youth, Apprenticeships and Disadvantage* National Youth Bureau, Leicester

Lee, G. (1984) *Trade Unionism and Race: A report to the West Midlands Regional Council of the Trades Union Congress* Birmingham

LO (1991) *Invandrarpolitiski program* Stockholm

Lochak, D. (1990) "Les discriminations frappant les étrangers sont-elles licites?". *Droit Social*, n°1.

Lochak, D. (1991) "Conseil National des Populations Immigrées. Groupe 'Egalité des droits' : Rapport". *Actualités-Migrations*, n°363.

Loontechnische Dienst (LTD) (1992) *Het Stichtingsakkoord etnische minderheden in de praktijk.* Ministerie van Sociale Zaken en Werkgelegenheid, Den Haag

Lustgarten, L. (1987) "Racial inequality and the limits of law" in R.Jenkins and J.Solomos (eds) *Racism and Equal Opportunity Policies in the 1980s* Cambridge University Press, Cambridge

Luthra, M. and Oakley, R. (1991) *Combating Racism Through Training: A Review of Approaches to Race Training in Organisations* Policy Paper in Ethnic Relations No.22, University of Warwick

Lutz, H. (1993) "Migrant Women, Racism and the Dutch Labour Market" in J. Wrench and J. Solomos (eds) *Racism and Migration in Western Europe* Berg, Oxford

Lyon-Caen, G. (1992) *Les libertés publiques et l'Emploi* Rapport au Ministre de Travail, de l'emploi et de la formation professionelle, La Documentation Française, Paris

MacDonald, H. (1993) "The Diversity Industry", in *The New Republic*, 5 July 1993.

Marrodán, M.D. y otras, (1991): *Mujeres del tercer mundo en España. Modelo migratorio y caracterización sociodemográfica*, Fundación CIPIE Madrid

Martens, A. (forthcoming) "Migratory movements, the position, the outlook: charting theory and practice for trade unions" in J. Wrench, A. Rea and N. Ouali (eds) *Ethnic Minorities, Migrants and the Labour Market: Integration and Exclusion in Europe* Macmillan

Martín, L., Gómez, C., Arranz, F. y Gabilondo, A., (1994): *Hablar y dejar hablar (Sobre racismo y xenofobia)*, Universidad Autónoma de Madrid, Madrid

Mason, D. and Jewson, N. (1992) "'Race', equal opportunities and employment practice: Reflections on the 1980s, prospects for the 1990s" *New Community* Vol.19 No.1

Mason, D. (1994) Employment and the Labour Market *New Community* Vol.20 No.2

Matuschek, H. (1985) "Ausländerpolitik in Österreich 1962-1985. Der Kampf um und gegen die Arbeitskraft" *Journal für Sozialforschung* Vol.25 No.2

Meggeneder, O., Ranftl, E., Moser-Zobernig, U., Wenidoppler, K. and Wimmer, M. (1992) *Betriebliche Arbeitszeit zwischen Wunsch und Wirklichkeit* Forschungsberichte aus Sozial- und Arbeitsmarktpolitik Nr.39, BMAS, Vienna

Meloen, J.D. (1991) *"Makkelijker gezegd.." Een onderzoek naar de werking van een gedragscode voor uitzendbureaus ter voorkoming van discriminatie* VUGA, Den Haag

Miles, R. (1993) "The Articulation of Racism and Nationalism: Reflections on European History" in J. Wrench and J. Solomos *Racism and Migration in Western Europe* Berg, Oxford

Mirza, Q. (1995) *Race Relations in the Workplace* The Institute of Employment Rights London

Mulder, F.E. (red.) (1991) *Positieve Actie; Een kwestie van beleid, Handreiking om de positie van vrouwen en allochtonen in de gemeentelijke organisatie te verbeteren.* VNG- uitgeverij, Den Haag

Nexus Research (1994) *Report of National Study on the Travelling Community.* Task Force on the Travelling Community, Dublin

Nys M and Beauchesne M-N, "La discrimination des travailleurs étrangers et d'origine étrangère dans l'entreprise" *Courrier Hebdomadaire*, CRISP, 1992, No.1381-1382

Overdijk-Francis, J.E. (red.) (1993) *Handboek Minderheden.* Bohn Stafleu Van Loghum, Houten

Owen, D. and Green, A. (1992) 'Labour market experience and change among ethnic groups in Great Britain' *New Community* Vol.19 No.1

Parnreiter, C. (1992) "'... alle Arbeitskräfte des Erdrunds.' Über den Import ausländischer Arbeitskräfte nach Österreich und ihren Nutzen für die Wirtschaft" in Prader, Thomas (ed.) *Moderne Sklaven. Asyl- und Migrationspolitik in Österreich* Promedia Vienna

Parnreiter, C. (1994) *Migration und Arbeitsteilung. Ausländerbeschäftigung in der Weltwirtschaftskrise* Promedia Vienna

Pattipawae, N. (1992) *Gedragscodes ter voorkoming en bestrijding van rassendiscriminatie.* Ministerie van Binnenlandse Zaken, Den Haag

Paulson, S. (1991) *Utvecklingsbehov för framtidens arbetskraft. En studie om invandrare på Göteborgs arbetsmarknad.* Göteborgs Näringslivssekrateriat, Göteborg

Penninx, R. and Roosblad, J. (eds) (forthcoming) *Trade Unions, Immigration and Immigrant Workers in Western Europe 1960 - 1993*, University of Amsterdam, Amsterdam

Peppard, N. (1983) "Race relations training: the state of the art" *New Community* Vol.6 Nos. 1/2

Phizacklea, A. and Miles, R. (1980) *Labour and Racism* Routledge and Kegan Paul, London

Pinto, D. (1993) *Onderwijs over cultuurverschillen. Effecten van cursussen Interculturele Communicatie.* Proefschrift, Rijksuniversiteit Groningen, Groningen

Pichelmann, K., Brandel, F. and Hofer, H. (1994) *Verdrängungsprozesse am Arbeitsmarkt* Occasional Paper No.345; Vienna: IHS

Praag, C.S. van (1989) *Werkloosheid en inkomens bij etnische minderheden*. WRR, Den Haag

Radin, B. (1966) "Coloured Workers and British Trade Unions" *Race* Vol. VIII No.2

Räthzel, N. and Ü. Sarica (1994), *Migration und Diskriminierung in der Arbeit. Das Beispiel Hamburg*. Argument-Verlag Hamburg/Berlin

Rea, A. (1995) "Social Citizenship and Ethnic Minorities in the European Union" in M. Martiniello (ed) *Migration, Citizenship and Ethno-National Identities in the European Union* Avebury, Aldershot

Regeringens proposition. 1993/94:101 *Åtgärder mot rasistisk brottslighet och diskriminering i arbetslivet*

Rex, J. (1992) "Race and ethnicity in Europe" in J. Bailey (ed) *Social Europe* London

Rhodes, E. and Braham, P. (1987) "Equal opportunity in the context of high levels of unemployment" in R. Jenkins and J. Solomos (eds) *Racism and Equal Opportunity Policies in the 1980s* Cambridge University Press, Cambridge

Roelandt, Th., J.H.M. Roijen en J. Veenman (1992) *Statistisch Vademecum 1992*. SDU uitgeverij, Den Haag

Room, G. (1995) "Exclusion, equality before the law and non-discrimination: old people, economically disadvantaged people, the unemployed" in *Exclusion, Equality before the Law and Non-Discrimination*, Proceedings of a Council of Europe seminar, Council of Europe, Strasbourg

Roosblad, J. (forthcoming) "Trade unions and immigrants: the Dutch case" in Penninx, R. and Roosblad, J. (eds) *Trade Unions, Immigration and Immigrant Workers in Western Europe 1960 - 1993*, University of Amsterdam, Amsterdam

Sales, R. and Gregory, J. (1995) "Employment, Citizenship and European Integration: The Implications for Migrant and Refugee Women" Paper presented to the *British Sociological Association Annual Conference*

Schaub, G. (1993) *Rekrutierungsstrategien und Selektionsmechanismen für die Ausbildung und die Beschäftigung junger Ausländer*. Berlin, BIBB. P. 58ff

Schierup, C-U (1992) Indvandrerne på det danske arbejdsmarked: strukturændringer, diskriminering, alternativer. *Vi Ta'r FAF, Artikelsamling om indvandrere i Danmark*. Forbundet af Arbejdere fra Tyrkiet (FAT)

Schierup, C-U (1993) *På kulturens slagmark - Mindretal og størretal taler om Danmark* Esbjerg

Schierup, C-U and Paulson, S. (eds) (1994) *Arbetets etniska delning* Carlssons, Stockholm

Seifert, W. (1994) Berufliche und ökonomische Mobilität ausländischer Arbeitnehmer - Längsschnittanalysen mit dem Sozio-Ökonomischen Panel.

Simpson, A. and Stevenson, J. (1994) *Half a Chance, Still?* Nottingham and District Racial Equality Council, Nottingham

SIV (1995/06) *Statens invandraverk, Statistik 1994* SIV Norrköping

Sivertsen, J. E. (1995) Høy arbeidsledighet blant innvandrere. *Samfunnsspeilet* 2/95 Statistisk sentralbyrå Oslo

Smeets, H.M.A.G. (1993) *Etnische minderheden bij de overheid, faal en slaagfactoren bij positief actie beleid.* ISEO, Rotterdam

Smith D.J. (1977) *Racial disadvantage in Britain: the PEP report.* Penguin, Harmondsworth

SOU. 1983.18 *Lag mot etnisk diskriminering i arbetslivet. Delbetänkande av diskrimineringsutredningen* Allmäna förlaget Stockholm

SOU. (1992) *Förbud mot etnisk diskriminering i arbetslivet* Allmänna förlaget Stockholm

SOU. (1995) *Arbete till invandrare.* Delbetänkande från Invandrarpolitiska kommittén

Speller, T. en A. Willems (1990) *Scholing en arbeidsmarktpositie van allochtonen.* Katholieke Universiteit Nijmegen

Statistics Norway (1994) *Ukens statistikk 31/32:94.* Statistisk sentralbyrå Oslo

Stöss, R. (1989) *Die extreme Rechte in der Bundesrepublik.* Westdeutscher Verlag Darmstadt

Tesser, P.T.M. (1993) *Rapportage minderheden 1993.* Sociaal en Cultureel Planbureau, Rijswijk

Thomas, R.R. Jnr (1990) "From Affirmative Action to Affirming Diversity", *Harvard Business Review,* March/April.

Thorud, E. (1985) *Norsk innvandringspolitikk og arbeiderbevegelsen: fra åpne dører til innvandringsstopp* Institutt for statsvitenskap, Oslo

Toksöz, G. (1990) "Arbeitsbedingungn und betriebliche Interessenvertretung der Arbeiterinnen aus der Türkei in der Bundesrepublik Deutschland". In: Fijalkowski, J. (ed.) *Transnationale Migranten in der Arbeitswelt.* Bonn.

Treichler, A. (1994) 'Ausländerarbeit und Ausländerpolitik in Einzelgewerkschaften' in Kühne, P and N. Öztürk, K-W. West (eds.) (1994) *Gewerkschaften und Einwanderung,* Bund-Verlagin, Köln

Tribalat, M. (1989) "Immigrés, étrangers, Français: l'imbroglio statistique". *Population et Société,* n°241.

TUC (1991) *Involvement of Black Workers in Trade Unions* Ruskin College/Northern College, Trades Union Congress, London

Uyl, R. den, Ch. Choenni and F. Bovenkerk (1986) *Mag het ook een buitenlander wezen?* LBR-reeks 2, Utrecht

Vasta, E. (1993) "Rights and Racism in a New Country of Immigration: The Italian Case" in J. Wrench and J. Solomos *Racism and Migration in Western Europe* Berg, Oxford

Veenman, J. (1985) *De werkloosheid van Molukkers.* Ministerie van Sociale Zaken en Werkgelegenheid, Den Haag

Veenman, J. (red.) (1990) *Ver van huis: achterstand en achterstelling bij allochtonen.* Wolters-Noordhoff, Groningen

Verweij, A.O. (1991) *Gelijke kansen voor allochtonen op ontslag? Een onderzoek naar uitstroom van allochtone werknemers.* In: Migrantenstudies, 1

Virdee S. and Grint, K. (1994) "Black Self Organisation in Trade Unions" *Sociological Review* Vol.42 No.2

Welsh, C., Knox J. and Brett M. (1994) *Acting Positively: Positive Action under the Race Relations Act 1976* Employment Department Group, Research Series No. 36, London

West, K-W. (1994) 'Industrielle Arbeit und Menschenrechte', in Kühne, P and N. Öztürk, K-W. West (eds.) (1994) *Gewerkschaften und Einwanderung*, Köln, Bund-Verlag

Wiener Intergrationsfonds (1995) *Bericht über das Jahr 1994* Wiener Intergrationsfonds, Vienna

Wimmer, H (1986) "Die Arbeitswelt der ausländischen Arbeitnehmer" in Wimmer, H. (ed.) (1986) *Ausländische Arbeitskräfte in Österreich* Campus Frankfurt

Wrench, J. and Solomos, J. (1993) "The Politics and Processes of Racial Discrimination in Britain" in J.Wrench and J. Solomos (eds) *Racism and Migration in Western Europe* Berg, Oxford

Wrench, J., Brah, H. and Martin, P. (1993) *Invisible Minorities: Racism in New Towns and New Contexts* Monographs in Ethnic Relations No.6, University of Warwick

Wrench, J. (1987) "Unequal Comrades: trade unions, equal opportunity and racism" in R. Jenkins and J. Solomos (eds) *Racism and Equal Opportunity Policies in the 1980s* Cambridge University Press, Cambridge,

Wrench, J. and Taylor, P. (1993) *A Research Manual on the Evaluation of Anti-Discrimination Training Activities* International Labour Office, Geneva

Wrench, J. and Virdee, S. (1996) "Organising the Unorganised: 'Race', Poor Work and Trade Unions" in P. Ackers, C. Smith and P. Smith (eds) *The New Workplace and Trade Unionism* Routledge, London

Yalcin, Z. (1995) *LO kontra Invandrare: B-uppsats Statsvetenskapliga institutionen* Stockholms universitet, Stockholm

Zegers de Beijl, R. (1990) *Discrimination of Migrant Workers in Western Europe* International Labour Office, Geneva

Zegers de Beijl, R. (1991) *Although equal before the law... The scope of anti-discrimination legislation and its effects on labour market discrimination against migrant workers in the United Kingdom, the Netherlands and Sweden.* International Labour Office, Geneva

European Foundation for the Improvement of Living and Working Conditions

PREVENTING RACISM AT THE WORKPLACE:
A report on 16 European countries

Luxembourg: Office for Official Publications of the European Communities

1996 – 196 pp. – 16cm x 23.4 cm

ISBN 92-827-7105-9

Price (excluding VAT) in Luxembourg: ECU 20